Fundamental of Library Science and Librarianship

Fundamental of Library Science and Librarianship

S.K. Kapoor

CYBER TECH PUBLICATIONS
4264/3, Ansari Road, Daryaganj, New Delhi-110002 (India)
Ph.: 011-23244078, 011-43559448 Fax: 011-23280028
E-Mail: cyberpublicationsdelhi@yahoo.com
Website: www.cybertechpublications.com

FUNDAMENTAL OF LIBRARY SCIENCE AND LIBRARIANSHIP

S.K. Kapoor

First Edition 2010

Published by :

G.S. Rawat for **Cyber Tech Publications**
4264/3, Ansari Road, Daryaganj, New Delhi-110002 (India)
Ph.: 011-23244078, 011-43559448 Fax: 011-23280028
E-Mail: cyberpublicationsdelhi@yahoo.com
Website: www.cybertechpublications.com

Printed at: Asian Offset Printers, Delhi-53

Preface

Library science is a old designation for a field of study. A problem associated with this label is that core issues related to the development of library services are not specific for libraries, but may be understood as principled common for other kinds of information systems, information services or documentation as well. For example is the indexing and representation of documents in bibliographical records not unique for libraries, and most of the relevant principles used today are not developed within the library communities, but by other communities. This goes both for technical and management issues, which have been developed by, among many others computer scientists, and this goes for content oriented issues, such as knowledge organization systems, which have often been developed by subject specialists. A core qualification of librarians is thus knowledge of literatures. On the other hand are there still research questions connected with the term "library" (such as library history, library management and the social roles of libraries), which may not be covered by "information" or "documentation" labels.

During the last one decade, librarianship has developed enormously not only in its traditional areas but also into new areas involving completely new techniques and the uses of the equipment which has been developed to enable more work to get achieved with the minimum of extra manpower. The Librarianship and Library Science has been an attempt to include some important topics of library science which are very much important and necessary in day to day functioning of library the topics which matters are, classification of library science; development of library and information science; manual of library cataloguing; management of library administration; research methodology in library science.

It is anticipated that this book will be useful to university, college, public and school librarians but that it will also find a place on the open shelves in reference libraries.

—Author

CONTENTS

1

Introduction

The study of library history, for a long time the province of antiquarians, has grown into a distinct field with distinguished authors, especially in the past quarter century or so. The founding of groups for those interested in the history of libraries within national professional associations was crowned by the establishment within IFLA of the Round Table on Library History in the late 1970s. By that time, several journals had begun to assume significance for the field, and since 1973 the *Annual Bibliography of the History of the Printed Book and Libraries* has appeared.

The proceedings of the international symposium, "Library History Research in the International Context," held in Wolfenbuttel, Germany, in April 1988, marked yet another benchmark on the road toward sophistication in the study of library history. Survey reports on the status of library history research were presented by scholars from 13 nations representing four continents. Though not all the news was uniformly encouraging, in general the participants and the readers of the printed text felt that there was hope for the future.

One of the conspicuous omissions from the 1988 Symposium was a report on the status of library history in India — a nation known for its ancient and medieval, as well as more modern, library establishment. Although the history and tradition of literacy and books among certain classes in what is now India is long–standing, the modern library movement has roots in the later 18th century with real growth appearing a century or more later. Programmes for professional library education developed in the principal centres of Madras in the 1930s and Bombay, Calcutta, and Delhi in the 1940s, with others following during the 1960s.

A number of relatively short surveys and monographic works dealing with Indian library history have treated various chronological periods, types of libraries, geographical areas, or a mix of these. Since the tradition is so rich, the library education programmes relatively strong, and the interest in pursuing national cultural history keen, questions that recur to the student of library history are: What is the status of library history in India? How can this be explained? What might the future hold?

One of the authors of the present article, Donald G. Davis, Jr., undertook a systematic overview of the situation in India during a five–week research tour in the summer of 1988 sponsored by the American Institute of Indian Studies. The project "aimed to study the current status of library history in India by cursorily reviewing the existing [English–language] bibliography, by surveying present activities, and by describing and evaluating the findings from an international and sympathetic point of view ". In addition to long stays in Calcutta at the National Library of India and in Delhi, the tour encompassed visits and interviews at eight library schools and nine other institutional libraries. The report that resulted was widely distributed in the following two years.

The findings of the survey included description of the literature, the historians, the organization structure, and the general attitude toward library history within the profession. The literature survey enumerated works written primarily as history, rather than description, and accounted for fewer than 100 significant monographs, dissertations, scholarly articles, chapters in collected works, and whole volumes of collected papers. These publications constitute a core bibliography for the field. Strengths include the public library movement, Muslim influence, the national library, and library associations; weaknesses include academic libraries, private libraries, library education, and comparative studies.

In library history, about a dozen persons were identified as productive researchers and writers. Several are in retirement, continuing their research after leaving professional employment; as these cease their labours, the profession will sustain a great loss. On the other hand, there is a good group of widely–scattered, younger historians who are just beginning to assume the responsibility of continuing the work of interpreting the profession to its society in historical terms; some of these live outside India.

The organization structure of research in library history is diffuse, with the best collection of printed materials at the National Library of India. Programmes in library and information science have not given much attention to library history; and even on the doctoral level, most of the dissertations that have appeared have been done in other departments or overseas. There are no identifiable groups that bring persons interested in library history together and not many conferences on the subject. The few historically–oriented articles that are produced appear in the general professional journals, or, more likely, in scholarly journals published abroad.

The general attitude of library historians seems to be discouragement. The elder scholars as well as their junior colleagues usually work in isolation, sometimes with academic colleagues in historical or literary studies. They see little professional recognition for historical research from their fellow librarians, despite the rich sources for explicating the role of libraries and information in the complex culture of a developing nation.

The survey concluded that despite the pessimism regarding the future of historical studies in librarianship, the outlook for the future is not without hope. The challenge of the coming years will be to find agreement about the nature of the unfinished agenda. Two questions are critical: First, is library history a luxury for a few aberrant and typically elderly members of the profession; or is it a topic that the whole profession, or a significant portion of it, can embrace with pride and enthusiasm? Second, is library history only the province of nations heavily influenced by the West, or it a mark of a maturing profession in any nation that is coming to grips with its role in the cultural life of the country and contributing its part to that cultural record?

Some possible steps envisioned for the future included formation of regional interest groups under the aegis of the Indian Library Association, regular programme meetings, an informal newsletter, occasional publications, and development of a model syllabus for library education programmes. Mention was even made of programmes at the forthcoming IFLA conference in 1992.

Essentially, little has changed since 1988. Yet there is evidence for hope. Some of the younger library historians are completing their doctoral degrees and have published their results. They need to be encouraged and to communicate more regularly with one another. Another major achievement is the splendid, two–volume compilation, *Humanities Information Systems and Centres* (1991), that presents capsule descriptions of 66 specialized institutions in the fields of cultural studies, many of them being archives or rare book repositories. Most of the entries, many prepared by scholars who might form a nucleus of a library history network, contain substantial historical notes on the founding and development of the institutions and their libraries.

The identification of potential research topics and subjects for investigation is a role that library historians can play in their profession. And when contemporary problems manifest themselves, historians can examine the evidence and help to explain their context, offering some insight into possible solutions and alternative courses of action. In the case of India, libraries represent all of the various types known to the human race, including those of the most advanced countries. Yet one must acknowledge that some outstanding examples may serve only as exceptions to the prevailing low status of libraries, and that fine looking organization charts and statistical tables do not always provide a clear picture of what the real situation is at the grassroots level. Among the many potential contemporary topics that might invite the attention of Indian library historians are the underdeveloped state of public libraries, the lack of genuine library consciousness in the library community, and the role of the profession.

On paper India appears to have a well–organized, functioning system of public libraries that attempt to supply the reading needs of all its citizens. In reality, the condition of most public libraries, large or small, urban or rural, city or village, is exceedingly poor. In fact, a case could be easily made that with few exceptions, genuine public libraries worthy of the name are yet to be established. Modern public libraries that are user–centred, service–oriented, and collection–balanced centres for graphic records are still in the future. The reasons for this extremely slow development, despite efforts in the early 20th century to approximate the kind of service available in Europe and North America, are surely worth exploring. While the effects of domination by colonial powers, primarily the British, may have produced a lack of concern for the vernacular–speaking and reading populace, local and more recent decisions about priorities are certainly involved as well. Comparative studies of individual states has only begun.

The issue of library and information consciousness in the nation is relevant here. One could receive the impression that a commitment to the value of reading, information, and libraries is not high among professional librarians and sponsoring agencies. Some in the library establishment are convinced that the government is interested in libraries and literacy on only a marginal level.

Though individual states differ greatly in their provision of library service, a prevalent idea seems to be that passing library legislation by itself will result in great advances, whereas funding and implementation have frequently failed to support legislation. Studies examining the comparative effect of library legislation in various states could yield some fruitful insights that might provide guidance to future efforts.

Another issue for investigation is the role of the Indian library profession. Judged on its past, the Indian library establishment has been unable to mount an effective effort to achieve some short–term and medium–term goals with respect to library development. The tension between the specialized libraries connected with government agencies and the commercial sector, and public libraries and libraries associated with educational institutions, has been one reason for the lack of success. The historian can examine actions taken, and not taken, by library associations to discover their impact on library progress. One persistent problem has been the creation of professional standards. Another has related to the proper duties and responsibilities of librarians.

In his 1987 presidential address to the Indian Library Association, T. S. Rajgopalan rightly remarked:

It is generally acknowledged that our libraries are underutilized in relation to investments being made in them. Non–use and low–use of libraries amount to wastage of facilities being made available. Maybe the literacy rate, lack of reading habits, etc., are the causes for low use from the side of patrons...User education programmes must be organized by libraries in a way that libraries are fully utilized. If library historians would address the roots and trends of library use issues, they would provide a valuable service to their profession and society.

With the centenary of S. R. Ranganathan's birth in 1992, it is an appropriate occasion to reconsider the expression of opinion that he offered in a radio talk in April 1956:

An account of the libraries in the first four periods (the Vedic, the Buddhistic, the Medieval, and the Muslim) must necessarily depend upon the historical research. This has not yet been done. The library profession is too small in India to spare a person to fill up this antiquarian gap. Those trained in the scientific method of tracing history are too preoccupied with dynastic and political history to spare sufficient time for cultural history in general and library history in particular. This statement no doubt reflects the feeling of many colleagues from India, but is it not possible now to fill the "antiquarian gap" in a way that will benefit librarians and those they serve?

TRENDS IN PHILIPPINE LIBRARY HISTORY

Since the purpose of this paper is to speak about trends from a historical perspective, the analysis concentrates on Philippine library history during the 19th and 20th centuries, the historical period in which the modern library revolution has taken place. An introduction to early libraries in the Philippines is included, with the hope of filling up a much-needed gap which also exists in many other Southeast Asian countries. Like other continents, Asia has had a complex history of freedom and domination which has in turn shaped contemporary events. Thus, we cannot isolate facts from their relationship to national, regional, and international history.

Sources, facts, and trends point to a clear division of this paper's topic into historical periods linked to events defining Philippine history. Colonial domination was guided by principles which varied from century to century and from power to power. The Spanish crown wanted first and foremost the conversion of the natives to the Catholic religion and supported this endeavor through missionary efforts. Much later, the United States experimented with democratic ideas in the Philippines, in an effort to modernize the country. And the newly established Philippine Republic aspired to achieve what a free nation could, without the control of previous powers.

Although historical changes have been sudden and radical, a gradual transition brought over into the next period something of the library tradition of earlier years. The Spaniards used Philippine syllabaries and the native languages together with xylographic printing, introducing typographic printing and a strong influence of the Spanish and Euro-continental library tradition-born in the Middle Ages and built upon scholarly libraries and private collections. The new library trends of the 19th century were carried over by Filipino scholars and library collectors from the Spanish to the American colonial period. They introduced a public library system, modernized printing, and established the foundation of the library profession as a science. Today modern library trends in the Philippines follow universal patterns but still carry lights and shadows of previous centuries.

This analysis breaks up Philippine library history into three periods: (1) ancient, (2) colonial, and (3) modern in their nature. Furthermore, Philippine modern library history may be divided into its (1) Spanish, (2) American, and (3) Republican periods.

ANCIENT PERIOD OR BEFORE HISTORY

The Philippines is a truly young nation. Ferdinand Magellan reached the island of Samar in 1521, leading to the formal occupation of the Philippines by the Spanish crown in

1572. Different accounts and testimonies speak about Philippine pre-Spanish culture. The first Western travellers reported different levels of knowledge of the art of writing among Southeast Asian inhabitants. There was a localized knowledge of reading and writing, but no trace of the existence of libraries. Later on, early Filipino nationalists were to assume that pre-Spanish documents were destroyed by the colonizers as the latter did in Mexico, but their arguments are not based on historical facts. Credible and coincidental accounts written by the first religious missionaries described a spectrum of native cultures separated by linguistic and geographical barriers. The art of writing was confined to specific areas in the archipelago, skilfully practiced mostly by women, and used for correspondence and note-taking. Writing in the Philippine syllabaries survived the first fifty years of domination as a means of religious instruction and in the wording of official documents, gradually disappearing during the following centuries and turning alphabetical.

THE COLONIAL PHILIPPINE LIBRARY PERIOD

Ferdinand Magellan sailed under the Spanish crown convinced of the existence of an alternative route to Asia. This new route was going to foster European-Asian trade, bypassing the control that the Portuguese exercised over Africa. But distance and expenses disheartened the intent of the Spanish Crown. Guided by a sense of mission, the King of Spain, Philip II, consented in the conquest and control of the archipelago for the spreading of the Catholic faith and the establishment of a closed trading port in Manila.

Thus, the conquistadores brought the sword, while the religious who accompanied them introduced the Catholic faith together with books to aid them in this new field of mission. Early ordinances given by the Spanish King clearly indicated that no secular literature was to sail into the new colonies. The Spanish book market then was flooded with tales of chivalry, but as far as we know, the law was strictly implemented and ships were thoroughly searched at the Manila harbour. Since, the King wanted no distraction from both conquerors and natives, only religious books found their way into the islands. The first collections came with the Spanish missionaries. The earliest records speak of a private collection in 1583. It was owned by Bishop Domingo de Salazar and was probably the first of its kind in the islands. But as so often happened during the first centuries of domination, this collection was reportedly lost in a fire. Other collections of an academic nature followed: those of the Augustinian Convent of San Pablo, the University of Santo Tomas, and the College of San Ignacio. To enrich their collections, the missionaries shipped books from Europe and engaged in book trading with Chinese merchants, most probably for the purpose of learning about the latter's culture and language. The introduction of printing was but a result of the zeal and sense of mission of these missionaries. Need and urgency made them use the xylographic method to produce the first printed book in the Philippines in 1593, the Doctrina Christiana. Printing skills were borrowed largely from China, and the first printer was a Chinese convert named Juan de Vera. Then in 1604, the first typographic press appeared, which, unlike the ones of Macao, Goa, and Japan, was manufactured in the Philippines. The libraries of the time collected, together with religious works, maps and manuscripts. This was specially the case in the Convent of San Agustin, whose collection was captured and brought to Europe by British forces during their occupation of the islands from 1762 to 1764. Private collections must have existed too, but no record has been found of substantial amounts of books in the possession of private individuals.

Philippine library developments during the 17th and 18th centuries had a common feature: the urgently felt need for books. Books from Europe seemed to have poured constantly into the Philippines, as attested to by news from different parts of the Philippine islands. Where are all these books? They were rarely collected. A strong demand and a devastating deterioration seemed to have consumed them all. After centuries of hardships, fires, natural calamities, and wars, no trace seem to have been left of them.

AN IDEA FOR A MODEST BUT MODERN PHILIPPINE LIBRARY

The roots of the modern Philippine library may be traced to the so-called Age of Enlightenment, which seized and dominated European thought during the 18th century. The Bourbon King of Spain, Charles III, had introduced a number of reforms which re-sulted in initiatives in every field-among them, the creation of Sociedades Economicas in Spain and the Colonies. The idea behind the Sociedad Economica was to create a forum for scientific and cultural ideas and to foster agriculture, industry, and craftsmanship by engaging in the distribution of books and the establishment of libraries. A parallelism could be established between these philanthropic ideas and the Mechanics' Institutes in England, towards the end of the 18th century, or the Mercantile Libraries in the US which were to appear during this same period. The trend was Enlightenment through humanitarian and political goals and social progress.

In the Philippines, the Sociedad Economica was established in 1781 by Governor Jose de Basco y Vargas, and it engaged mostly in the free distribution of books. Although the libraries of the Sociedad did not yield any record of holdings until 1877, its creation signaled the beginning of a new era in Philippine library history: popular and public reading.

The concept of public libraries had taken different shapes in the history of many nations, but the foundation of today's modern public library was inspired by the famous law of 1850 in England which established public libraries through public taxes. In Spain, the first regulations for the establishment of public provincial libraries were issued in 1812, but it was too early a start for Spain and its colonies which still had to weather a century of war and anarchy. Nonetheless, the eventual social impact of this concept in Spain and in most of Europe came under different names and entailed different praxes. The concept of a public library was somehow mixed. In 1858, the Spanish government defined as public libraries the national library, university libraries, provincial libraries, and all those which addressed public education in general.

The mixing of public libraries gave rise to the idea of popular libraries, which reached the Philippines in 1871. Prestigious teachers were to be rewarded with books for the establishment of popular libraries. The holdings of these libraries were to be informative and educational, and their management entrusted to teachers. Recommendations encouraged group reading and allowed the circulation of books. The funding for the library was to come from the local government and their collections from the central government. The tenor of this attempt followed a tradition: popular libraries were attached to public instruction to maximize the use of personnel and facilities.

Although the Sociedad Economica had performed the function of a public library during the later part of the 19th century, popular or public libraries did not leave any record in Philippine territory until 1887, when the Museo-Biblioteca de Filipinas was established. Most probably, the 12 public libraries reported at the end of the Spanish period, which held 4,019 books, were in reality popular libraries established in educational religious institutions.

One of the more significant facts in 19th century Philippine library history was the royal order of August 12, 1887. This law established the Museo-Biblioteca de Filipinas in Manila under the Department of Civil Administration. It was a true public library which counted on public funding, had a Filipino scholar, Pedro Alejandro Paterno, as director, and a modest professional staff. The library had published a catalogue and the first library bulletin in the history of Philippine libraries-the Boletin del Museo-Biblioteca de Filipinas. Everything in the Museo-Biblioteca was innovative: regulations, organization, and circulation. Vested with legal authority and directed by a Filipino, this institution was the humble beginning and the foundation stone of the Philippine National Library. Its history ended with the outbreak of war in 1898, and its holdings, around 1,500 titles, were integrated into the American Circulating Library in 1901.

The introduction of the press, the increasing political and ideological tension in the archipelago, and modern trends in the arts and sciences had created a thirst for reading, reflected in the libraries of a number of recreational societies and private individuals. Societies like the Circulo Nacional Recreativo, the Manila Club, the Casino Espanol, and others had libraries for the exclusive use of their members. A culture of reading, created in the highest strata of Philippine society, motivated the collection of books in private libraries by Filipino scholars and heroes of the 1896 and 1898 Philippine War of the Independence. This passion for collecting books and the growing interest in library management carried over a library tradition to the 20th century: the scholarly library.

Libraries in religious schools and the new secular academic institutions had also grown in importance, pushed by political and ideological forces, but lacking in means and handled by nonprofessional library staff. Religious instruction and basic general education had emanated from parishes and convents distributed all over the islands and contained modest collections of books to aid the parish priests in their tasks. Parishes had collections of 200 to 500 books, covering a wide range of subjects but following the selective criterion of the parish priest.

Literacy and religious instruction was common and extensive, often admired by travellers, but primary education was only imparted in Manila and a few regional capitals. The three seminaries of the Islands, the religious schools in Manila, and the new secular institutions, like the Escuela de Artes y Oficios, had libraries supporting their curriculum.

The University of Santo Tomas had a collection of 12,000 titles, the largest in the archipelago. The library's holdings reached 20,000 by the beginning of the 20th century. The scholarly nature of libraries in most of the central houses of the religious orders expanded academic resources. All these orders had library collections, but the biggest were owned by the Franciscans (8,000 volumes), the Recollects (7,000), and the Dominicans in the Convent of Santo Domingo (5,000).

Historical facts of the 19th century indicate the influx of new ideas. Modern trends began to influence libraries and readers, but needed a cooperative effort, based on training, and a change of mentality. Librarianship all over the world was still in the designing stage, the internal mechanisms of which process we can better understand with the help of Philippine library history.

A TURNOVER IN PHILIPPINE MODERN LIBRARY

The Spanish-American war of 1898 opened a new chapter in Philippine history. Commodore George E. Dewey destroyed the Spanish fleet at Cavite on May 1, 1998. Then on February

6, 1899, the US Senate voted in favour of the occupation of the Philippines. The Philippine War of Independence, which started in 1896 against the Spaniards, turned against the Americans and ceased in September of 1902.

Amid this turbulent environment, it is surprising to read the following notice in the August 1899 issue of The Library Journal: "A free library and reading-room has been opened in Manila, chiefly for the use of American soldiers and sailors. Many books and periodicals have been given and further contributions will be welcomed." The newly opened library was the American Circulating Library, which after its integration into the collection of the Museo-Biblioteca and further additions from private collections and government offices became the Philippine National Library. Library trends prevailing abroad were now channelled through the new colonial power into the Philippine library culture.

The economic growth that the US experienced after the American Civil War (1861-1865) established the foundation of what we know today as librarianship. In the last quarter of the 19th century and in the beginning of the 20th, a wide range of ideas took root in the American library culture, through the support of tycoons like Andrew Carnegie. Public libraries and circulating libraries multiplied. The American Library Association was founded. Charles Coffin Jewett introduced his cataloguing rules, and Melvil Dewey his classification System. The Library Journal was published and the first courses on librarianship organized. Most of these ideas were to reach the Philippines through the sacrifice and effort of a handful of pioneers.

The American government was committed to the establishment of a public education system and a strong public service in the Philippines, two areas in which library development made an impact. Libraries in government offices found financial support from the very beginning, but school libraries needed a determined and strong woman like Lois Stewart Osborn as a catalyzer. All other library developments were made possible through the initiative and effort of the American scholars and librarians who came to work for the US public service and the Filipino scholars who carried a tradition from the previous century. Government officials sought innovation through a solid public service and prioritized the establishment in 1901 of what would later be called the Scientific Library. It was designed as a component of a central laboratory to serve various bureaus and departments of the Philippine Insular Government and given the appropriation of 46,290.66 dollars for its establishment. It grew fast, was always short of shelving space, and in 1934 subscribed to 2,519 journals and contained 149,360 bound and unbound volumes, rising to 357,000 before the outbreak of World War II.

The American government's major thrust in the field of education sought to introduce democratic ideas through a modern and public educational system. The wholesale restructuring of society and its values was to be accomplished with a teaching force of around 3,700 teachers. Schools would number 4,531 in 1910, 5,944 in 1920, and 9,393 in 1948.

School teachers started working under difficult conditions and with very limited resources. The few available books were of no use to the new teachers. Aware of this need, Lois Stewart Osborn, an English teacher assigned to the provincial capital of Pampanga, started a personal campaign that culminated in the establishment of the first Philippine school library system. By 1932, there were 4,947 libraries in the public schools with a total of 2,215,796 books in their shelves. Still, standards were not the same in all the school libraries, but 30 years of work had yielded an impressive record.

Perhaps the development of a public library system was not that rewarding. Public libraries had grown intimately linked to the National Library since 1916. Reliable reports, in an effort to clarify confusing statistics, stated that the National Library in 1934, with its 15 branches and 11 travelling libraries, had 188,474 bound volumes plus pamphlets and manuscripts. In 1941, there were 18 provincial and city libraries all over the Philippines. How can we possibly compare this number with the 4,947 public school libraries of 1932? A rather meager budget for both the development of a National Library and a public library system had forced a policy of priorities. Although the Law of June 3, 1908, provided for the establishment of a Philippine Public Library, it was only intended for the development of a National Library as a repository of Philippine history and culture. In 1908, the law appropriated the sum of 3,000 pesos for the acquisition of new library materials and another 3,000 pesos for securing suitable quarters. By 1934, the annual budget had gone up to only 7,700 pesos. Necessarily, the National Library had to secure additional funding from the Insular Government, which helped increase the collection to 733,000 volumes in 1941. The National Library had built a collection, but the public library system could do very little with severely limited resources.

Nonetheless, a revolution in Philippine library culture had started. American pioneers introduced modern library standards, while Filipinos contributed with their collections, scholarly support, and leadership. The scholarly approach to libraries was a tradition in Filipino bibliophiles and scholars like Josi Artigas y Cuerva, Teodoro Kalaw, Trinidad Pardo de Tavera, Epifanio de los Santos, and others. But the foundation of Philippine librarianship was forged by Lois Osborn, Mary Polk, and James Robertson in 1914, through the establishment of library courses in the University of the Philippines and the Philippine Normal School. These courses were intended to supply new libraries with trained staff, but it was necessary to complete the formation of selected students in professional schools outside the country. Then, Lois Osborn and Mary Polk worked to obtain fellowship grants from the US government. In 1919, four fellow scholars or pensionados (Gabriel Bernardo, Eulogio Rodriguez, Cirilo Perez, and Jose Munda) left the islands to continue their studies in the University of Wisconsin. Others followed, preparing the new graduates to assume leadership in the country.

The merging of modern trends and the rise of Filipino librarians consolidated through the initiative of Trinidad Pardo de Tavera, culminating in the establishment of the Philippine Library Association (PLA) in 1923. PLA was intended to be a forum and a regulatory body, but needed some time to gain recognition and experience. The organization of the first national convention for librarians and the first national book week in 1934 set two milestones, but better communication between the private and public sectors was wanting. PLA gave priority to the need for professional librarians, funds, and library services in libraries under government control and was then unable to reach a poorly represented private sector.

The universe of the private sector comprised an expanding number of schools and universities, a few business libraries, private collections, and libraries in the houses of religious institutions. In 1941, there were 19 private colleges and universities. Their libraries had grown from small collections, managed by working students and faculty, to comprehensive holdings, maintained by trained librarians and organized according to the new trends. With a few exceptions, however, this transformation was slow. The exceptions were the University of Santo Tomas-which started offering library courses in 1932; the Ateneo de Manila-praised as one of the best organized libraries in the Philippines; the College of San Beda and a few others. Again, the problem was basic: the need for professional staff and training courses. Private school were in similar straits.

As far as we know, the libraries of the religious institutions were mostly scholarly collections, which together with their archives maintained a more traditional library organization. Private collectors, following similar patterns, emphasized rarity and curiosity. Both were managed by non professional staff.

At the conclusion of this chapter, the historical analysis shows a refreshing change of pace: librarianship is fostered by library pioneers, nurtured in library schools, and consolidated through association.

MODERN LIBRARIES FOR THE PHILIPPINE REPUBLIC

Gregorio Zaide, a qualified eyewitness of World War II in his capacity as a historian, testified: "The outbreak of World War II in the Philippines in December 1941 tolled the death-knell of almost all the rich depositories of Filipiniana materials in the country. At war's end, the Philippines became a desolate country of ruins, the ex-tent of the devastation being equalled only by the extensively-bombed city of Warsaw in Poland."

The National Library saved only 36,600 volumes out of 733,000. The Scientific Library was totally destroyed. The same fate befell the collection of the University of the Philippines, which out of 147,000 volumes recovered only 3,000, returned by borrowers after the liberation. Other government libraries, school libraries, and scholarly collections in religious houses, and in most of the private universities were also destroyed or looted. (The University of Santo Tomas was one of the few that had the great fortune of weathering the armed conflict and saving its collection.) The almost total destruction of these libraries during World War II severely depleted the country's scholarly resources and turned the second half of the century into a harrowing journey towards modernization.

The Republic of the Philippines was solemnly inaugurated in the morning of July 4, 1946. But, the newly constituted nation had to struggle for years to recover part of her historical heritage and to build up the new library institutions of today. During this half-century, libraries in the Philippines had undergone re-establishment, organization, and modernization, three stages that provide a fitting division of our analysis into historical periods.

Postwar rehabilitation posed grave problems, and libraries were among the last in the scale of priorities. Without the benefit of a clear library rehabilitation plan, the first initiatives collected books through the United States Information Service (USIS). The books distributed among the public libraries did not suit the needs of readers, but the University of the Philippines obtained three large shipments of important publications through the University of Michigan and the University of Southern California at Los Angeles.

Within the Philippine Council for US Aid (PHILCUSA), a different initiative shaped up in 1951. Statistical experts found a disorganized library, which held back the progress of rehabilitation projects. To solve the problem, the conference of 1952 proposed a plan for the improvement of library services outlined in a five-stage draft: (1) regular meetings; (2) cooperative organization and cataloguing; (3) the compilation of a union catalogue and a union list; (4) the publication of a monthly listing of combined acquisitions; and (5) cooperation with other government agencies. The implementation of this plan was assigned to a new department, the Interdepartmental Reference Service (IDRS), which spearheaded the establishment of the Association of Special Libraries of the Philippines (ASLP) in 1954. ASLP was represented by government and private libraries and established a linkage between the private and public sectors.

The implementation of rehabilitation programmes relied heavily on training and cooperation. From 1950 to 1970, the Philippines developed library training programmes and courses, completed with master's degree studies abroad, and constituted associations, cooperatives, and regulatory bodies. Schools offering library courses were usually absorbed by the academic departments of Liberal Arts and Education. As the number of universities offering library sciences courses grew, little by little professional librarians replaced non professional staff in postwar Philippine libraries. In 1961, through the creation of the Institute of Library Science in the University of the Philippines, the foremost leading and innovative educational institution in the country, the first master's-degree programme was offered in the Philippines. Soon after, other library schools followed. It is not surprising to see how the growing body of library professionals has influenced librarianship in the country, establishing or reinforcing the Philippine Library Association (PLA), the Association of Special Libraries of the Philippines (ASLP), the Philippine Association of School Libraries (PASL), the Philippine Association of Colleges and Universities (PACU), the Philippine Accrediting Association of School, Colleges and Universities (PAASCU), and others. Many of them became accrediting bodies, starting a campaign for standards, which were very much needed in a country that had suffered from natural calamities, a weak infrastructure, and the devastating effects of World War II. This on-going campaign has already yielded many fruits but still needs continued support. The latest fruit is Republic Act No. 6966, which regulates the practice of librarianship through a board examination, thereby raising the profession to public recognition and scrutiny.

Library growth and development in the Philippines has shown the profession's determined will and passion. The National Library has grown to over a million volumes from a salvaged collection of 36,600 titles, rebuilding much of the Philippine historical heritage by purchasing private collections. There are now 545 public libraries, still few for a country like the Philippines, comprising a collection of over 700,000 volumes.

The University of the Philippines System boasts of 900,000 titles in its holdings. The University of Santo Tomas has 400,000 volumes in the library of its Espana campus. Other university libraries have an average collection of 150,000 volumes, and colleges 50,000. Public and private special libraries have multiplied by the hundreds, showing good control over their resources and offering extensive and sophisticated services to their patrons. Over 200 libraries contain rare Filipiniana materials, enhanced by private collectors who have built impressive scholarly collections. Then there are thousands of private and public school libraries which, with varied holdings and standards, need close supervision by accrediting boards to ensure curriculum support.

New forms of regional and international cooperation have resulted in the involvement of libraries of government agencies in regional and international projects. Through research and information sharing, these agencies collaborate with the Association of Southeast Asian Nations (ASEAN), the Agricultural Bank for Asia (AIBA), Food and Agriculture Organization of the United Nations (FAO), United Nations Educational, Scientific, and Cultural Organization (UNESCO), and others in the process of project planning and implementation. This new phenomenon is growing fast and has inspired collaborative initiatives within the country.

Technological progress has introduced a new library trend in the Philippines: the automation of library services. Library automation is not really new (it has been available since the 1970s), but only a few libraries could afford expensive computer systems and hardware. The economic growth of the Philippines during this decade and the commercialization of computer software have prepared the ground. Special libraries were the first ones to prioritize automation in their budgets, and academic institutions have since followed. The country is still far from offering highly technical services as a whole, but the phenomenon of library automation is spreading fast and the demand for library automation systems increasing.

At the turn of the millennium, the collections and services of Philippine libraries reflect both the national identity and the country's level of technical development. Much still needs to be done. The immediate need in the Philippine Republic, as a young nation of only half a century of existence, is a supportive plan of modernization in non-urban areas, comprising training, funding, and cooperation. History speaks for itself. The enthusiasm of a few can change a country when their efforts are channelled into training, cooperation, and association. And a strong will is necessary when circumstances are most trying.

CASE STUDY: MANAGEMENT OF INFORMATION

Management Development and its Practice in Chinese Library and Information Services

Management, as a human organized activity, has been in existent e in organized society throughout all civilized history, although its systematic study as a branch of science is fairly recent. It emerges and develops along with the development of social productivity and obviously the management approaches have become more advanced and progressive to correspond with the progress of human society.

That is to say the management approaches have a very close relation with social productivity and the economic formation of society. The library as a part of the social fabric, has existed in all ages of organized society. Management approaches in business, industry and social administration have inevitably influenced library management, and 50 would the past approaches influence the recent grits. The influence between one part of the world and other parts is extremely evident in modern society because of the advanced means of transportation and communication.

According to some hooks on management, the development of management in western countries can be roughly divided into four periodis: the prescientific period (before 1800), the scientific period (1800 1927), the human-relations period (1927 50) and the synthesis period (1950 present). Library management practice has generally followed the same pattern of development, several years later than business and industry. A study of the development of management in China and in Chinese libraries has revealed that it by and large follows the same basic lines. Therefore, it would be beneficial to take a short look at the development of business and library management in western countries first before dealing with the management approaches in China in general and in Chinese library and information services in particular.

The prescientific management approach existed during the period of slavery and feudal society. The word for these periods would be autocratic. To become a manager throughout these periods one only needed authority, power and coercion. There were no human rights as we speak of today, no willing participation and cooperation between manager and the managed. The industrial revolution beginning with the invention of Watt's steam engine and the spinning Jenny promoted the development of modern industry in the eighteenth century and brought with it the first glimmer of understanding in terms of management skill.

Many principles and methodology of modern sciences were applied to problems of administration. In this context, the scientific management approach came into being. But most of the managerial concepts of the time emphasized organizational aspects, especially those relating to the production of goods. Attention was focused on production, efficiency, and the prevention of waste. Human factors were neglected. In contrast to this, the main emphasis of the human relations approach was on the individual and the informal group in the formal organization. This approach was concerned with integrating people into a work environment. The phrase "personnel administration" came into prominence at this time, and increased efforts towards democratization and staff participation were evident.

This period was a reaction against the overemphasis on productivity during the scientific management period. In order to overcome the one-sidedness of both the scientific management approach and the human relations approach, most of the effort expended in developing management thinking and concepts has, since the early 1950s, been toward refining the work started by F. W. Taylor (the scientific approach advocate) and 1,. Mayo (the human relations approach advocate) and combining elements of both with ideas from other fields such behavioural sciences. Thus management theory and practice has entered into a new stage the synthesis period. This approach pays more attention to individual ego needs besides economic and social needs for work motivation and also attaches importance to the work situation which consists of three elements: people, organization and environment. Only if all these six factors are in balance can a harmonious and pleasant work situation be achieved and increased productivity as well.

The development of library management can also be roughly divided into three basis periods, *i.e.* pre-1937, the scientific (1937-1955) and the human relations (1955 present). However, these time divisions art somewhat arbitrary, as the overlap between one period and another is very great, although there is some evidence that the periods identified do represent an effort on the part of library administrators to pick up some of the ideas coming out of the disciplines of business management and public administration.

Most libraries in the period before 1937 tended to be small. As the concern was simply to keep the libraries open, there was very little need to be concerned about costs and management. The chief librarian was expected to run the library and to make the decisions in almost all stages of its operation. Libraries had been run with a rather traditional and conservative approach. In the late 1930s, a number of changes in library services took place and in some respects there were great strides forward. Studies on cost analysis, technical services, cataloguing and use of edge cards appeared about this time.

Then people began to look seriously at some of the work done by Taylor and others to see whether or not there were sonic techniques applicable to the library, situation. After the Second World War, with the rapid development of science and technology, and the urgent needs for scientific information and education, the budgets of libraries increased as well as new library building and collections. To cope with this new situation, libraries began applying a combination of the scientific management approach of the Taylor school with some of the new mathematical operations research techniques developed during the War and began to emphasize, efficient operation. However, being administrators of non-profit making institutions they had little or no idea about how much it cost to carry Out various library activities during this period, until in the mid-

1960s computer application and systems analysis became more feasible for the library situation. The human relations school in library management came into being about 1955 and has had a continuing influence on library administration up to present time. In most libraries, human relations management means democratic administration, participative administration and involvement in the decision-making process, although there are several difficulties and problems in its practice.

More and more evidence demonstrates that the synthesis management approach is not only a theoretical concept, but a practical method employed in many libraries in recent years. As a matter of fact, no library administrator confines himself to one definite management style or school, but usually combines several styles or schools with scientific approach as the core. The Introduction of computers and modern facilities of communication and other electronic technology into libraries has had a profound effect on library management. No doubt, library management will continue to improve. Managers or administrators of libraries will have the background to make better selections from the developments in management and related fields. As this takes place the libraries should become a more basic part of the community arid a pleasant environment in which to work.

Management Development

As stated above, management development has a close relationship with social development. T. F. Mention's great contribution to social sciences is his discovery, that human society in all parts of the world has by arid large gone through the same stages of social formation. Management development in China can also be roughly divided into three basic periods as in western countries, but with some differences. The main differences are: firstly, the prescientific period is rather long in China and the approaches of that period have strong influence on the approaches which followed, because of the long history of feudal society in China and the long dominant influence of Confucianism on Chinese ideology and ethics. Secondly, China went through semi-feudal and semi-colonial society, *i.e.* a mixed social formation of feudalism and colonialism, in the last century, which makes the scientific approach in China during this period somewhat different from the western one. Thirdly, the new democratic and socialist revolution in China inevitably marked a new stage of management development in China.

As for the temporal divisions, the whole period of Chinese slavery and feudal societies is prescientific; the scientific period began with the first attempt at introducing techniques of capitalist production (called the-Westernization-Movement-initiated by comprador bureaucrats in the latter half of the nineteenth century) till the founding of the People's Republic in 1949. Then began a new approach of socialist scientific management which is a different concept, but somewhat similar to human relations or synthesis approaches, and is the one that still needs to be developed and perfected.

Being one of the most ancient civilized countries in the world, China was outstanding in administering state affairs, organizing military operations and managing great projects such as the Great Wall and the Grand Canal in ancient times. Administrative affairs were systematized arid regularized as early as Xia Dynasty, (21-16th century, BC.) according to historical recordings. During the periods called the Spring and Autumn, and Waring States (770-221 BC), there was a period of time called the "Contention of a Hundred Schools of Tought Of, these schools, Legalists and Confucianists were in a dominant position and had a strong influence alternatively on the approaches of state administration.

Legalists advocated reform and-"ruling by law". Qin Xiao Gong, the Duke of the State of Qin appointed legalists as his senior officials and carried out reform. Very soon, his state became stronger than the other states and finally defeated all of them. In the end, the whole of China was reunited by his grandson Qin Shi Huang, the noted first emperor of the Qin Dynasty in 221. Confucianists advocated "Following the previous kings' practice" which was rather conservative. Because of the needs to consolidate the centralized feudal monarchy, Emperor Wu of the Han Dynasty (206BC-AD220) implemented a policy of "Banning the other schools of thought and solely esteeming Confucianism". Since then, Confucianism dominated Chinese ideology for about two thousand years. The doctrine of obedience and loyalty to superiors benefited the ruling classes, but hampered people's initiative and creativity and fettered the productive forces. That is the reason why China could not move from a feudal society to a capitalist society in modern history, though the seeds of capitalism emerged long before they did in western countries, *i.e.* the thirteenth century, at the end of the Yuan Dynasty and the beginning of the Ming Dynasty. Autocracy in tile feudal society of China was so strong that even successive peasant uprisings could not shake its foundation until the invasion of foreign imperialism in the last century.

The repeated defeats in the wars between feudal China and foreign aggressors completely exposed the corrupt nature of the Qing Dynasty. These events on the one hand promoted the Reform Movement within the ruling classes and bourgeois democratic revolution of the people, and on the other hand introduced the ways and techniques of capitalist production and management. The rising of comprador-bureaucratic capitalism and the presence of foreign capitalism turned feudal China into a semi-feudal and semi-colonial country politically and economically. Management approaches in industry and business in this period were, in the main, scientific ones, but more autocratic. Workers had to work long hours, for low wages and in poor working conditions. Management in some enterprises during this period still relied heavily on coercion.

In discussing management in new China, two facts that make the nature of management differ from the western one must be noted. One is that China had abolished feudalism through land reform and later, capitalism through socialist transformation. All land, natural resources and means of production now belong to the people. Another fact is that the working people are politically masters of their own country. The principle of "cadre participation in collective productive labour and worker participation in management" ensures their position in production being equal to that of managers. Most of them work conscientiously and enthusiastically. This was especially true during the 1950s when planning, efficiency and economic results, in a sense, were emphasized, while labour emulation and voluntary labour were also encouraged. People were motivated mainly by spiritual reward in the early years. The participation in decision making. and the supervision over the management by workers are the striking characteristics of socialist management.

In the early 1950s, China stood politically on the side of the Soviet Union and learnt economically from the Russian. To some extent, China just copied the Soviet model in management as in other fields, which did not quite accord with China's real situation in many respects. It is wise for any country to learn from others' experiences and apply them in a creative way so as to develop her own. The "Charter of the Anshan Iron and Steel Company" was a systematic and comprehensive set of management regulations in industry stipulated by China in the early 1960s, which was then summarized into "70 Regulations" called Management Regulations for Industries, Mines and Enterprises-. Unfortunately, these regulations, influenced by left political idea had several defects. For example, while exaggerating the situation of class struggle in socialist society and overemphasizing the importance of mass movement in industry, scientific rules and methods were not respected adequately.

The authorities concerned were simply after a high production quota, high output and quantity, while quality, efficiency, cost unit, economic results and the law of value were overlooked. That is what people usually called "too much enthusiasm and too little scientific consideration". However, for many years since the early 1950s, Sun Yefang, the former director of the Institute of Economics of the Academy of Social Sciences and a noted economist, has established a series of socialist economic principles in management in the context of China, such as those on achieving maximum economic results with minimum labour consumption; on paying attention to the law of value and profits in a planned economy; on enlarging enterprises' rights of management; and on the correct application of economic levers and raising the position of profit in management. His theories divined correctly that the mechanical copying of the Soviet model and the "left" deviation policies would do no good to Chinese economy. Unfortunately, Sun's theories were not accepted by the former authorities, and instead, he was criticized and accused of being revisionist just at that time, scientific laws and economic rules were not fully observed and people's socialist enthusiasm was abused, thus causing two great setbacks during 1959-61 and 1966-76 in economic construction.

The penalty for that is heavy: the huge waste of time, natural resources and human energy, especially the people's enthusiasm. The most successful enterprise in the early 1960s was Daquing Oil Field which was regarded as an example of scientific management in industry by the whole of China for many years. One of its management principles, the system of personal responsibility, is still adopted by all factories.

In recent years, things have been changing a lot. Scientific management is reemphasized in addition to economic system reform and technical transformation. Efficiency and economic results are again the vital norms for evaluating the success of a unit's management. People's material interests are linked with production. They are encouraged to do more work, get more pay and be well off before others. Since individual interests have a lot to do with the interests of the units, every one is very much concerned with what is going on in his units and has a great say in decision making. Equalitarianism is rejected in the salary system nowadays. Instead, differentials are established according to kind of work and the quantity and quality of work done, and thus the socialist principle of product distribution, *i.e.*

"from each according to his ability, to each according to his work", is really carried out. People are thereby motivated and inspired, and the relations between the managed and managers, and among colleagues and follow workers, are thus improved. On the other hand, each production unit has more rights of self-management. That is to say it is more independent than it was, and assumes sole responsibility for its own profits and losses, which directly concern the income of both managers and staff. Under this situation, the initiative and enthusiasm of the people are brought into full play and thereby productivity is raised and output increased. China is now experiencing a period of transformation through which some defects in the existing system will be overcome and some new approaches suitable to China's specific condition will be found on the basis of other management approaches for her modernization. Library and information services, as part of society, are sure to apply some of the principles of industry and business management to their own management, with some modifications in order to suit their own needs.

Library Management

The existence of libraries in China can be traced back as far as the Shang Dynasty (1600-1100 BC). Although China has been noted for her prosperous imperial and private libraries for thousands of years, the main function of these early libraries was to collect and keep books, as in other countries. The use of these libraries was restricted to imperial families, senior officials and noted scholars, not for the general public. However, the prosperity of Shu Yuan (academy) libraries and private libraries in the Ming (AD 1368-1644) and especially the Qing Dynasty (AD 1644-1911) played an important role in spreading literacy and knowledge and in preserving rare editions of ancient books. The former libraries were designated only for the reference use of teachers and students. Books could not be taken out of the library premises.

The latter were merely for book collection, but sometimes could be consulted by friends and noted scholars. These collectors were usually bibliographers or experts on textual criticism, examination and correction and were sometimes also book publishers. Book lending was generally impossible. Because of the relatively small size of most private libraries, almost all operations could be done by one person. A few private libraries such as the Tian Yi Ge and the Xi Gu Ge which had existed for several hundred years, had very, large collections by the standards of those years. For example, the Tian Yi Ge had 70000 volumes and the Xi Gu Ge 84000 volumes. Unfortunately, war, damage and financial problems made the existence of these libraries very difficult in old China. Finally, all of them were taken over by the state. There are few records about the management of imperial libraries, and yet the development of Chinese classification such as the *Si Bu Fa* (the Four Division Classification Scheme), the compilation of large encyclopaedia such as the *Yong Le Da Dian*, and national bibliographies such as the *Si Ku Quan Shu* in feudal China indicate certain success in managing these libraries.

Modern libraries in China began with the establishment of the first public library in Wuhan, Hubei Province and especially the founding of the Metropolitan Library, now the Beijing National Library, in 1910. The transition from traditional library functions to modern ones took place thereafter. The main trends during this period are as follows:

1. The functions of the library were no longer merely for collecting and keeping but also for using books.
2. Libraries were gradually used by everyone and not only by the privileged few.
3. The collection of books on modern sciences and technology rather than the Chinese classics was stressed.
4. Better service and satisfaction for users were required.
5. Books were no longer classified by languages but by subjects.
6. More attention was paid to the division of work and specialization as well as professional training in management.

The open shelf system was popular in many libraries. Book from catalogues were replaced by catalogue cards. Modern decimal classification, *i.e.* Dewey's scheme was introduced to replace the traditional Chinese *Si Bu Fa*, which was no longer suitable for modern scientific and technical literatures. Library science was also introduced into China and studied during this period. Many noted scholars and librarians made great contributions to the development of librarianship and library services in old China. For example, Professor LI Dazhao, one of the earliest propagators of Marxism-Leninism in China, was the former director of Beijing University Library from 1918 to 1922. He strongly advocated that the library should not be a book storage, but a place for research, and education; a librarian should not be a book keeper, but a researcher and instructor; the library should open to the labouring class free of charge. He took a lead in introducing open shelves in his library for the convenience of students. For this purpose, he changed shelving from traditional dictionary form, or alphabetical order into subject classification and organized catalogue cards of books in western languages by following Dewey's classification. He also paid great attention to statistics in order to improve the quality of service and satisfy the users needs.

Tile great contributions of the Beijing National Library to tile culture of modern China lies in its effort and success in collecting, preserving and sorting out Chinese classics, rare editions of ancient books and important documents, and in building a large collection of scientific and technical literatures in foreign languages, despite foreign aggression, civil wars, disasters and the corruption of previous governments. As for management during this period, it was mainly traditional.

Library Management

Library services in new China have expanded rapidly in the last thirty years and a national network has been formed. Now, there are already about 20000 libraries of various types with more than 100000 staff. Take the public library and the university library as examples. By 1981, there were 1731 public libraries above county level with a staff of 19641 and 670 university libraries with a staff of 17000. Both types of libraries have total collections of about 190 million volumes. By comparison in 1956 there were only 96 public libraries above county level, with 3714 staff and 28-9 million volumes and 212 university libraries with 3568 staff and 37-28 million volumes.

The Administrative Bureau for Library Services at the Ministry of Culture, a central agency for the planning and coordinating library development of all types, was set up in 1981 to suit the new situation brought about by the modernization drive in China. Furthermore, each type of library has a central unit for coordinating its activities, *e.g.* the Beijing National Library for public libraries. The Academy of Sciences Library for science libraries, and the Ministry of Education for university libraries. The expansion of library services in China demonstrates that libraries have played an important role in economic construction and education and are already an indispensable part of society.

At the same time, Chinese librarians have gained some experience in library management and made some progress in the study of librarianship. For instance, the central authorities concerned have in the last two years sponsored a number of conferences, at which several working regulations have been formulated or revised respectively for public libraries, science libraries and university libraries in order to improve working efficiency and the quality of service. Another important event is the promulgation by the state Council in 1981 of "The

Temporary Provisions of Professional Titles for Library, Archive and Information Personnel", which is of tremendous significance for improving personnel management and inspiring stair enthusiasm.

Standardization of documentation is the key link for library management. Since its founding in 1979, the National Documentation Standardization Technical Committee of China has done a lot in this field. It has sponsored several workshops in cooperation with the China Society of Library Science and the China Society of Scientific and Technical Information to examine "The National Standard Entries for Cataloguing" prepared by the Standardization Group of Beijing National Library, "The Abstract and Title-list Entry Formats for Retrieval journals" prepared by ISTIC, and suggest the use of "The Classification Scheme for Chinese Libraries" (including both the detailed version of the-Classification Scheme for Documents" and the simplified version) and of-The Chinese Thesaurus".

This Committee also worked out-Tape Formats for Catalogue Information Exchange",-Name Codes for Nations and Regions", "Sex Codes for People", "The Codes for Administrative Regions of PRC" and-The Standardized Codes of Chinese Characters for Information Exchange". The latter two, already Chinese National Standards, are being prepared for submission to ISO/TC97/SC2 for approval as international Standards. Research in information methodology, and in the theory and practice of library science were started years ago. There is a Section for Information Methodology in ISTIC and 12 research groups under the China Society of Library Science including those for research in fundamental theory, bibliography, classification, cataloguing, reader service, staff training, rare and ancient books, standardization, information: services, children's library and foreign library work. Some progress has been made in recent years. Scientific management, efficiency and economic results and the application of computers in libraries and information institutes are also receiving great attention and sonic initial successes have been achieved in these respects.

In summing up past experiences and lessons, library services in China have suffered setbacks twice during the last thirty years. One was in the years of so-called "Great Leap Forward", another in the "Cultural Revolution". Both were caused by the trend of neglecting scientific management as in industry and by the influence of a depressed economy as well. There is not a slightest doubt that scientific management in China is as important as in any other country. As everybody knows, the fact that the rapid advance of science and technology produces large amounts of documents, makes it more difficult for librarians to select, collect, process, store and report, and for users to access them quickly and precisely. Only scientific management and scientific methods in addition to modern facilities can solve this problem to some extent.

The library itself is an integrated system consisting of different functional departments doing different jobs. The coordination and cooperation between departments and jobs, and the contact between the library and users are essential for a library to fulfil its social functions or to attain its objectives; and the library services or library undertaking in this country as a whole, including different types of libraries, also from an integrated system. Centralized planning with overall consideration for healthy development, rational geographic distribution, and effective cooperation among different or same types of libraries demands the introduction of scientific ways to analyse the needs and possibilities of the economic situation as important basis for allocating funds and facilities.

From a long term point of view, it is imperative for a nation like China with so large a territory and the biggest population in the world, to establish a retrieval network which includes data bases, communication systems and terminal facilities in order that a quick and precise service can be offered to users, as in the United Kingdom and the United States. This is the aim of the modernization of the Chinese library and information services. But first of all, they must be well managed. Without good management, any resource cannot be given full play, no matter how intelligent the staff, how advanced the facilities and how large the collections.

Owing to the fact that some Chinese librarians are fully aware of their weakness and the importance of scientific management in libraries, they have been vigorously committing themselves to the study of its theory and practice in recent years. A number of seminars have been held to discuss its definition and principles, especially in the Chinese situation. Here is a-definition of scientific management based on recent discussion. It is defined as "giving full play to manpower, material and financial resources in order to raise operational efficiency and the quality of services by applying the principles and methods of modern science and technology and observing the objective laws of librarianship, for the purpose of achieving optimum social results of services". This definition includes two concepts: efficiency and the social results of service.

As a matter of fact the first one is the means and methods, the second is the objective of scientific management or the objective of library services. There is a controversy about the measurement of efficiency and social results. In fact, the measurement of efficiency is possible for most of library work, *e.g.* the repetitive and mechanical routines such as ordering, cataloguing, cards filing, binding, circulation and shelving. But social results are more difficult to measure. The satisfaction of users and the application of new technology or the improvement of education and culture in localities may be generally regarded as social results of library services. Cost and profit cannot generally be taken as criteria to measure the performance of libraries as they are for business, but these factors must be taken into consideration for good management.

As far as scientific management itself is concerned, this means good planning, rationalization and standardization of library work and documentation It also involves highly organized activities relating to administrative, professional, personnel and equipment management, such as planning, organizing, stalling, budgeting and directing.

Scientific management in Chinese libraries and information services is ideally characterized by the following principles.

(1) *The Principle of Centralization and Unification:* China is a country with a planned economy. The development of her industry, agriculture and all other public services is carried out in a planned way. Therefore, the expansion of library and information services in this country cannot go beyond the ability or remain behind the needs of her

economy. It is necessary to give overall consideration to the priority and geographic distribution of different libraries in order to make the best use of limited resources such as funds, manpower and facilities, to organize a rational national network and technically to realize standardization and unification of library work and documentation such as classification, cataloguing and automation for sharing resources nationwide.

(2) *The Principle of Democracy:* Staff and some users expect to be asked to speak their views or make suggestions in the process of policy making, decision making and planning. There are two ways to do so in practice. The authorities make the draft or outline of a plan first, and then consult staff and sometimes users. This way is called "From top to bottom". Otherwise, staff and sometimes users, are asked to discuss first. Then, the authorities concerned summarize their suggestions and ideas as a basis for drawing up their plan or making decision. This is called the "from bottom to top" method in policy making. Sometimes, these processes go through several times from top to bottom or from bottom to top before a decision is made if it is not urgent. Moreover, staff and users are encouraged to make complaints or suggestions at any time in the process of carrying out of a plan or a policy in order to correct unexpected errors and mistakes because of the changing situation or carelessness when making this plan and policy. Democratic management helps the authorities overcome subjectivism and bureaucracy and inspires staff enthusiasm, initiative and creativity because their personality and opinions are respected. In addition, problems can be found and solved in a timely way. Relations between management and stair are improved and the ties between library, users and society at large are thereby strengthened.

(3) *The Principle of Economic Results:* Unlike business, libraries are non-profit-making institutions. It is difficult to measure their economic results in the from of unit cost and profit. However, it is possible for libraries to use their funds as economically its possible, assign staff

tasks as rationally as possible and utilize facilities as effectively as possible. It is also possible to establish a series of optimum systems fur literature collection, storage and service, and to formulate some rules and regulations that serve the needs of these systems with the aim of costing less money to get more documents that users need most, taking less people and time to process more documents and providing users with better service. The waste of human energy, money, time and material resources is incompatible with the principles of scientific management and must be lessened or totally avoided if possible.

(4) *The System of Personal Responsibility:* The social functions and relations of library with society were never so important as they are today. Society supports libraries, libraries serve society. The quality of library services directly affects both users and the whole of society. Conversely, social needs or users' needs also promote library services. Therefore, elaborate division of labour, and frequent contact and mutual dependence between departments are very important in order to offer a better service to society. Jobs in each department and in each link of an operation must be done well. That means that everyone must be sensible of his responsibility and get his or her job done on time, in the required quantity and quality. This responsibility system, like the one used in business provides standard to assess the performance of staff and the departments and enhances their sense of responsibility in work. A better management and service can thus be achieved in the end.

The above principles are general guides or aims to be sought for better management in library and information services. As for tire present situation so far, it is not quite the case yet. There are still a lot of things to do before reaching these aims.

Some Suggestions for Improvement of Chinese Library Services

In comparison with other countries, planning and management in Chinese library services do have some strong points, but on the whole, the managerial level is relatively low as it is in industry and for the same reasons. Some factors which affect the efficiency of library services should be improved in order to serve the information and education needs of this country and at the same time modernized library services themselves.

(1) *Geographic Distribution:* For historical reasons, there are more libraries providing better services in big cities and economically developed areas than that in rural and remote areas. It is incredible that some counties even have no library services at all. Irrational distribution of libraries is of course a common problem in many other countries, and it was riot so urgent to solve this problem some years back in China because the needs for information and education in rural and remote areas were very small. Things are quite different nowadays. The new economic policies for industry and especially for agriculture, stimulate economic development in these areas. People are becoming well off and want to learn. Small rural factories need information for technical transformation and innovation in order to increase the quantity and improve the quality of products or change the line of their products to some which may be more profitable. Peasants need information and knowledge for scientific farming. Scientific and technical books and other materials are in great demand and hard to get in many rural areas. People call this situation "science fever" which could riot be seen before. It is reported that many peasants invited experts from their neighbouring areas or professors from colleges to transfer technology, or attended technical seminars and "technical fairs" themselves sponsored by local authorities. From a long term viewpoint, perhaps, the more effective and economical way to satisfy the information and education needs in rural areas is to improve library services. The general accepted LA standards for the provision of branch libraries are that: a population of under 1500 in a catchment area is usually better served by a mobile library; an isolated population of over 1500 normally needs a trailer library, sub-branch

or branch library; in urban areas a branch should be provided in each major shopping centre. China is unable to reach these standards at present, but can do her best to improve the county central library service and at the same time to provide branch libraries in most districts and sub-branches, or mobile libraries or reading rooms of some sort at some town level grass roots. Agriculture is of vital importance in China's economy, arid about 80% of her population are peasants living in rural areas. No one in China can afford to neglect their demand if he wishes to see agriculture well developed and enough food to feed the 1000 million people or to tap the resources in remote areas. The provision of library services must be taken into consideration by the local leadership in those areas where there are still no such services, when planning overall development in their localities. The central library authorities, on the other hand should urge the local authorities to give enough financial arid manpower support to the establishment of library services.

(2) *Regional Cooperation:* Organizationally, China has already had a national library network consisting of different types of libraries. The problem is that these libraries lack close cooperation with information services, between different or even similar types of libraries, especially on a regional scale. The tasks of information services in China's situation differ from that of library services in some respects, and each type of library has its own tasks and objectives. However, their cooperation on a regional scale is very important to improve the efficiency arid quality of services and to utilize resources in a more economical way. The United Kingdom arid some other countries have set some examples in library cooperation. Their experience is helpful for China in projecting regional networks and cooperation with Beijing National Library and ISTIC as backups like the British Library's position and functions in Britain. Regional cooperation including acquisition, cataloguing, staff training and resources sharing between libraries and information services would be organized, with

provincial arid county public libraries arid local information institutes as centres. Some libraries, for instance university libraries, may have their own cooperation, like those in Changsha, Hunan Province in recent years. It should be emphasized that for a country with the biggest population in the world, regional and local networks arid cooperation in China are more important than in any other countries. Users should first rely, on their local libraries, then central libraries in this region. National centres are the last resort. Therefore, the collection of regional central libraries should be relatively large and comprehensive according to local conditions and needs, and regional union catalogues containing holdings of the participating libraries should be prepared for this purpose and for avoiding duplication of labour. Regional cooperation is the infrastructure of national cooperation and the basis of library modernization. China should exert much effort in the establishment of regional cooperation in order to make the best use of her resources and to modernize her library services.

(3) *National Referral Services:* On the basis of regional library cooperation and regional information networks which already exist, two national referral centres should be established according to the actual existing situation: one mainly for monographs on social sciences and natural sciences as well in the Beijing National Library and one mainly for scientific and technical serials in ISTIC in order to improve the exploitation of existing resources nationwide. In doing that, the preparation of the national bibliography, catalogues of different types of literature and regional union catalogues should be hastened. Abstracts and indexes, other retrieval and reference books and directories published at home and abroad should be collected as comprehensively, as possible. At present, referral services are offered only, by mail or by personal visits. It is quite possible technically and economically, now for China to carry out these services by, direct telephone and ISTI links with big libraries and local information institutes. When conditions are

ripe, these two centres will be national data bases for automatic retrieval equipped with computers linked through telecommunication systems with terminals all over the country. It is recommended that the centre in ISTIC also provide a business information service for the needs of foreign trade and economic cooperation with foreign companies. Local information centres should provide local product arid market information. For tins purpose, market research reports, company cards, trade and professional directories, trade and business journals from major developed countries and business publications published at home should be collected, and specialists for guiding the use of these publications should be trained.

(4) *Open Access and Opening Hours:* Because of management problem and the fear of the loss of books, open access is still not popular in most libraries and information institutes except for periodicals, newspapers and children's books. Experiences have repeatedly proved that open access is the best way to facilitate users' needs and exploit literature resources. Rare books, valuable editions and manuscripts and some other materials are not suitable for open shelves. Open access to standard materials, patent literature and trade literature has been carried out in ISTIC libraries in recent years. Monographs and technical proceedings, research reports in big libraries such as Beijing National Library and ISTIC are difficult for open access, because the shelving is arranged by accession numbers or serial numbers, riot by subjects for saving the trouble of reshelving resulting from the huge daily intake of publications. Nevertheless, this call be done in medium and small size libraries, especially ill university libraries, school libraries and local public libraries.

As for opening hours, the internationally accepted standards for urban main libraries are 60 hours per week; for branch libraries 18-60 hours per week. Urban libraries and information institute libraries in China open only eight hours a day, 48 hours per week. No services are available on Sundays and national holidays.

Children's libraries arid rural libraries usually open on Sundays. It is recommended that science libraries and urban public libraries with science open 10 hours a day, 60 hours per week. Opening hours for information documentation centres and university libraries may be longer depending on the users' real needs, and if possible, board and accommodation should be provided for those who cannot get home on the day of a visit. ISTIC Chongqing Branch Library has offered this service for several years. Other libraries should do the same if necessary and conditions permit.

(5) *Publicily and Users' Survey:* Besides reporting Journals, exhibitions arid lectures, guides and pamphlets about each kind of service and how to gain access to them and other information should be published in libraries and information centres. This is not only for the convenience of the users, but would also save much trouble for the staff and as a result, would save time for both users and stall'. Publicity relating to user service is a weak point ill Chinese library arid information services. Most libraries do not even have a sheet of printed material for presentation to users and foreign visitors. Compare this with some other countries where libraries, even smaller ones, provide various types of pamphlets free of charge explaining their services and holdings. The results are good. Users feel quite at home, especially fresh visitors and timid users who are not confident about what to do. Publicity is very important in user services arid each library should have someone in charge of this work.

Surveys and investigations on users' needs and the level of satisfaction by existing services should be carried out regularly by specialists ill order to improve the quality of services. Little has been done about this to date in most Chinese libraries and information centres. This kind of survey is very necessary and should he done by various means such as telephone, questionnaires, individual correspondence or even personal interview. When this is done, library policies and plans will be built on a more realistic foundation. Better services can then be achieved.

(6) *Library Education:* The fact that China lacks qualified librarians is serious, especially in local libraries. This situation can perhaps be illustrated by the following statistics. Among 100000 library staff in 20000 libraries, only 3000 graduates were from the Departments of Library Science of Beijing University and Wuhan University and another 1500 persons had received correspondence courses by the end of 1980 since 1949. This figure accounts for a very small proportion of the total staff, not more than 5% on the average even in university and science libraries and public libraries above provincial level. Eighty-one percent of the stair began working in libraries just during or after the "Cultural Revolution" (1966-76). Eighty percent among them only had middle school education. On the other hand, quite a few technicians and research workers do not quite know how to use the library to search for documents. Of course, many staff can become professionals by training and working practice, and users get familiar with the use of the library by frequent visits or by the guidance of the staff. However, the lack of systematic library education and training for the stair would inevitably affect the efficiency of operation and the quality of services and for the users, the effective search for useful documents and literatures or other materials for the purpose of reference and education or entertainment.

Happily, the central authorities have done something to change this situation in recent years. For example, there are already 19 universities and colleges having departments or specialities of library and archive studies. Wuhan University even has a speciality of information science in the Department of Library Science. Correspondence courses continue to be given to some stair. On-the-job and off-the-job training in Beijing National Library, ISTIC and other big libraries has been continuous except during the. years of "Cultural Revolution". The guide for users was improved recently.

This is really encouraging, but not enough for a country like China with so many libraries and staff. A radical solution to this problem would be to enhance library education. It is recommended firstly that one or two colleges of library and information science be set up for undergraduates as well as postgraduates to do research in order to supply libraries and information institutes with qualified librarians and staff and to raise the academic level of librarianship and information science. Secondly, all college and university undergraduates, science undergraduates in particular, should be given library and courses in order to make them ready to use library and information services when they become users, especially after graduation.

(7) *Personnel Management:* For librarians and library stair, as part of the Chinese intellectual stratum, their social position was low, and their labour was not fully understood by society sometimes in the past. Things are getting much better now, their contributions to society are generally acknowledged and appreciated by both people and government. However, present personnel management is not conducive to bringing stair initiative and creativity into full play. Most stair are not quite satisfied with the existing cadre system, promotion and salary systems. For example, officially there are four conditions for stair promotion and salary increment: education, length of service and experience, professional ability and contribution or performance. Generally speaking, it sounds good. In fact it is very complicated to implement. Most leaders used to emphasize the second one, *i.e.* the length of service and experience, because it is easy to measure and saves labour and argument. This "iron rice bowl" (job security) and "big pot rice" (equalitarianism) system are accepted by many people because the assessment system for stair performance is far from perfect. For quite a long time, "be red and expert" was supposed to be the lofty realm of accomplishment and the only standard for a perfect librarian, as for other intellectuals. Actually, "be red" was always overemphasized and distorted while "be

expert" neglected or even criticized. Today, this slogan is given some new meanings and some more concrete standards are adopted for evaluating the performance of stair.

Following the reform in economic areas, a reform is abcut to be carried in libraries and information institutes. In the context of library and information services, this reform should, firstly, change step by step the life-tenure system of leadership into an election system, at least partly, so that more younger professionals may have the opportunity to play their parts and make their contributions in management positions. Non-professionals and aged leaders should conscientiously give up their posts to younger ones for the interest of the country. Secondly, the state assignment system should, at least partly, be replaced by a recruitment system so that the quality of staff can be controlled. Their specialities can thus be matched to the job and more willingness they will give to their assignments thereby. Thirdly, working regulations and the personnel assessment system should be improved and perfected. For instance, the following factors should be considered in personnel assessment: professional knowledge, professional skill, managerial ability, working attitude, service quality and achievement. Quality of service and achievement or working results would be always put into first place so as to encourage people to work hard and learn well. This assessment should be done in some cases by examinations, or by colleague appraisal with reference to work records. The appraisal of the leading person which in most cases is crucial and decisive should be. as fair and impartial as possible without personal prejudice and discrimination. Proper material and spiritual reward is necessary for those who have good performances. When this is done, staff enthusiasm will be inspired and no or less complaints will be found then.

(8) *A Library Act:* Many countries in the world have formulated library acts and practised them for many years. China does not yet have one. The history of library development has proved that it library act is

very necessary and important for the healthy development and the perfection of library services. China should by all means have a library act to stipulate legislatively the principles, social functions, financial sources, scope of activities and the forms of services of libraries; the natures and functions of the library committee and the system of leadership and administration and their tasks so that library position and development can be guaranteed by law. For instance, library services in China were always the first ones to have their funds cut and the last ones to have their funds increased in the past. Some local governments never allocate enough funds for local libraries. This situation would not have happened if there had been a library act, or at least things would not have been so bad.

The implementation of a library act, on the other hand, reflects government concern about people's welfare and their rights to enjoy education and entertainment. It also reflects the level of the development of library services of a country.

Conclusion

China is very aware of her current weaknesses in management both in industry and in library and information services. The existing management systems do not quite fit the new Situation created by the modernization drive. The current reform of economic systems and technical transformation, the new economic policies at home and the open-door policies towards the outside world require it reform in management systems and a lot of managers with both theoretical background and practical experience of management.

Just for this end, 1-6 out of 7 million leading cadres, managers and technicians in industrial and communication departments have received management training during the past three years, which includes economic policies, basic economic theories and fundamental techniques of business management. In addition, the China Society of Management was set up, the *Journal of Management* has appeared and a number of academic conferences on management were held during the same period. Considerable attention is also being devoted to foreign management techniques. While sending some people to study abroad, an industrial, scientific and technical training centre was jointly inaugurated in 1980 by China and the United States in Dalian, Northeast China.

Many leading cadres of libraries and information institutes have been trained at this centre. These training programmes will help library and information services improve management techniques, raise the quality of service to society, and provide a major impetus to the modernization of library and information services as well as to the nation.

2

The Crisis of Democracy and the Public Library

Public libraries account for a miniscule portion of government expenditures and are the first to be cut when budgets fall short. Government policymakers view public libraries as a dispensable supplement to the public school system, an inessential social service for the unemployed, or even as frivolous entertainment at public expense. So why should we care if barbarians crash the gates of the public library? Of what great significance to the state and its public would that be?

The answer is that government policymakers have missed the most important function of a public library, which is to promote and sustain the knowledge and values necessary for a democratic civilization. Conversely, the condition of public libraries may be taken as a litmus test for the state of democratic civilization. Any threat to the core values of a democratic civilization will be reflected in the state of its public libraries; and, any threat to public libraries will weaken democracy.

The main body of this work is occupied with an analysis of postmodern consumer capitalism and its effects on democratic civilization. We will find that postmodern consumer capitalism threatens the public sphere of rational discourse and that the healthy functioning of this sphere is essential to democracy. Postmodern consumer capitalism transforms discourse into a private consumer product and as such reduces knowledge to mere information or entertainment. But since public libraries play such an important role in maintaining the public sphere of rational discourse I have framed my analysis of postmodern consumer capitalism with a discussion about the public library.

The public library may be like the proverbial canary in the mine—the first to go when the air is poisoned. It is uniquely positioned to feel the effects of a declining democratic civilization; and it is the first to go when knowledge gets reduced to information and entertainment.

In March of 1998 the American Library Association (ALA) published an article by Steve Coffman in which he proposed that public libraries be run like corporate chain bookstores. The following issue of the ALA's magazine American Libraries hosted a large number of letters from librarians who objected to Coffman's proposal that libraries be run like bookstores. The author of one letter explained that a library is "a democratic, egalitarian centre" that "provides a wide spectrum of information to anyone who wants it, regardless of their background." A bookstore, on the other hand, "has no mission, morality, vision, or even stake in the community; its only purpose is to get middle-class people to spend money."

Several years later Coffman's article looks more like a forecast or description of trends affecting public libraries than a radical proposal for change. Some libraries are already moving in the direction of imitating the organizational and procedural structure of corporate chain bookstores. The chain bookstores don't hire librarians. They hire low-paid clerks to help patrons fetch books. There is no reference service. Book ordering is centralized and automated. There is no discrimination between "good" literature and "bad" literature; there is no mission to serve the public good; there is no mission to promote democracy or education; the sole criterion for selecting books is sales/circulation. The most extreme example of this trend may be the branch libraries of east London which have been renamed "Idea Stores" (Lane, 2003; Ezard, 2003). The Idea Stores employ supervisors and customer service representatives, but no librarians. There are cafes near the entrance to each Idea Store but no reference service is available. Corporate designers and advertising agencies seek to draw "customers" into the Idea Stores by creating an appealing brand image. "The project—described as retail-inspired—is based on the conviction that 'in our increasingly retail-focused and lifestyle-conscious world' commerce is now the ruling influence on the lives of younger people. This group, it is felt, is far more likely to borrow books or use educational services if the ambience reminds them of a superstore or, as with the colours and signs at Bow, the departure lounge at Gatwick airport." (Ezard, 2003). In the United States, the public library system of Riverside County, serving a million people in California, was turned over to a private contractor in 1997 (Hanley, 1998: B6). The mayor of Jersey City's attempt to privatize his city's public library was beaten back by librarians and public spirited citizens in 1998, as was the Hawaii State Library's attempt to outsource book selection to Baker & Taylor in 1997 (Hanley, 1998). But GATS (General Agreement on Trade in Services) and the WTO could some day require all of the world's public libraries to privatize in the interest of neoliberal market reforms (Rikowski, 2003).

How did we get to the point of having libraries without librarians? How did we lose the 'public' in 'public library'? And why should we care? To answer these questions we will have to delve into the history of libraries and librarianship as well as explore larger trends in politics and the economy. We will need to think about the mission of a public library and what distinguishes it in a fundamental and essential way from a private market business. We will need to think about the difference between entertainment and education, pandering and edification, a market economy and democracy. What we will find is that democracy, civil education and the public good are the three pillars supporting the public library. Postmodern consumer capitalism threatens all three and with them the institution of the public library.

DEMOCRACY AND PROFESSIONAL LIBRARIANSHIP

In a recently published history of libraries, Battles (2003) explains that prior to the nineteenth century libraries were by necessity limited to a small collection of classics because, in spite of the invention of the printing press, books remained difficult and expensive to produce. Book selection was therefore a simple process, since there was little to choose from, and it constituted a small part of librarianship. With the development of the mechanical mass production of books in the nineteenth century librarians were for the first time faced with the task of deciding which books from among the thousands produced they should add to their collections.

Most of the first generation of public librarians were concerned about the flood of trashy popular literature made possible by mechanical mass production in the nineteenth century. They conceived their role to be "gatekeepers" of the culture and defenders of such public goods as democracy, education, and morality. Some wanted to separate the wheat from the chaff and maintain a collection of great works. Others were willing to allow works of lesser value into their collections in the interest of providing their patrons with the first rung on a ladder of development that ascended toward the classics of western civilization. In either case, librarians maintained a collection of great works and understood their role to be that of educators who serve the public good.

Although Melvil Dewey accepted the same Victorian values as his colleagues, he did not believe that librarians should have the authority to instill those values in their patrons by directing their reading. Dewey's primary contribution to librarianship was to improve the efficiency of libraries by adopting the techniques and strategies of mass production in factories. One such technique was standardization. Another was to dumb down skilled workers. Just as scientific management in factories dumbed down skilled craftsmen by putting all intelligent decision making into the hands of managers and turning workers into virtual automatons (such as Charlie Chaplin parodied in the classic film Modern Times), Dewey dumbed down professional librarians.

Dewey was no pioneer in women's rights, in spite of admitting women to the school of library science at Columbia. On the contrary, according to Battles (2003: 144), Dewey used the hiring of women in libraries to define the profession down. Since women in Victorian society were generally subordinate to men and lacked professional autonomy, by installing women in libraries Dewey hoped not to raise the status of women but to lower the status of librarians. By installing women in libraries Dewey wished to insure that librarians would defer to male professionals such as himself. For Dewey the role of librarians was akin to that of factory workers. Their role was to execute a mechanical work process in the most efficient manner possible, as determined by their managers and other experts, not to design or direct that process. The role of librarians was to get books into the hands of their patrons as efficiently as possible by following Dewey's scientifically designed work procedures. As mere technical functionaries Dewey did not believe that librarians should have the authority to direct the reading of their patrons by selecting books they deemed best.

The Carnegie Corporation, which funded so many of America's first public libraries, had a similar view of the role of librarians. Andrew Carnegie himself shared the prevailing moral views of his age. In his 1889 essay "Wealth" Carnegie "stated why he believed he became rich: his mental and moral capabilities would enable him to use money to serve the public good." (Jones, 1997: 12). In a 1920 biography Carnegie was quoted as saying "I think I'm doing a whole lot for the morality of the country through my libraries." (Johnson, 1996: B8). But he repeatedly stated that his public library buildings weren't philanthropy because they "only help those who help themselves." (Jones, 1997: 11). On November 18, 1916 a Mr.

Johnson submitted a report to the trustees of the Carnegie Corporation stating that "it was the librarian's training and aptitude that defined the impact of each library" and recommending, among other things, that the Carnegie Corporation should "spend money to support the academic training of librarians." (Jones, 1997: 101). But the trustees, led by Mr. Bertram, rejected Johnson's proposals. According to Johnson's autobiography, Bertram said that with regard to "librarian training, Mr. Carnegie... believed in having books where anyone could get ahold of them... a librarian's business is to hand out books, and that doesn't require a long expensive training." (quoted in Jones, 1997: 102).

However, in spite of these challenges to the professionalism of librarianship, however, librarians did receive academic training throughout the twentieth century, and for most of the twentieth century they conceived the primary mission of the public library to be the promotion of democracy through education. In her review of the history of the way in which librarians in the United States have understood their role in supporting democracy, Kathleen de la Pena McCook (2001) identifies four major publishing events: the histories of the public library by Jesse H. Shera and Sidney Ditzion, the reports of the American Library Association's Committee on Post-War Planning, and the set of volumes issued by the ALA's Public Library Inquiry.

The histories by Shera (1949) and Ditzion (1947) were the first major histories of public library development. As McCook (2001) emphasizes, both Shera and Ditzion recognized education and democracy as central to the mission of the modern public library throughout its history. According to Shera (1949: vi): "The modern public library in large measure represents the need of democracy for an enlightened electorate, and its history records its adaptation to changing social requirements." Ditzion (1947:74) states that during the latter half of the nineteenth century public libraries in the United States continued "the educational process where the schools left off, and by conducting a people's university, a wholesome capable citizenry would be fully schooled in the conduct of a democratic life." The National Plan for Public Library Service (1948) was the final part of the work of the American Library Association's Committee on Post-War Planning. The Public Library Inquiry was carried out and published between 1947-1952. Both of these reports of the American Library Association emphasized that democracy and enlightened citizenship would be just as important to the mission of the public library in the years going forward as they had been in the century prior to World War II.

Over the course of the 1960s and the 1970s, however, the Public Library Association moved away from prescribing national standards toward introducing a planning process by which each local library could develop its own mission. As McCook (2001) explains: "Once the Public Library Association developed the planning process, each public library had a methodology to use at the local level to develop its own mission, goals and objectives in collaboration with community and staff. The 1980 manual, Planning for Results, and the 1982 Output Measures for Public Libraries provided the tools for planning and measurement. The role of the public library in serving democracy was no longer a value imbedded in a formal public library standards document, for no such document existed at the national level." As we will see later, this shift from national standards to locally defined objectives corresponds to a shift in consumer capitalism from the homogeneous mass markets of the 1950s to the segmented markets and marketing strategies of the 1960s and the 1970s. Although the American Library Association continues to make statements in support of democracy up to the present day, and although the local determination of a library's mission could contribute to greater democracy rather than less, it should be noted that the quantitative nature of the Output Measures for Public Libraries (Zweizig, 1982) creates a bias toward measures of success in the public library which mirror measures of success in the capitalist economy.

For example, circulation mirrors sales. Both circulation and sales can be easily measured in quantitative terms. But if democracy and an enlightened citizenry were the goals of the public library, then we would measure success not merely by how many items we circulate, but by how many readers we have helped to become better citizens. That in turn depends on the quality and diversity of material we circulate as well as their number and highlights the need for professional judgement in collection development. In fact, the decline of qualitative measures of success at the national level reflects the rise of consumer capitalism during the postwar years and the decline of the ideal of the democratic nation state. As we will see later this decline culminates in the 1990s with the rise of neoliberalism (Barber, 1995) and the notion of a market democracy (Frank, 2000) in which the consumer replaces the citizen as the primary agent of "democracy" or of what is being called democracy.

KNOWLEDGE MANAGEMENT IN LIBRARIES

Knowledge economy is a knowledge-based economy. In the knowledge economy era, the management refers to effectively identify, acquire, develop, resolve, use, store and share knowledge, to create an approach to transforming and sharing of tacit and explicit knowledge, and to raise the emergency and innovation capability by utilizing the wisdom of the team. Since knowledge has become the driving force for social development, the attention of the society to information and knowledge is rising and people's demands for information and knowledge are increasing step by step. This has provided a good environment for library development. Moreover, as information and knowledge has become an important productive factor for the modern economic system, the society will inevitably require intensified management of information and knowledge. How to manage knowledge will become an important subject facing libraries in the near future. Knowledge management in libraries should be focused on effective research and development of knowledge, creation of knowledge bases, exchange and sharing of knowledge between library staffs (including its users), training of library staff, speeding up explicit processing of the implicit knowledge and realizing of its sharing.

CHARACTERISTICS OF KNOWLEDGE MANAGEMENT

The role of knowledge management in libraries will become more and more important along with the development of knowledge economy. It is a new management mode, boasts the following superiority and characteristics incomparable with conventional management:

Human Resource Management is the Core of Knowledge Management in Libraries

The most important resource in the knowledge economy system is the talents who grasp knowledge. The talent competition has become the focus of market competition in the knowledge economy era. In the knowledge economy era, the libraries will attach importance to vocational training and lifelong education of library staffs to raise their scientific knowledge level and ability of acquiring and innovating knowledge. They also will and fully respect the human value, guide and bring into play wisdom potentialities of library staffs, take developing knowledge resources in the brains of library staffs as an important way for rising work efficiency. An all-round improvement of library staff's quality and positioning of the human value will become important objectives of knowledge management in libraries.

The Objective of Knowledge Management in Libraries is to Promote Knowledge Innovation

Knowledge innovation is the core of the knowledge economy society. As bases for collection, processing, storage and distribution of knowledge and information, libraries represent an indispensable link in the scientific system chain, an important link in the knowledge innovation. Secondly, libraries take part in scientific research process directly. The library work is a component of knowledge innovation. Thirdly, libraries must pay attention to diffusion and conversion of knowledge. They act as bridges for turning the results of knowledge innovation into realistic productive forces. Knowledge management in libraries is to promote relationship in and between libraries, between library and user, to strengthen knowledge internetworking and to quicken knowledge flow. In the knowledge economy era, libraries will carry out researches on development and application of information resources, construction of virtual libraries, protection of intellectual property rights in the electronic era etc., thus founding the base for knowledge innovation.

Information Technology is a Tool for Knowledge Management in Libraries

Knowledge acquisition is the starting point of knowledge management in libraries. The application of information technologies enlarges the scope of knowledge acquisition, rises knowledge acquisition speed and reduces knowledge acquisition cost. It is impossible to accomplish such important tasks by using man's brains only in the modern society in which the knowledge changes with each passing day. It will be possible to link closely knowledge sources and knowledge workers by computer networks, thus constructing knowledge networks in libraries based on realization of single-point informatization. The knowledge acquired must be accumulated and converged into knowledge warehouses of libraries. The priority of information technologies in the field of knowledge storage not only finds expression in quantity, but also in retrieval, sorting and security of the knowledge. Information technology is also indispensable in the application and exchange of knowledge and other fields. It functions as a source and tool for knowledge innovation.

CONTENTS OF KNOWLEDGE MANAGEMENT IN LIBRARIES

As a completely new method of management, knowledge management in libraries leaves much to be desired in its theoretical system. In my opinion, knowledge management in libraries should include such respects as follows:

Knowledge Innovation Management

Knowledge innovation management in libraries refers to the management of the production, diffusion and transfer of knowledge as well as of the network systems constructed by related institutions and organizations. It includes three aspects, namely, theoretical innovation management of knowledge, technical innovation management and organizational innovation management. Theoretical innovation management is to enrich and enlarge the theoretical and practical research fields of library science and information science through pursuing the latest development trends in library science the world over. Technical innovation management is to manage the network systems constructed by institutions and organizations that relate to the full course of technical innovation. In their evolution from conventional libraries to electronic libraries, or digital libraries, Libraries should make technical breakthroughs and progress and build up technical facilities to support knowledge management. Organizational innovation management is to create a set of effective organizational management systems adaptable to the requirements in the electronic library era to support and strengthen knowledge management activities, by optimizing the functional departments and operation procedures of libraries.

In these systems, it firstly requires that leaders who take charge of knowledge management activities should undertake to formulate the management plans and coordinate all knowledge management related activities. Secondly, it requires establishment of special leading groups of knowledge flow for accomplishing all tasks relating to knowledge management activities. Electronic resources committees are established composed of various types of specialists to take charge of evaluating, procuring and creating the electronic resources on the one hand, and coordinating activities of business departments and spurring them on to close cooperation in such fields as procurement and organization of the electronic information resources as well as providing services on the other hand.

Knowledge Dissemination Management

Knowledge dissemination is of equal importance as compared to knowledge innovation. Knowledge creators do not have much time and energy to look for knowledge users. Though there are a multitude of knowledge users, it is very difficult to acquire knowledge that already exists in the minds of knowledge creators as restricted by various objective and subjective conditions. Therefore, libraries may play the part of knowledge tosser, use diverse media and channels to disseminate various new knowledge. In the 21st century, the Internet, with its mass information and extensive contents, will provide people with the main approach to searching knowledge and acquiring information. But now there emerge absurd, salacious, false and uncivil information resulting from seeking for commercial profits and political objectives on the Net. Therefore, it is necessary to strengthen knowledge dissemination management in libraries as follows:

1. uninterruptedly strengthening the creation of libraries' own document resources and deepening the development of document information resources;
2. continuously raising the quality of libraries' staffs and strengthening continuous engineering education of working staffs;
3. giving full play to the special role of the expert system in knowledge dissemination;
4. making a comprehensive utilization of all media to ensure security of operation of networks, and prevent online criminal activities and online dissemination of inapropriate information.

Knowledge Application Management

In the 21st century libraries should also attach importance to provision of services for people to acquire knowledge and achieve maximum functions and efficiency of knowledge information. Therefore, knowledge services based on high-speed information networks should be carried out by:

1. Setting up virtual libraries or information centres for enterprises, governments, public organizations and scientific research institutions. It is difficult for an

enterprise or a social organization to put sufficient manpower, material and financial resources on information gathering, organizing and developing. It is also impossible and unnecessary to spend a large amount of funds on information resources for their own use. Libraries can create virtual libraries or information centres for these organs separately according to their respective information requirements by using abundant information resources on the high-speed information networks.

2. Setting up digitized knowledge services which is actually a development trend of libraries in the 21st century. This presupposes: creating step by step the users-oriented information service systems such as information dissemination, information search and special supply of information; quickening the creation of digitized libraries; studying the methods, means and techniques of information distribution and search with the Internet as the base and WEB technique as the core.
3. Digitizing libraries' resources. The electronic libraries or digitized libraries are the technical modes and development trends of libraries in the knowledge economy era. The knowledge services of libraries in the future will start with creation of databases comprising electronic journals and books in different languages that have discipline features and can operate on high-speed information networks. Great efforts should be made to transform all existing large non-electronic information resources into electronic information and integrate them into electronic libraries.

Human Resources Management

Human resources management takes it as its basic starting point to train high quality specialized talents and to revitalize the library undertaking. In practice, we should pay full attention to diversity and variation of library staffs' requirements, strengthened management of different library staffs by applying contingency management approach. That is, to some people, rigid management method is applied, rigorous supervision and control imposed, and quantity and quality requirements of work according to regulations and procedures are made clear. And, to the rest of people, more flexible management method is applied to let them participate in decision-making and consultation and undertake more jobs so as to bring their management abilities into full play and realize organizational and personal objectives. Doing well in continuous engineering education of specialized staffs, which should not only focus on the theory of library science and related disciplines, but also cover the latest technical knowledge. And strengthening professional ethics education.

TECHNOLOGIES FOR LIBRARIES

One of the aims of knowledge management in libraries is to promote the knowledge exchange among library staffs, strengthen innovation consciousness and abilities, arise the library staffs' enthusiasm and abilities for learning, making the knowledge most efficiently applied to business activities of the library, and rebuilding the library into a learning organization. Therefore, the main train of thought in realizing knowledge management of libraries is a rational design of the organizational structure and business procedures of libraries, and cultural fostering, as well as modernized information support, thus creating an environment and incentive mechanism forinnovation, exchange, study and application of the knowledge.

In the Field of Organizational Structure, Business Processes and Culture of Libraries

(1) *Introducing the CKO System:* The Chief Information Officer (CIO) is a conspicuously high management position that has emerged successively in the government departments and large organizations in Western countries since the 1980s. The Chief Knowledge Officer (CKO) is the highest-ranking person in charge of knowledge management, which has evolved from CIO along with the transition of information research management into knowledge management. The CKO system represents the latest development trends of the information management system of the organizations, and marks the transition of information management from the stage of information resources management to that of knowledge management..

(2) *Realizing seamless combination of library business management with knowledge management during the business process reorganization of libraries:* Knowledge management integrates itself with the whole process of knowledge exchange, sharing, innovation and application of the organization, and becomes the key driving force for the knowledge innovation, exchange and application of the organization. The implementation of knowledge management will inevitably give rise to organization of library business process. This reorganization will also be the process of further combination of library business management with knowledge management.

(3) *Rebuilding the library culture by using the theory of knowledge management:* Knowledge management will inject new blood into the library culture. The main contents include: mutual trust, open exchange, studying, sharing and developing knowledge operation mechanism of libraries, enjoying the knowledge management process. In a word, to make full use of knowledge, it is necessary to foster a new type of library culture suitable to its requirement. This is high level requirement of realizing technology of knowledge management.

In the Field of Information Technology

The main information technologies relevant to knowledge management includes: Internet, Intranet and Extranet; storage architectures; database management systems; metadata; data acquisition and gathering; dissemination, messaging; push and pull; information retrieval; information resources sharing; groupware; middleware; online analytical processing; multidimensional analysis and data mining. How to convert data to the object of knowledge management-knowledge is also relevant to some basic information technologies, mainly including data processing, reporting, networked communication, document management, information search and retrieval, relational and object-oriented databases, electronic publishing, work flow and help desks.

In addition, because of the differences in architecture, usage and characteristics between information and knowledge, the storage and management of knowledge are more complicated than those of information. The storage architecture technology, database management system technology and metadata are also the key technologies in knowledge management.

Conclusions

Economic environment and information environment is changing quickly today. Knowledge management has become a powerful tool for promoting innovation and realizing reengineering the various walks of life. It occupies very outstanding position in the creation of the knowledge innovation systems of a country. How for the library circles to meet the challenge of knowledge economy and to build the knowledge management systems of libraries is a subject that demands our urgent study and solution.

LIBRARIES AND LIBRARIANS

The information age is here with many challenges and risks for the information generator and the information disseminator. The challenges before libraries and information centres are manifold. The main challenge will emerge from the expected change in the very nature of future libraries and information centres.

LIBRARY SCENARIO

The diversity of the Indian library scenario is an important aspect for consideration while speaking about a vision for the 3rd millennium, since different library sectors in India are in various stages of development and no single solution or approach will be relevant in the Indian situation.

Indian library and information sector can be divided into five major areas: the National Library sector; Academic library sector; the Special and Scientific library sector, Government library sector; and the Public library sector due to various factors the scientific and special library sector is much more developed and modernized than the other four sectors.

The challenges which Indian libraries and librarians will encounter in the 3rd millennium are manifold but the most important challenge will be the change in the very nature of libraries and librarians *i.e.*, the libraries must change from collection oriented institutions to service oriented organisations and librarians have to change from custodians of books and documents to information managers and disseminators. In this changing scenario IT will play the most important role. While taking advantage of the different components of information technology the libraries of each sector will have to ensure the following:

1. take stock of the actual need of the library and its users;
2. bring about change in the functions of the library to make it service oriented rather than collection oriented;
3. resource sharing and networking of libraries;
4. consider both preservation and access as vital components of library service;
5. marketing of information and library services;
6. development of library professionals to cope with the new environment;
7. utilization of management techniques for dealing with the new objectives.

At the decision-making level India will need a National Policy for libraries and information centres within the changed socioeconomic environment keeping in mind the new requirements of the different sectors within the field of librarianship. It will now be worthwhile to analyze the present Library and Information scenario before preparing a vision for the 3rd millennium in each sector of librarianship in India.

THE NATIONAL LIBRARY SECTOR

The National Library sector in India can be divided into two types of libraries. The first one comprises the National Library, Calcutta and the recipient Public libraries under the Delivery of Books Act *i.e.*, Delhi Public Library (DPL), Connemara Public Library, Chennai and the State Central Library, Mumbai. These are the depositories of the printed cultural heritage of India under the Delivery of Books Act.

The depository libraries are a very important part of the National Library sector because India is a very vast and multilingual country with rich linguistic heritage. The 3rd millennium will have to see the cooperation between all these four libraries with the National Library at the apex. This can only be implemented if all these libraries are modernized at the same scale and have compatible systems to ensure resource sharing and networking. As these are financed by the Department of Culture (DoC) of the Government of India (GoI), the standards for modernization laid down by the DoC will be applicable to all these libraries.

The other part comprises the National level subject specific libraries such as National Science Library, National Medical Library, etc. In both these parts the National Library stands out as the largest single library which acts as the depository as well as the repository of all published material of India. The 20th century saw the development of all these national level libraries in isolation. The main challenge in the 3rd millennium in the national library sector would be to bring about close coordination between all these national level subject libraries and the National Library of India.

ACADEMIC LIBRARY SECTOR

The Academic library sector comprises school and college and the university libraries. While evolving a vision for university libraries for the millennium, the main focus should be on the role of the existing university library in addressing the national issues. Since most university libraries in India work in isolation some information need to be collected and collated before preparing such a perspective plan.

1. Data regarding the actual functioning of the library, its collection, user approach, library facilities, IT application status, library manpower status, etc.
2. A national agency may be identified for undertaking this work.

A major aspect of the new millennium will be cooperation at all levels starting from the local to the global level. Cooperation is a pre-requisite for all types of networking for resource sharing. Therefore, the following must be ensured before preparing the plan for linkages between university libraries.

1. Institutional commitment to accept the given measures.
2. Fund and support resource sharing solution.

3. Attitudinal changes in library staff to undertake additional responsibility in resource sharing environment.
4. Training of library staff to understand and appreciate the changed situation.

If these pre-requisites are made available the university libraries could plan for resource sharing programmes, apprenticeship in libraries for learning new skills and IT training programmes, consultancy in retro-conversion and in developing IT infrastructure. All these put together will be the basis of preparing a perspective plan and evolve a vision for university libraries in the country.

SCHOOL AND COLLEGE LIBRARIES

Excepting very high brow private schools, most schools in India do not have a library per se in the present situation. This area of librarianship is very neglected and needs immediate and continuous attention. As regards college libraries, most colleges have libraries but other than very well known colleges in each state, the ordinary colleges do not run libraries of any consequence. Therefore, India faces the challenges of actually preparing a perspective plan from scratch *i.e.*, from collection development to networking through IT solutions, and will need a complete blueprint to develop these two types of libraries during the coming centuries.

India has set up the Information and Library Network (INFLIBNET) under the University Grants Commission (UGC) as the inter-university agency on library modernization to take the initiative and address the issues required to implement the perspective plan for the Academic sector. Each university and its affiliated college libraries also should be part of the overall scheme of development.

DISTANCE EDUCATION

India has developed a well organized distance learning system through the Indira Gandhi National Open University (IGNOU) to achieve a high percentage of educated citizens as a prelude to an ultimate knowledge based society. The diversity and geographical distance of India need a strong, well-planned distance learning system for all citizens of the country. To make distance learning worthwhile the information base of the library sector will be equally responsible to be able to cater to the information need of Indians different societal levels. IGNOU has started some unique services for students with the help of IT but unless the rich collection of reading material available in different libraries in India are accessible to the younger generation the aim of distance learning gets nullified. Therefore, the academic sector has to be so inter-connected that it will also cater to distance learners.

PUBLIC LIBRARY SECTOR

The Public library system in India has developed over the years for more than a century, initially under the patronage of the aristocracy. However, the new independent India which developed a democratic society, recognised the need for public libraries which will work for the common good and will build a strong foundation for a democratic set up.

According to the Constitution of India, Public library development is a State responsibility. Therefore, all states are vested with the mandate to set up libraries within the state at different levels. But due to the diversity in the level of state-wise development, the Department of Culture, Government of India has set up Raja Rammohun Roy Library Foundation (RRRLF) to act as a nodal agency for development of public libraries in India.

Though library legislation is almost a pre-requisite, all the Indian states have not yet passed the library legislation. Therefore, RRRLF is also working towards a model Public Library Bill which may be able to encompass all the facets needed for development of public libraries to suit the new changing environment. Moreover, in the rural sector the local governments have been made responsible and accountable for the development of public library facilities through new constitutional amendments. Also, the Central Government is taking well-considered steps to make dissemination of information the main activity in all sectors which deal with rural and social development. The 3rd millennium will see a drastic change which will ensure cooperation and collaborative efforts between the information generating agencies (whether government or NGOs) and the libraries and the information dissemination sector. The government is seriously considering to bring about conceptual change in the rural library sector by coordinating its activities along with the continuing education schemes of the National Literacy Mission (NLM).

The RRRLF has also been given the responsibility of resource mobilization for modernisation of the state and district central libraries, the development of infrastructure and training of personnel. The Department of Culture through the Central Secretariat Library (CSL) has laid down standards for library development software and networking as well as for bibliographic description to ensure standardization both in infrastructural development as well as retro-conversion of library catalogue in machine readable format.

GOVERNMENT LIBRARIES

Government libraries in India were developed mainly during the British period to cater to the needs of the decision-makers and the bureaucrats. These libraries have always been institutionalised within the departments of the government. All these departmental and ministerial libraries have collected government documents mainly of their respective department/ministry and have restricted their acquisition to the need of the departmental staff alone. The Central Secretariat Library (CSL) has, however, worked within a broader spectrum being the main library in the ministerial and bureaucratic set up.

During the last 50 years some of the government libraries have been developed into well-organised collections which can cater to an informed clientele. Since government information started being handled by the National Informatics Centre (NIC), the use of information technology became the key word in the government sector. The Department of Culture, which is the nodal agency for library development in India, has taken viable steps towards resource sharing and networking of the libraries under its supervision. This includes the National Library, Calcutta, Central Secretariat Library and National Archives of India library, libraries under the Archaeological Survey of India and the Anthropological Survey of India, etc.

SPECIAL AND SCIENTIFIC LIBRARIES

The special libraries and the libraries under Science and Technology group are in a much better developmental stage compared to the other four sectors. A good number of these libraries use current IT products and systems like computers, email, CD.ROMs and online storing and retrieval.

Libraries and information centres of research institutions such as those under Council of Scientific and Industrial Research (CSIR), Defence Research and Development Organisation (DRDO), Indian Council of Agricultural Research (ICAR), Indian Council of Medical Research (ICMR), Department of Atomic Energy (DAE), Indian Space and Research Organisation (ISRO), Department of Science & Technology (DST) and Institutes of higher learning like the Indian Institutes of Technology (IITs), Indian Institute of Science (IIS), Indian National Science Academy (INSA), Indian Institutes of Management (IIMs), are modernized and have been given the necessary resources for development.

LIBRARY NETWORKS

Other than INFLIBNET, there are a number of networks which have developed in the past decade. These are either city networks or activity subject specific networks. Developing Libraries Network (DELNET), Calcutta Library Network (CALIBNET), Madras Library Network (MALIBNET), Management Library Network, etc., are important and useful ventures for networking and resource sharing. Future of Library Development and the Challenges in the 3rd Millennium The details given above actually picturizes the latest situation encountered by Indian librarianship till the end of the last millennium.

The main challenge in the Indian situation is to visualise the present situation and bring about changes so as to nullify the observations made in the World Information Report, 1997-98, which are as follows:

- The bulk of the population is not information-dependent in day-to-day work and living.
- A large proportion of the population cannot consume information, especially if it is delivered in written form.

- The vast majority of the population does not have the means to access information.
- People in general are not accustomed to pay, cannot pay or are unwilling to pay for information. In fact, information does not even figure in their list of wants.
- The existing pattern of economic activities does not favour a growth in information consumption.
- The countries do not have sufficient capacity to invest in infrastructural development

Therefore, the future of Indian librarianship lies in descending from its ivory tower of catering to only a select few and the literate minority and to create a system which will penetrate into the actual information need of the majority of Indian people. So, there has to be a major paradigm shift to deal with the information needs of the vast majority of the population who at present do not have means to access information. Specially, the public library system in the country needs to be rejuvenated and re-modelled to cope with the present situation and the future trends.

There will be need to change the following on a broad-based basis in all types of libraries:

a. Library environment

b. Fragmented and isolated services

c. Organisational structure

d. Library collection

e. Information based infrastructure

f. Information and knowledge management

The first step towards this direction has been taken to a certain extent as the Report of the Working Group of the Planning Commission on Libraries and Informatics for the 9th Five Year Plan 1997-2002 addresses some of the challenges which confront Indian librarianship The Challenges and Risks for Librarians and Information Specialists in the 3rd Millennium The biggest challenge for Indian librarianship is to bring about attitudinal change among both library staff and users. Libraries and librarians are still the lowest priority in the decision making process and the librarians are the least visible persons. If this main challenge is confronted by librarians and libraries in real earnest it is only then that one can expect all the necessary changes within the system itself.

Libraries will also have to cope with the initiatives developed in the society in the changed IT environment. Libraries can no longer afford to remain institutionalized passive spectators. All the activities will now have to be tailored to give long distance and often home delivered information.

OPPORTUNITIES AND RISKS

The new millennium will open up unprecedented opportunities for information professionals. Employers will no longer look for the traditional career requirements but a flexible work force which can take on different roles and responsibilities as and when required. In this context the following changes are to be brought about in India:

1. Change the teaching curricula in the field of library and information science.
2. Utilize the traditional expertise and apply them effectively in the new situations by understanding the actual requirements and applying these skills.
3. Content generation to suit the new fields of study with the help of IT.
4. Play the role of information managers by utilizing the new technology to give access to the rich resources available in libraries.

Tomorrows information professionals will be knowledge navigators instead of information collectors. In the Indian situation the new generation of librarians will have to face these challenges and risks to remain in the information business in all the sectors. Inter-changeability and capabilities to adjust from one sector to the other will be the biggest challenge for Indian librarians.

NATIONAL POLICY FOR THE NEW MILLENNIUM

To fructify all that has been stated above there is a felt need to frame a National Policy of Libraries and Information Systems and Services, suited to the new environment. The DoC had framed a National Policy on Library and Information System (NAPLIS) during the late 1980s which is a very good foundation for preparing a new policy which will encompass the futuristic viewpoints for the library sector as a whole. It has to spell out all relevant issues, challenges, threats and opportunities which are envisioned for the new millennium.

India is on the threshold of major changes which will be possible only if a worthwhile and modern information system is set up at the right time, with the help of right infrastructure and is administered by the right type of qualified people.

Summary

Ms. Kalpana Dasgsupta completed her higher studies in India and in the United States. She has a Post Graduate degree in Political Science from Patna University, India and Master of Science in Library Science from Syracuse University, New York State, USA. Her career as a librarian started in 1965 and she has worked in the largest libraries in India. Her career graph has gone up from a Library Assistant in a special library to the Librarian and Head of the National Library of India. She is presently the Director of the Central Secretariat Library of the Dept. of Culture, Government of India (GOI). She has also acted as Director of the Delhi Public Library which is the largest public library system in India. With 35 years of professional experience she acts as a technical advisor to many activities of the GOI.

She is also consultant to the Prime Minister's Office for its library development. With her vast experience in management and technical development of libraries she has been acting as member of various high-powered committees of the GOI. She has more than 30 professional articles and has authored and edited several books in the field of library information science. She is presently the President of the Indian Library Association (ILA) for a period of 2 years (2000-2002) which is the largest national association in the field of librarianship in India.

3

Networking of Astronomy Libraries and Resource Sharing

Astronomers have always had a special need for rapid communication over long distances. More recently the increase in international collaboration has given an incentive to explore the latest electronic innovation, namely the electronic mail and internet access for faster communication. These have become an integral part of scientific organisations and libraries (Rajashekar & Sreenivasa Ravi, 1993)

Previously, communication among libraries and library personnel was through traditional methods like the post and teleprinter links. In some cases, the telephone link was used in urgent cases. Now, the internet concept has changed the scenario even in Indian libraries. Libraries are able to access databases outside the country without much difficulty. This has revolutionized not only the information seeking behaviour of the scientists but also the role of the librarians.

Librarians are working towards maximum utilization of resources available and in this context we are thinking of networking all astronomy libraries in India.

WHY NETWORKING

1. For better resource sharing
2. To reduce costs
3. For speedy delivery of documents
4. To keep abreast of new developments
5. To give access to advice from colleagues with similar problems through a newsletter.

PARTICIPATING LIBRARIES

There are eight scientific institutions in India, for which astronomy is the major research area.

Indian Institute of Astrophysics Library (IIA)

It is more than 200 years old and has a rich collection of books and journals in Astronomy and Astrophysics. Some of the astronomical journals start from volume 1 dating back to the nineteenth century. The library has most of the old observatory publications. They form an important part of the collection as many astronomical catalogues are published here which are still used by our scientists.

Inter-University Centre for Astronomy and Astrophysics Library (IUCAA)

It is an autonomous institute, located in Pune, and has been established recently. The main areas of research are Astronomy and Astrophysics, General Relativity and Gravitation.

Though the library of this institute is new, it has succeeded in building up a very good collection of books and journals in Astronomy and Astrophysics. The majority of astronomy journals are received by airmail at IUCAA.

National Centre for Radio Astrophysics Library (NCRA)

It has a wide collection of materials on radio astronomy and astrophysics. This institute is located in Pune, close to IUCAA.

Nizamiah Observatory Library

This Observatory is very old and functions under Osmania University, Hyderabad. The present library was established in 1961 and it has a fairly good collection of old books and journals. The Observatory has been receiving reprints and publications from the beginning of this century from all over the world on exchange basis, so the library is rich in old material.

Physical Research Laboratory Library (PRL)

The Physical Research Laboratory, located in Ahmedabad, has a library, funded by the Department of Space. The Institute carries out research in many areas of Physics. In addition, it also concentrates on Astronomy and Astrophysics, Infrared Astronomy and Radio Astronomy.

Raman Research Institute Library (RRI)

The Raman Research Institute Library has been developed around the library started by the nobel laureate Prof. Raman and is also located in Bangalore. With his diverse interests in different branches of science and deep interest in reading, Prof. Raman had added invaluable books to the library. It has a rich collection of astronomy and astrophysics books. Its preprint collection is also a valuable resource for sharing.

Tata Institute of Fundamental Research Library (TIFR)

Tata Institute of Fundamental Research Library, Bombay was established in 1945. In addition to books in various branches of physics it has a large collection of books and journals in the areas of astronomy, astrophysics and space physics.

Uttar Pradesh State Observatory Library

Located in Nainital, the library has built up a vast collection of books and journals in astronomy in the short span of 45 years and is very keen on expanding its collection and services.

WHAT TO SHARE

Books	Policy Decisions
Journals	FORSA Forum
Observatory Publications	Current Events
Preprints	Newsflash
Catalogues	
Lists of Publications	
Recent Additions	
Newsletters	

Table below gives the total collection and the services offered by the individual libraries. The table shows that four libraries have automated their library catalogues using the same library software called LIBSYS and two libraries use a software called SLIM. LIBSYS is a fully integrated multi-user library system designed to run on a wide spectrum of hardware and software platforms and it can also import databases built on other software (*e.g.* SLIM). This is one of the important criteria which will make this networking feasible.

Resources and Services available at FORSA libraries

No.	Library	Software	Coll.Books	Coll.Jour.	Jnl.Sub.
1.	IIA	LIBSYS 3.X	13,300	18,400	142
2.	IUCAA	SLIM 2.0	10,000	4,000	150
3.	NCRA	SLIM 1.1	5,400	3,300	104
4.	NIZA.OBS. Library		5,340	3,995	10
5.	PRL	LIBSYS 3.1	16,500	25,000	197
6.	RRI	LIBSYS 3.X	19,613	23,273	137
7.	TIFR	LIBSYS 3.2	55,000	56,000	656
8.	U.P.State Obs.Lib.	Acquiring LIBSYS	8,273	8,061	76
		Total	133,426	142,029	

From table, it is evident that the collection of books and journals of all the libraries put together is not very large and will occupy less than 2 GB space.

NETWORKING MODELS

1. Interconnecting all astronomy library homepages.
2. Creating an integrated library database.
3. Establishing connectivity using search-engine architecture.

Model I

In this model, which is the simplest, the home pages of the participating libraries will be linked.

Many research organisations in India have designed their home pages and libraries are also a part of their homepages. Similarly, member libraries of FORSA also have their independent web pages and they are accessible on the internet. Since these web pages will exist independently, a scientist looking for a document will be able to trace it eventually, if not immediately (Madalli 1998). At present, only six libraries out of the eight FORSA libraries have internet connection, but we hope that the other two libraries will be able to get their home pages soon.

Model II

In this model, the databases of all individual libraries will be merged. Since the total collection of books is 133,426 and there are 142,029 journal volumes we will not be requiring more than 2 GB space for an integrated database. The merging of books and journals will be effected with the help of a unique feature like the ISBN numbers. Since the physical location is one of the fields in the data entry form, it is not difficult to reflect it in the merged database. This has a major advantage from the user's point of view. It will be less time-consuming, since the scientist will have to access only one server where the inte-grated database will be located. The LIBSYS software, used in most of the libraries, has the facility to display the availability status of the document. It is mandatory for the library personnel to maintain, rather than update this integrated database.

It could either be a commitment from an exclusive group of people or it could be done remotely from individual locations. We are also planning to create a profile of all member libraries as the common web page, which will be linked to the integrated database. In the event of any exclusive feature of a particular library being listed, it is easier to access that feature from the common web page. For example, in our library we have many old documents, which will be catalogued in a database and any individual interested in the archival material can access that database from the common web page. The availability of electronic journals will be another feature which could be accessible only by the individual institute's scientists, though it will be a listed item in the common web page. Incorporating too many icons and graphics in a web page is a time-consuming factor at the time of retrieval.

Keeping all this in mind, we will design soon our common web page to facilitate an easy navigation and retrieval through the internet, not only for our scientists, but also for the international community. We are also gearing up our library staff to undertake training in handling the network, especially hypertext linking. Though we have a very good technical support from the software company, we are getting equipped with basic knowledge of software maintenance and also the optimum usage of the features of this software. Funding for this joint project is envisaged from member libraries and also from the Department of Science & Technology of the Government of India.

Model III

In model III, which is a sophisticated model, the databases will be connected with the help of search-engine architecture. In the March 1997 issue of Scientific American, Lynch (1997) describes one such model called HARVEST which derives indexing terms using software called "Gatherers" that reside at web sites. By doing so, the search engine can avoid downloading all the documents from a web site which would burden the network traffic.

The search engine's server takes the help of the Gatherers to create a file of keywords that can be processed into an index for querying by users. Lynch says that "eventually, the librarian's classification and selection skills must be complemented by the computer scientist's ability to automate the task of indexing and storing information. Only a synthesis of the different perspective brought by both professions will allow this new medium to remain viable." If this concept can be applied to the library database, it will be an efficient tool for future retrieval and international cooperation.

Conclusion

India has taken advantage of the wide range of scientific information available through computerised networks. It has already geared up to having modern communication facilities (including satellite communication), adequate electricity, subsidised communication costs, rationalisation of taxes on computer equipment, etc., which gives us a thrust to fully participate in the new information age. The astronomy librarian of Australian National University has expressed a desire to be a part of this network, thus extending the network to the Asia Pacific region. When this network is realised, it will have a broader subject coverage to include physics and mathematics, along with astronomy. Eventually it will be an international cooperation with more new ideas and suggestions.

DIGITAL LIBRARIES AND EDUCATION

This article builds on work in the past few years, triggered by Ticer course [Roes, 1999] and consulting activities, notably for the Dutch Open University and the Amsterdam University for Professional Education. It attempts to identify strategic issues for libraries wishing to pursue a more active policy with regard to the changes affecting higher education due to the increased use of information and communication technologies (ICT). The article starts out by sketching the changes currently occurring in education.

A study of the literature, carried out while preparing a new strategic plan for the libraries of Amsterdam University for Professional Education, identified five major areas in which libraries can develop strategies to enhance services for their patrons. The following domains are discussed: digital libraries and digital learning environments; digital portfolios; information literacy; collaborative course design; and the relation between physical and virtual learning environments.

Next, possible implications for library staff regarding the changes are discussed. The article concludes with thoughts on alignment between library strategy and the strategy of the library's parent institution.

THE CHANGING WORLD OF EDUCATION

Undoubtedly, there are profound changes going on in the educational system. These changes are needed because of ever growing pressure in the school systems themselves, partly because society itself is changing into one in which knowledge work becomes ever more important, and partly because of the very information and communication technologies which are transforming our economies.

Both of these factors evoke change and offer a solution to the problems with which the educational system struggles. Carol Twigg and Michael Miloff [Twigg and Miloff 1998] analyzed the changing learning situation in the United States, and their analysis is also to a great extent valid for the European situation. By confronting trends and technological developments, they arrive at a vision of a "global learning infrastructure" in which the role of schools and universities will be drastically changed, a radical transformation of the educational system. They see the following trends:

- The number of students is still growing.
- Different types of students are asking for education; participation of women, older students, and students from ethnic minorities is growing. Different students bring different experiences with them.
- Increasingly, work and study are combined, and that leads to a need for more flexible learning arrangements in which the campus or school building is no longer central to the educational process.
- More generally, there is a trend towards lifelong learning.
- Lifelong learning leads to an emphasis on "learning to learn". Knowledge becomes obsolete at an ever-increasing rate in a knowledge economy, and knowledge workers need to be able to refresh their knowledge on a regular basis.
- Because of the differences between students, there is a need to accommodate different learning styles, customization and alternative learning routes. Courses have to take more into account the different experiences and backgrounds of students.
- Higher education institutions have long had a monopoly in providing education, but increasingly, companies and public bodies possess knowledge that can be reused for educational purposes, partly for in-house training (knowledge management) but also to offer to external markets.
- Education is under constant budget pressure, thus there is a need for more efficient and effective education.
- Students more and more are behaving like consumers who want to make informed choices about how and where they want to be educated, which implies students are no longer committed to one institution.

- Teaching staff will exhibit more job-hopping behaviour than they did in the past.
- There are too many dropouts in the current educational system.

Information and communication technologies (ICT) have the potential to offer a solution for at least part of the problems mentioned above. According to Twigg and Miloff [Twigg and Miloff 1998]:

- Through the Internet, course material can be offered independently of time and place. Modularization makes it possible to offer different and flexible learning routes.
- An ever-increasing number of students have access to the Internet, whether at home or on campus. Costs of Internet access will continue to drop.
- More and more information is made available through the web. Search engines assure the accessibility of this material. Groupware allows (a)synchronous communication between teachers and students—worldwide.
- Online market research is quick and easy, and this market information can be combined with transaction log data allowing institutions to monitor consumer (*i.e.*, student) response on an ongoing basis.
- In principle, a worldwide competition for education is possible and it is already apparent in the market for MBA courses. Carol Hughes [Hughes 2000] also foresees increasing competition in the delivery of information services for higher education, implying that libraries might lose their monopoly position in information services to their parent institutions. (Hughes' e-book company, Questia Media, is an example of a new competitor.)

In summary, Twigg and Miloff [Twigg and Miloff 1998] envisage a global learning infrastructure. One might envisage learning environments of the future as:

- being student-centred
- being interactive and dynamic
- enabling group work on real world problems

- enabling students to determine their own learning routes
- emphasizing competencies like information literacy to support lifelong learning

Through these elements listed above runs a common theme: the adoption of more active learning styles in which students take more responsibility for their own learning goals and for the ways in which to realize these objectives. Active learning implies that students don't limit themselves to resources supplied by their instructors, but also that the students search for new materials themselves in order to solve problems at hand and to develop their competencies continuously. Since libraries in higher education find their *raison d'être* in supporting research and education, a relevant question is how libraries can and should transform themselves in order to cope with the changes in our educational systems. The following five strategic areas will be discussed in the next sections of this article:

- digital libraries and digital learning environments
- digital portfolios
- information literacy
- collaborative course design
- the relation between physical and virtual learning environments.

DIGITAL LIBRARIES AND DIGITAL LEARNING ENVIRONMENTS

Digital libraries seem, no, *are* natural complements to digital learning environments. They are able to integrate the freely available information on the web with the more formal literature for which (increasingly consortium) licenses on electronic versions are arranged with publishers. These licenses enhance and replace traditional collection development policies. Digital libraries facilitate time and place independent information services for students, needed especially if active learning styles become more commonplace [Barnard 1997, Beagle 2000].

Digital libraries are already available 24 / 7 from anywhere in the world, offering flexible arrangements for students / knowledge workers. Much work done over the past decade in developing digital libraries will have an important pay-off for educational innovation. The main issue, of course, is whether more active learning styles will become the norm, since many of today's courses are of a rather "self contained" nature in which educators present students with texts to work through in a linear way and assessment is too often based on whether or not a student is able to reproduce the texts prescribed by the teacher. Two approaches in this respect can be identified. The first one, which takes the needs of specific courses as point of departure, can be seen mainly in the UK in projects like INSPIRAL and ResIDE [INSPIRAL and ResIDE]. INSPIRAL is a research project in England that investigates issues involved in linking virtual (or digital or managed) learning environments with digital libraries.

It looks at technical, institutional and end-user challenges, with an emphasis on the last two aspects, and analyzes stakeholders' and learners' needs. Its point of departure seems to be how teaching staff can best be supported when designing digital learning environments and enriching these environments with resources available in digital libraries. This tailor-made approach is very much apparent in the ResIDE project where the focus is on the teachers and their courses. This model can be seen as analogous to the work of reference librarians putting together reserve collections to support courses.

Another approach, apparently more popular in the United States, has a different, more macro way of looking at digital library support for learning environments and concentrates on learning resources in general. An example of this approach is the National Science Foundation (NSF) national science, mathematics, engineering, and technology education digital library (NSDL) programme [Wattenberg 1998, Zia 2000]. This programme seeks to bring together a vast, centralized collection of learning resources supporting all possible kinds of education, ranging from K-12 to graduate and lifelong learning, into one big library for the nation—and even beyond. As such, the NSDL approach is consistent with the large scale of many of the other NSF digital libraries projects.

To libraries and librarians, the NSDL approach seems more threatening; however, I think in both options there will still be a need for library staff to support educators with respect to the selection of adequate resources for a given course.

Librarians pursuing this aspect are well advised to learn more about the standards (*e.g.*, IMS / Instructional Management Systems) being developed to protect investments in content development from the rapid developments in technology used in digital learning environments [Bacsich et al. 1999]. The issue here is that instructional content should be easily transferable from one platform to another. Related issues are integration with administrative systems and authentication.

Donald Beagle [Beagle 2000] warns that another, related question, *viz.* compatibility of digital learning environments and library systems, is a neglected issue so far. The main problem seems to be managerial short-sightedness. In the Netherlands, for example, the common opinion of administrators seems to be that work on digital libraries doesn't need special attention anymore—for which some valid arguments can be put forward—and that the subject of ICT in education is an entirely different one from the subject of digital libraries. The point, of course, is that this view fails to incorporate the advantages of digital libraries, which are natural complements to digital learning environments.

DIGITAL PORTFOLIOS

Digital portfolios are new tools for student assessment and they are more than that as well. Initially, digital portfolios were developed as an alternative way of assessing student progress, with more emphasis on the learning process and the material results a student achieves throughout a course of study. By showing material results, the student can demonstrate that certain competencies have been acquired. At the same time, as a personal tool [Tillema 1998] the portfolio offers students the ability to closely monitor their own progress and to set new learning goals in the planning of their education. Additionally, a portfolio, which continues to grow during training, can be used in job interviews to show prospective employers the candidate's background in a much richer way. Digital portfolios work especially well in situations where students work with assignments to solve real-life problems and are free to manage their own learning process. In discussions with educational innovators at Amsterdam University of Professional Education, the idea surfaced that (elements of) digital portfolios can be of wider use than just for assessment of an individual student's progress. Since the portfolios contain material results, these results might also be of interest to future students on which to build, much in the same way as the information chain works in scholarly work. By taking a knowledge management approach to digital portfolios, these results can be shared over the Internet or, more likely, the intranet. This implies a new task for the library in the management and indexing of these student portfolios in such a way that they too can be integrated with other information resources offered by the library. In this sense, digital portfolios are an extension of the first domain identified—digital libraries and digital learning environments—but now include the intranet. The emphasis here is on the institution as a knowledge organization, and the integration of that knowledge with other information resources.

INFORMATION LITERACY

Adding digital portfolios to the ever increasing amount of information available leads to a third domain in which libraries can play a more active role in support of educational innovation: information literacy. The concept of information literacy can be traced back to the 1970s and was originally connected to democratic ideals. Throughout the years, the view of information literacy has evolved towards a more technical one and has been connected to the development of the information society [Webber and Johnston 2000], a term which is now being replaced by the notion of the knowledge economy. A well-known definition of information literacy is the one developed by the American Library Association [ALA 1998]:

"Information literate [people] are not only able to recognize when information is needed, but they are also able to identify, locate, evaluate, and use effectively information needed for the particular decision or issue at hand. The information literate person, therefore, is empowered for effective decision making, freedom of choice, and full participation in a democratic society." There are many more definitions of information literacy, but they all share an emphasis on personal competencies, which are usually broken down by the chain: recognition of an information need, development of a search strategy-query formulation and selection of sources, evaluation, synthesis, and effective use of the new information. Sometimes, correct citing is also seen as a crucial competency. In addition, information literacy is often mentioned together with the concept of critical thinking skills. Notice also how information literacy is conceptually closely linked to terms like "active learning", "problem-based learning", "student-centred learning", "lifelong learning", and "learning to learn".

It is impossible to imagine an information *illiterate* knowledge worker. Hannelore Rader [Rader 1997] remarked that "[l]ibrarians are uniquely qualified to assume an active role in the new teaching environment because of their skills in collecting, evaluating, organizing and providing access to information." Information literacy can be seen as building on, but going way beyond, traditional library instruction. Increasingly, librarians will be involved in teaching classes—sometimes in close cooperation with faculty, sometimes in general skills courses. An important trend in the last few years is that library staffs are developing internet-based instruction modules. The Texas Information Literacy Tutorial <http://tilt.lib.utsystem.edu/> is an excellent example of this latter approach, which has gained widespread recognition in the library community.

COLLABORATIVE COURSE DESIGN

Of course, librarians who are building expertise in developing web-based course material can also use this expertise in a more broad sense. The idea here is that—in contrast with the traditional situation in which teaching staff develops courses on their own, and choose the way they teach and assess student progress (the teacher as king of his class)—learning environments of the future will be designed by multi-disciplinary teams of experts. Experts in developing course material, programmers, graphical designers, and experts in assessment, all will work together in designing rich modularized learning environments that offer alternative learning routes to different types of students.

However, many learning environments build on a model for which origins can be traced back to early distance education. In this model, students are given a "box" containing all the material for a course they need to master, so-called self-contained courses. An approach that, of course, made sense in traditional distance education where library support has always been a rather cumbersome issue [Unwin, Stephens and Bolton 1998]. Alan Bundy [Bundy 2000] remarks that digital learning environments lead some educators to use the technology to gain even more control over students.

But if the emphasis is on developing competencies needed to become knowledge workers, and if work and learning are more interconnected, one might expect that learning environments will become more open. Students in such a model are expected to go beyond the primary learning materials offered by teaching staff and are expected to explore independently other information sources as well.

Again, if more active learning styles become the norm, then one can foresee a role for librarians in the multi-disciplinary teams developing learning environments such as those mentioned above. Librarians can add links to the resources—print and electronic—available in their collections and on the web. They can explain how information resources in a particular subject field are organized and how students can find their way in subject areas that are relatively new to them.

A nice example of this approach is the module DEsite <http://cwis.kub.nl/~dbi/instruct/eu/> developed at Tilburg University to explain the complexities of the decision making process in Europe. The module was developed in close cooperation between legal scholars and library staff. Lawyers explain the technical and legal aspects of the decision making process, and library staff show how to trace the many documents produced in this process in the jungle of European Union databases and web sites.

Together they have built a learning environment that individually they could not have produced easily. The DEsite model shows the synergy that is possible, and the result is a rich learning environment for students and an electronic reference tool for lawyers active in this field.

PHYSICAL AND VIRTUAL LEARNING ENVIRONMENTS

Techno-enthusiasts tell us that virtual learning environments will suffice to satisfy the needs of future students. This is not to imply that people won't be working together, but they will do this work time and place independently using groupware. This picture of a world of students and knowledge workers lonely behind their desktops denies the important social aspects of learning and working. John Seely Brown and Paul Duguid [Brown and Duguid 2000] remind us of the importance of the social context in which people give meaning to information and refer to (real, not virtual!) communities of practice as ideal learning environments. Noriko Hara and Rob Kling studied student frustrations with purely web-based learning environments [Hara and Kling 1999] and the results of their study reinforce this point. Students encounter many technical problems and miss the direct feedback inherent to class room situations where even the body language of the teacher gives important clues. Next to virtual learning environments, the physical learning environment will remain of importance too, and the two will probably coexist for generations to come.

The (physical) library is a learning environment ideally suited to support more active learning styles. Kerstin Friden [Friden 1996] studied the effects the introduction of problem-based learning had on the use of the library. She found that students made use of the library much earlier in their training, and the use was more intensive and more equally spread over the year.

If we look at recent developments in library architecture in the United States [American Libraries 1999] some trends in library functions become more visible. There is a clear trend towards more client-centred buildings instead of the collection-centred ones of the past. Some libraries experiment with lounge-like facilities and offer pleasant reading rooms, not just for individuals but also for groups. Integration of libraries with computing facilities is a clear trend, one that will present even more of a challenge now that multimedia computers are becoming the norm. Increasingly, the term "learning environment" or "learning centre" is used for this kind of facility.

It shows that, next to digital learning environments, there is also a need for physical learning environments where students and teachers find a wealth of resources and facilities, and where they can work, on their own or together, in order to learn and teach.

IMPLICATIONS FOR LIBRARY STAFF AND ORGANIZATION

The linking of digital libraries to digital learning environments, standards issues, knowledge-sharing, support in education, more active support of educational processes, classroom instruction, development of course modules in multi disciplinary teams, rethinking and redesigning library buildings—all these issues have obviously profound implications for library personnel. Richard Biddiscombe [Biddiscombe 2000] sees a strong need for the library itself to become a learning organization. We might add that, now more than ever, lifelong learning becomes important for library staff.

Hannelore Rader [Rader 1999], a pioneer in this field, emphasizes leadership and innovative attitude of library personnel. She stresses the importance of developing partnerships between library staff and faculty. This requires a proactive approach: look at what is going on in education in your institution and show where library resources can enhance learning environments. In her view, library staffs have an advantage: they can build on their expertise in digital libraries, and they have a head start in using modern technology. Ultimately, in Rader's view, librarians should become partners in educational innovation.

Patricia Iannuzzi [Iannuzzi 1998] reported on developing library-faculty relationships at Florida International University. Organizational culture is the main obstacle in developing these relationships, and it takes time to change this culture. At Florida International University, the introduction of information literacy was seen as an opportunity for rethinking the role of the library. Iannuzzi warns that librarians think too much about how to integrate information literacy in new initiatives, instead of wondering how information literacy can help these initiatives to succeed. Finally she gives some practical advice: keep informed, meet the key people, and get involved.

It can be expected that more active library support of educational innovation will give rise to new types of jobs. Some early examples are the academic technology specialists at Stanford University in the United States <http://acomp.stanford.edu/atsp> and the learning technology officer at the University of Edinburgh in the United Kingdom [Alexander 2000]. The academic technology specialist is a hybrid function, combining library and ICT expertise, and the specialist's task is to support teaching staff in the use of new technology. Most of the time (about four days a week), these specialists work with faculty in their offices and classes, the remaining day of the week is used to exchange experiences. Edinburgh's learning technology officer acts as a bridge between library and academic staff to ensure that library expertise is properly exploited, a definition that seems a bit too library-centred.

On a larger scale, there could be organizational consequences. Much in the same way that digital library projects have led to closer cooperation, and sometimes mergers, between libraries and computer centres, educational innovation leads to closer cooperation between libraries, computer centres and educational support units. Examples of such cooperation include the University of Newcastle, Australia [O'Brien and Sidorko 2000], and the DINKEL Institute of Twente University in the Netherlands <http://www.dinkel.utwente.nl/dinkel_en.html>. Another option is to explore the possibilities of networked organizations in order to mobilize and combine the many different competencies spread throughout higher education institutions.

INSTITUTIONAL AND LIBRARY STRATEGIES

This article has sketched interesting challenges for librarians wishing to pursue a more active role in educational innovation. An important final question is whether there are organizational and strategic preconditions that must be met in order to succeed. In their reports on the America Library Power project, Carol Collier Kuhltau [Kuhltau 1999], and Norman Webb and Carol Doll [Webb and Doll 1999] stress that the most important condition is that there is a basic agreement between administrators, teachers and library staff on what kind of education an institution wants to give. Those schools advocating more active learning styles will benefit especially from increased cooperation. The pay-off for students is an increase in information literacy and critical thinking skills, core competencies for knowledge workers.

Even if there is no shared institutional vision on education, there is no excuse for librarians to wait and see. It just implies that they have to find alternative routes. One nice thing about networked organizations is that one can build them without the consent of administrators. With or without an institutional strategy, it is still a librarian's task to support teaching and learning, and to develop relationships with faculty further and in the direction of supporting their teaching. Librarians should talk with students and find out in which ways librarians can best accommodate student learning. Librarians can start small and develop ideas and projects in close cooperation with their patrons.

Looking at examples of colleagues at other institutions to find out what works and what doesn't—and why—is a good place to begin. Librarians have, and can develop further, unique skills to support educational innovation and they have the opportunity to act as role models within their institutions. After all, library work *is* knowledge work.

EMERGING DEVELOPMENTS OF AUDIOVISUAL AND MULTIMEDIA

In developing countries today, there is a gradual emergence of the realization that knowledge and information will be the engines to drive their economies in the 21st century. Kenya is no exception. Libraries, places where information has always been stored and offered to users, have been affected the most by current technological developments.

For long, most Kenyan libraries (both academic and public) have based their strength on the 'presence' of print information offering textual information whose use is connected with actual presence in the libraries themselves. However, the emerging trend points to the realization that these libraries exist in an era of information explosion, hence must make use of the current technological developments in providing a variety of new formats through which information can be stored and disseminated. The Kenyan libraries are therefore beginning to be confronted with the information explosion created by new technological developments. The capacity of the book as the only carrier of information is beginning to burst its seams. This has made many Kenyan libraries to contemplate and redefine their positions within the current information trends.

The Kenyan library organization has the following four categories: academic, public, special, and school libraries. Their systems of information provision have distinct borders as they are oriented towards specific areas of focus.

Academic Libraries

These comprise 5 state university libraries, 8 private university libraries, 4 polytechnic libraries, several teacher training and institute libraries. These libraries serve to support research, teaching / learning and other literature work oriented toward specialized scientific areas of the users.

Public Libraries

The bulk of Kenyan public libraries is formed by the Kenya National Library Service (KNLS) branches. The others are City and Municipal libraries. The KNLS was established through an Act of Parliament in 1965. Its functions include: offering mobile library services in rural and remote areas, reference services, free advisory services to schools, services for the blind, conducts national book week exhibitions, and also have AIDS corners.

School Libraries

These comprise primary, secondary, and special school libraries. They serve primary and secondary school children who, through promotion strategies, are encouraged to explore school library collections for learning and leisure. They support the Kenyan educational system.

Special Libraries

These comprise Private, Research, Diplomatic Mission, Parliament and Government Ministries libraries. They function to provide specialized information specific to their organizations.

The Emerging Developments

Times have changed considerably since the late 1980s, when the demand for audiovisual librarians to establish collections particularly in public and academic libraries, was the faintest idea in Kenya, though simmering. The emerging trend in these libraries today, is portraying a move towards AV. and Multimedia resourcing as the volume of information has become the deciding factor in modern library collections.

Resourcing in Academic Libraries

Changes in Kenya's educational system have engendered changes in teaching / learning approaches and pre-empted a shift in practice in the resourcing requirements in academic libraries. Factors motivating the shift include: the prolification of courses, the expanding student population, the gradual recognition of student sophistication with the use of media audiovisuals, the increasing demand for continuing education and distance learning, requiring a wider utilization of information in various formats.

According to the author's research findings, the following range of AV. and Multimedia resources were available in most of the libraries visited: slides, audiotapes, radio, microforms, computers, photocopiers, videos, films telephones, televisions, internet access, fax, CD-ROMs, CD-I, OPACs.

A good number of new technology is being acquired by these universities to provide the users with ready reference they need, computer data banks and OPACs of library collections are popularly used for research purposes.

Resourcing in Public Libraries

The AV. and Multimedia resourcing in these libraries is still minimal. The integration of technological advances in these libraries is therefore, still dismally slow. While the condition may be attributed to the government imposition of financial constraints on organizations using public funds, the other worrying factor is the librarians misconception concerning budgetary needs for stock acquisition-too often the " book-fund-first syndrome" prevails. A survey of the users of these libraries indicated that their literacy levels also contribute to the poor

AV. and Multimedia resourcing. In fact, the majority of the users in regional branch libraries are primary and secondary school going children. Those who visit them for leisure reading have minimal educational levels, though in some regions graduate school teachers also make extensive use of these libraries. Though the old trend of media resources centre not being associated with public libraries still holds, the generation user profiles are causing ripple effects making librarians to think of establishing AV. and Multimedia resources as a means of retooling for better services.

Currently, the KNLS headquarters in Nairobi is adequately equipped with AV. and Multimedia resources. The library services here serve users with higher literacy levels and with varied information needs.

Media resources commonly found in most of the KNLS branches include radios, and cassette recorders. Whether full use is made of them, is not clear. But when the author made two visits, one to a branch library in Eldoret and another in Kisumu, she found in each of them a radio, cassette receiver, and a television set working in the children's sections. This was encouraging. The main claims that can therefore be made for the Kenya public libraries (*i.e.* KNLS branches and city libraries) are: that shortly after Kenya's independence in 1963, though dominated by print, they have made along history of providing both information and leisure for the local communities in Kenya; such services have attracted many people into their reading rooms and made the public to identify libraries as important points for information search and important component of the society.

STAFFING FOR MULTIMEDIA RESOURCES

In both academic and Public libraries, there is a shortage of qualified personnel to ensure the best collection of AV. and Multimedia materials and maximize the potential of technologies and other facilities. The evolution of new tools in capturing, storing, retrieving and disseminating information have caused a considerable shift in the roles of librarians. Thus, the demand for qualified librarians with skills for management of AV. and Multimedia resources is at present high in Kenyan academic and public libraries. And the increasing demand for academic and Public libraries to cater appropriately for the disabled, especially the blind, justifies the AV. and Multimedia resourcing in these libraries. It means then that the roles of the librarians must change and be proactive.

THE MODERN LIBRARY

Modern libraries, in addition to providing patrons with access to books and other materials, often publish lists of accessions and may maintain a readers' advisory service. Interlibrary loan services, lecture series, public book reviews, and the maintenance of special juvenile collections are other important recent developments. Three systems of book classification are widely used to facilitate access to library collections: the Dewey decimal system of Melvil Dewey, the system of Charles Ammi Cutter, and the Library of Congress system. Since the 1930s public library systems have had several technological tools at their disposal, including microphotographic techniques for copying, computer data banks enabling the storage of far more information and the search of indexes and catalogs far more quickly than ever before, and computer networks that provide instant access to materials in libraries throughout the world and to the Internet and its increasingly rich resources.

Major university libraries in the United States must work to meet an enormous demand for research materials and spend nearly $5 million a year for books and related supplies such as binding materials. Preservation of pulp-based paper, which becomes brittle after a few decades, has become a major drain on library resources; many libraries will no longer acquire books that are not printed on acid-free paper. Such libraries typically have private endowments as well as receive federal and state support. Other libraries throughout the world operate on far smaller budgets, frequently with severe financial handicaps.

The architectural design of modern public libraries in the United States has placed the highest priority on functionalism. Outstanding examples of library construction include the central housing for collections in New York City (1911), Los Angeles (1926; major renovation 1993), Baltimore (1932), and San Francisco (1996) and university buildings at Columbia (1896;

no longer a library) and Harvard (1915). Modern buildings tend toward modular construction and smaller, separate housing for special collections.

EVOLUTION

The earliest known library was a collection of clay tablets in Babylonia in the 21st cent. B.C. Ancient Egyptian temple libraries are known through the Greek writers. Diodorus Siculus describes the library of Ramses III, c.1200 B.C. The extensively catalogued library of Assurbanipal (d. 626? B.C.) in Nineveh was the most noted before that at Alexandria. The temple at Jerusalem contained a sacred library. The first public library in Greece was established in 330 B.C., in order to preserve accurate examples of the work of the great dramatists. The most famous libraries of antiquity were those of Alexandria, founded by Ptolemy I, which contained some 700,000 Greek scrolls. The library at Pergamum, founded or expanded by Eumenes II, rivaled those at Alexandria.

The first Roman libraries were brought from Greece, Asia Minor, and Syria as a result of conquests in the 1st and 2d cent. B.C. Caius Asinius Pollio established (c.40 B.C.) the first public library in Rome, but the great public libraries of the Roman Empire were the Octavian (destroyed A.D. 80) and the Palatine (destroyed c.A.D. 190) and the more important Ulpian library, founded during the reign of Trajan. In addition to these public collections, there were many fine private libraries by the time the Roman Republic was ended in 27 B.C. Of these there remain only fragments of one at Herculaneum.

The early Christian libraries were in monasteries; the Benedictines amassed a fine collection at Monte Cassino. The Romans had brought book collections to the British Isles, but important early monastic libraries were founded in York, Wearmouth, Canterbury, and elsewhere in England and Ireland by Anglo-Saxon monks. Some of the finest manuscript illumination was produced in these libraries. On the Continent, St. Columban and other missionaries founded monastic libraries in the 6th cent. Most of the ancient Greek and Latin texts that have survived until modern times were preserved in medieval European monastery libraries. The Arabs in the 9th to 15th cent. collected and preserved many libraries, and the Jews and the Byzantines also developed fine libraries during the medieval period. In the 14th and 15th cent. Charles V of France, Lorenzo de' Medici, and Frederick, duke of Urbino, all formed fine libraries; part of the Urbino library is now in the Vatican Library. In the 15th cent. the Vatican Library, the oldest public library in Europe, was formed. In 1475, Platina, as its first librarian, made a catalogue that included 2,527 volumes. In 1257 the Sorbonne library at Paris was founded, and in 1525 the erection of the Laurentian Library in Florence, designed by Michelangelo, was begun. Many of the great university libraries (*e.g.*, Bologna, Prague, Oxford, and Heidelberg) were opened in the 14th cent.

In the United States a circulating library, the Library Company of Philadelphia, was chartered in 1732 on the initiative of Benjamin Franklin. A public library had, however, been opened in Boston as early as 1653. Other early subscription libraries included the Boston Athenaeum, the New York Society Library, and the Charleston (S.C.) Library Society. In 1833 the first tax-supported library in the country opened at Peterborough, N.H. The American Library Association was formed in 1876, and this organization spurred improvements in library methods and in the training of librarians.

Libraries in the United States and Great Britain benefited greatly from the philanthropy of Andrew Carnegie, who gave more than $65 million for public library buildings in the United States alone and strengthened local interest by making the grants contingent upon public support. Among the innovations of the late 19th cent. were free public access to books (involving elaborate classification schemes) and branch libraries or deposit stations for books in many parts of cities; in the early 20th cent. travelling libraries, or "bookmobiles," began to take books to readers in rural or outlying areas.

NOTABLE LIBRARIES

Among the chief modern public and university libraries are the Bibliothèque nationale and the Mazarine, Paris; the British Museum, London; the Bodleian Library, Oxford; the Vatican Library, Rome; the Ambrosian Library, Milan; the Laurentian Library, Florence; the Russian State Library, Moscow; the Huntington Library, San Marino, Calif. the Library of Congress, Washington, D.C.; the New York Public Library; the libraries of Chicago, Columbia, Harvard, Princeton, Yale, and other major American universities; and the Newbery and John Crerar libraries in Chicago.

There are several sorts of libraries in the United States and elsewhere that exist apart from the public and university systems. Three'major categories of these are private libraries, usually housing special collections, *e.g.*, the Pierpont Morgan Library in New York City of rare books in the humanities and the Folger Shakespeare Library in Washington, D.C. presidential libraries, which contain the papers of past presidents not held in the Library of Congress, *e.g.*, the Jimmy Carter Library, Atlanta, Ga., the Dwight D. Eisenhower Library, Abilene, Kans., the Gerald R. Ford Library, Ann Arbour, Mich., the Rutherford B. Hayes Library, Fremont, Ohio, the Herbert Hoover Library, West Branch, Iowa, the Lyndon Baines Johnson Library at the Univ. of Texas, Austin, the John Fitzgerald Kennedy Library, Boston, the Franklin D. Roosevelt Library, Hyde Park, N.Y., and the Harry S. Truman Library, Independence, Mo.; and industrial libraries formed by many corporations to house research works relevant to their business.

AUTOMATED DIGITAL LIBRARIES

The Cost of Access to Research Information

Libraries are expensive and research libraries are particularly expensive. Even in the United States, few people can afford good access to primary scientific, medical, legal and scholarly information. Members of major universities have excellent library services. So do people who work in teaching hospitals, or for drug companies or rich law firms. Others have access to information only through the tedious, inefficient system of interlibrary lending. In less affluent countries the situation is worse; even the best universities cannot afford good libraries. Must access to scientific and professional information always be expensive, or is it possible that digital libraries might change this sad situation?

The costs of a conventional research library fall into three main categories: facilities (which include buildings), library materials and staff. In digital libraries, the facilities costs are small, since digital libraries avoid the need for expensive buildings. Digital libraries require computers and networks, but these are relatively inexpensive, and the costs to users are shared with other services, such as electronic mail and word processing.

To build digital libraries that are inexpensive for users requires dramatic reductions in the costs of materials and of staff. Progress is being made in reducing material costs. Open access materials on the Internet are making many primary materials available at no cost. Some open access materials are identical to those that are available commercially. Others provide an acceptable substitute, such as Amazon.com as an alternative to *Books in Print*. For several disciplines, the open access materials are already good enough to support research. In an earlier paper, I discussed the economic forms that are supporting these open access publications and the strong economic reasons to believe that the volume of open access materials will increase.

Hence, the key to inexpensive access to information lies in lower staff costs, which is the subject of this article. Big libraries are labour-intensive. Although salaries are low, staff costs are the largest item in most budgets, typically about half. The libraries at Harvard employ a thousand people and the Library of Congress more than four thousand. If professional and research information is to be available more widely, either users must bypass libraries, or libraries will have to employ fewer people. Over the past thirty-five years, libraries have automated routine clerical tasks, such as circulation or filing catalogue cards. Is it possible that, at some future date, computers might assume the skilled tasks that now require professional librarians?

The term "automated digital library" can be used to describe a digital library where all tasks are carried out automatically. Computer programmes substitute for the intellectually demanding tasks that are traditionally carried out by skilled professionals. These tasks include selection, cataloguing and indexing, seeking for information, reference services, and so on. The common theme is that these activities require considerable mental activity, the type of activity that people are skilled at and computers find difficult. Automated digital libraries should not be confused with library automation, which uses computing to reduce routine tasks in conventional libraries.

Equivalent Library Services

The remainder of this paper discusses the question of whether automated digital libraries can give good service to users. The short answer is that many aspects of automated libraries are a mirage—always just over the horizon—but some are surprisingly close or actually with us today. The underlying question is not whether automated digital libraries can rival conventional digital libraries today. They clearly cannot. The question is whether we can conceive of a time (perhaps twenty years from now) when they will provide an acceptable substitute.

Quality of service in automated digital libraries will not come from replicating the procedures of classical librarianship. More likely, automated libraries will provide users with equivalent services that are fundamentally different in the way that they are delivered. For example, within the foreseeable future, computer programmes are unlikely to be much good at applying the Anglo American Cataloguing Rules to monographs. But cataloguing rules are a means to an end, not the end itself. They exist to provide services to users, notably information discovery. Automatic methods for information discovery may not need traditional cataloguing rules. The criterion for evaluating the new methods is whether the users find what the information that they require.

Consider the contrast between web search engines and conventional abstracting and indexing services or library catalogs. Almost everything that is best about a library catalogue is done badly by a web search service. The selection of which materials to index by a web search engine relies on arbitrary considerations, the indexing records are crude at best, authority control is non-existent, and the elimination of duplicates leaves much to be desired. On the other hand, web search services are strong in ways that catalogs are weak. While cataloguing is expensive, indexing the web is cheap. The leading web search engines index several hundred million web pages every month, more than the total number cf MARC records that have ever been created. It is wrong to claim that conventional catalogs or indexes are superior because of their quality control, and it is equally wrong to claim that the web search services are superior because of their coverage and currency. The value to users depends on what the user wants to achieve.

For medical research, no web search engine can approach the National Library of Medicine's Medline service. Medline has over 11 million references and abstracts. It is built by a team of indexers who have knowledge of bio-medical research, using indexing rules and MeSH subject headings that have been developed laboriously over decades. In contrast, web search services such as Google are entirely automated. The indexes are built by a team of computers with no knowledge of what they are indexing. Google has the advantage over Medline of indexing hundreds of millions of web pages, and doing so repeatedly every month. It is quite useful for finding general information on medical topics, but it does not index the major scientific journals, its indexing records are crude, it has no understanding of medical terminology, and makes no attempt to separate sound medicine from quackery. It is a long way from being a substitute for Medline.

On the other hand, consider the trade-off between Google and Inspec, which is the leading abstracting and indexing service for computing. I used to be a regular user of Inspec, but have largely abandoned it in favour of Google. In many areas of computing, Google's restriction to open access web materials is relatively unimportant, since almost every significant result first appears on a web site and only later reaches the printed journals, if ever. Google is more up to date than Inspec, its coverage is broader and its indexing records are good enough for me to find what I am looking for. But its greatest strength is that everything in its indexes is available online with open access. In computing, substantially the same information is often available from several sources. Google provides a direct link to an open access version. Inspec references a formally published version, which is usually printed or online with restricted access. For my purposes, Google's broad coverage and convenient links more than compensate for its weaknesses.

This discussion highlights important differences between disciplines. For example, a scientist judges a library catalogue simply as a tool for information discovery, while, for a humanist, the catalogue may be a bibliographic source in its own right. Any predictions of the future value of web search engines compared with conventional abstracting and indexing services depend heavily on the publication and reading habits of people in different disciplines. However, as we look ahead twenty years, the most difficult part of the comparison is to guess how the automated tools will develop. We know that they will improve dramatically and we can anticipate that research habits will accommodate themselves to the new tools, but only a fool would attempt to forecast the precise changes that will occur.

Brute Force Computing

The first serious study of what is here called automated digital libraries was at MIT in the 1960s, under the leadership of J. C. R. Licklider, and discussed in his 1965 book "Libraries of the Future". This remarkable book described the design of what he called "procognitive systems" for the year 2000. It envisaged digital libraries based around "information-processing schemata" that would be free from the physical constraints of books and library shelves. He listed twenty-five desiderata listed for procognitive systems. Many of these are definitely in the realm of artificial intelligence. For example, one of his desiderata was, "Converse or negotiate with the user while he formulates his requests and while responding to them."

At the time that Licklider was writing, early experiments in artificial intelligence showed great promise in imitating human processes with simple algorithms. (For a contemporary view of this work, see Feigenbaum and Feldman, "Computers and Thought".) Therefore, Licklider was optimistic that, within thirty years, advanced algorithms in fields such as natural language understanding would enable intellectual processes to be carried out automatically.

Thirty-five years later, we can see that many of the results that he predicted have come to fruition, but not all and not in the manner that he expected. The development of sophisticated natural language processing has been slower than hoped, with general-purpose software still on the distant horizon. However, while Licklider and his contemporaries were over-optimistic about the development of sophisticated methods of artificial intelligence, they underestimated how much could be achieved by brute force computing, in which vast amounts of computer power are used with simple algorithms.

The rate of progress in computing power is described by Moore's Law, that the number of transistors on a semiconductor doubles every eighteen months. This is roughly equivalent to saying that computing power increases 100-fold in 10 years or 10,000-fold in 20 years. Few people can appreciate the implications of such dramatic change, but the future of automated digital libraries is likely to depend more on brute force computing than on sophisticated algorithms.

Many of the most successful methods of artificial intelligence apply simple methods to huge volumes of data. An interesting example comes from the computer programmes that play chess. The IBM system that is now equal to the world's greatest grandmasters is descended from Deep Thought, a student project at Carnegie Mellon University. The members of the Deep Thought team were not chess experts. Their breakthrough came from expertise in developing exceptionally fast hardware, which could analyze immense numbers of chess variations.

The potential for automated digital libraries lies in the simple observation that:

Simple algorithms plus immense computing power often outperform human intelligence.

Moore's Law tells us that the computing power will be available.

THE STATE-OF-THE-ART IN AUTOMATED DIGITAL LIBRARIES

The introduction of automated digital libraries is a continual process, much of it happening outside conventional libraries. Here are some current examples.

Information Discovery: Information discovery illustrates the complementary skills of computers and people. Humans are skilled at reading a few thousand words and extracting complex concepts. Faced with a billion pages (roughly the size of the web), they are helpless. Computers can index every word in a billion pages and search the indexes for simple patterns almost instantaneously.

The web search services represent the state-of-the-art in automated information discovery. Within each service lie a number of separate processes, each of which is carried out automatically, and each of which is constrained by the current state of computing. To build the indexes, a web crawler must decide which pages to index, eliminate duplicates, create a short index record for each page and add the terms found on the page to its inverted files. To search the index, the search engine must convert the user's query to a search command, match it against the inverted files, rank the results and return them to the user.

To anticipate the potential of automatic systems to rival the functionality of Medline in all disciplines, we need to examine the components of a system like Google and see how they could be improved. Moore's law predicts that computers will be 10,000 times more powerful in twenty years. With such computer power available, we know that the automatic search systems will be extremely good, even if no new algorithms are invented.

For example, to decide how closely a document matches a query would seem to require human judgment, yet standard methods of information retrieval do remarkably well. They use the power of computers to match simple patterns as a surrogate for the human ability to relate concepts. As humans, we use our understanding of language to observe that two texts are on similar topics, or to rank how closely documents match a query. Computers can estimate closeness of match by comparing word frequencies. One basic concept, developed by Gerald Salton at Cornell University about 1970, represents each document as a multi-dimensional vector and uses the angle between their vectors as a measure of the similarity of two documents.

Evaluating the importance of documents would appear to be another task that requires human understanding, but Google's ranking algorithm does remarkably well entirely automatically. The idea behind this algorithm is simple. Google ranks web pages by how many other pages link to them. It gives greater weight to links from higher-ranking pages. Calculating the ranks requires the algorithm to iterate through a matrix that has as many rows and columns as there are pages on the web, yet with modern computing and considerable ingenuity,

Google performs this calculation routinely. As a result, Google is remarkably successful in presenting a user with the most important page on a topic or a well-respected overview. This algorithm was developed as part of the NSF-funded Digital Library Initiative.

Archiving and Preservation: The Internet Archive, directed by Brewster Kahle, provides a topical example of the economic advantages of automated digital libraries. The Internet is an extremely important part of modern culture and contains many materials that should be preserved for future generations. Each month, a web crawler gathers every open access web page with associated images. The Internet Archive preserves these files for the future and mounts them on computers available for scholarly research today.

The Internet Archive is not perfect. Only HTML pages and images are collected, no Java applets or style sheets; the materials are dumped into a computer system with no organization or indexing; broken links are left broken; and access for scholars is rudimentary. Yet the simple fact is that without the automated approach of the Internet Archive, these materials would already have been lost. Attempts to catalogue and collect web materials using skilled librarians and archivists have floundered on the scale of effort needed to do even a rudimentary job.

Citations, Hyperlinks and Reference Linking: Citation analysis is a long-standing success story of applying computers to library information. Inspired by the efforts of Eugene Garfield, the founder of Science Citation Index, there is a long tradition of using citations as bibliographic measures. Hyperlinks are the web's equivalent to citations. Since they are already in machine-readable form, they are amenable to algorithmic analysis. Google's ranking algorithm can be seen as applying the concepts of citation analysis to the web.

Hyperlinks refer to items or copies of a work, but citations normally refer to the work itself or a specific manifestation. Automatic systems are becoming capable of extracting a reference from a document and linking it to the digital object that it references. Currently, the most fully automated system for reference linking is the SFX system, created by Hebert Van de Sompel and colleagues at the University of Ghent. Reference linking is one of the building blocks that are being used to build large-scale automated digital libraries. ResearchIndex is a digital library of computer science materials, created entirely automatically by Steve Lawrence and colleagues at NEC. It makes extensive use of citation analysis and reference linking. It downloads papers from the web. If they are in PostScript or PDF, it converts them to text. It parses the papers to extract citations and the context for the citation. It provides users with services such as searching the entire text or the citations, listing the references within a paper, following the citation links, or displaying the context in which references appear. An interesting aspect of ResearchIndex is that it provides a way for users to submit corrections, automatically of course.

Beyond Text: Metadata is one of the foundations of librarianship. There are a number of projects that extract metadata from digital objects automatically. Perhaps the most remarkable is the Informedia project, led by Howard Wactlar at Carnegie Mellon University. Informedia has the extremely ambitious goal of providing access to segments of video, such as television news, entirely automatically. Thus it includes algorithms for dividing raw video into discrete items, for generating short summaries (called "skims"), for indexing the sound track using speech recognition, for recognizing faces and for searching using methods of natural language processing. Each of these methods is a tough research topic and, not surprisingly, Informedia provides only a rough-and-ready service, but overall it is surprisingly effective. Moreover, many of the weaknesses of Informedia could be overcome by applying huge amounts of computing power. Informedia was another project of the Digital Library Initiative.

REFERENCE LIBRARIANSHIP

The job of a reference librarian ranges from helping users with the mechanics of using a library to tasks that require deep intellectual understanding. The ugly term "disintermediation" is used when users perform for themselves tasks that used to be carried out with the help of a librarian. Could we conceive of an automated digital library that disintermediates all the services that reference librarians now provide?

Information retrieval provides a good test case. The mechanics of searching have been almost completely assumed by computing. The current generation of scholars never experienced the tedium of reading through long lists of abstracts, searching huge card catalogs and following citations laboriously from journal to journal. Searching a card catalogue required skill. Because of the labour in creating and filing cards, only a small number of entries were provided for each work. Since few users ever mastered the complex rules for the main and supplementary headings, or the intricate filing conventions, serious users turned to reference librarians for help.

Automated digital libraries can clearly help with the mechanics of searching, but information seeking is more complex. Some years ago, I wanted to find data to support Moore's Law. Specifically I wanted to compare the rate of progress in semiconductors, magnetic media and telecommunications. After searching for half an hour using the standard online tools, I gave up and asked a reference librarian. Half an hour later she provided me with the data that I wanted. There was nothing magical about the methods that she used. She simply had more expertise in the idiosyncrasies of the information available and how to navigate through it. Automated libraries are a very long way from providing such insights.

In disciplines with complex organization of information, searching for information remains a skilled task. Often, knowledge of the subject matter is paramount and the experts develop their own skills. For example, carrying out legal research online is a basic skill that every law student learns. Historically, most doctors needed the help of a medical librarian to carry out an in-depth search. Now, even in medicine, the tools available to the user are sufficiently good that most searches can now be carried out directly by the user. It seems that automatic tools are steadily reducing the need for reference librarians in these fields.

However, consider a problem once set to a student by Marvin Minsky of MIT. How would we create a computer system to answer questions such as, "Why was the space station a bad idea?". For many years, we have had computer systems that can search enormous collections of text for the phrase "space station", or simple variations. For this purpose, computers clearly out-perform human searching for both speed and accuracy. But consider the concept "a bad idea". What is the possibility of computers being able to examine any arbitrary text and look for such abstract concepts within it? The recognition that no existing computer could address such questions stimulated the student (Danny Hillis) to design new computer architectures and to found the company Thinking Machines, but even with the most advanced parallel computers, nothing on the horizon approaches human judgment in understanding such subtleties.

COST

This article ends as it began, with cost. Undoubtedly the greatest advantage of automated digital libraries is cost. Computing power is much cheaper than human expertise, more so every year. When money and time are available in abundance, skilled professionals have no equal. But they are always in short supply. In the United States, the National Library of Medicine is funded by the government and provides open access to Medline, but only rich lawyers can afford to use the legal services provided by Westlaw and Lexis.

Because of the cost, traditional library systems are selective. Indexing and abstracting services restrict their coverage to a carefully selected set of publications. Catalogs do not include potentially useful information from monographs, such as individual items in anthologies, subheading, captions, and so on. There are essentially no attempts to catalogue the content of web sites, below the level of the whole site. Even so, these services are very expensive.

Automatic systems have no trouble with being inclusive; they have problems when they attempt to be selective. Their weakness is lack of precision. They exhibit what, in a human, would be called very poor judgment. Both ISI's Web of Science® and ResearchIndex provide users with interlinked scientific documents. Web of Science is a splendid service, but its production is not fully automatic, since ISI relies on skilled personnel for election and for key parts of the input process. Because the ResearchIndex methods are automatic and are applied to raw data, ResearchIndex inevitably has errors, while the skilled staff at ISI eliminate almost all errors, but at a cost. A library subscription to the Web of Science costs $100,000 per year. ResearchIndex is free.

To conclude, automated digital libraries combined with open access information on the Internet offer to provide the Model T Ford of information. Nobody would claim that the Model T Ford was a peer to the handcrafted cars of its generation, and automated digital libraries cannot approach the personal service available to the faculty of a well-endowed university. But few people could afford a hand-built car, and few people have easy access to a major research library. The low cost of automated digital libraries is already bringing scientific, scholarly, medical and legal information to new audiences.

4

Management and Preservation of Digital Publications

Executive Summary and List of Recommendations

There is an urgent need for Australian libraries and collecting institutions to collectively address the management and preservation of Australian physical-format digital publications which form part of the national documentary heritage. While information delineating the problems of dealing with digital publications is abundant, useful accounts of actual projects are limited. Australian libraries need to invest some funding and effort on practical investigations that will address preservation and access issues.

Australian participation in the development of international standards relating to the preservation of physical-format digital publications is important, and the National Library proposes to provide a continuing role in coordinating Australian developments.

A cooperative approach to the collecting of Australian physical-format digital publications by the legal deposit libraries is required to make sure that this material is comprehensively represented in Australian collections. As part of this, the designation of the National Film and Sound Archive as a legal depository is an essential step. Increased reporting of holdings to the National Bibliographic Database is another desirable development.

Fair dealing and library provisions should apply equally to physical-format digital publications, and legal deposit libraries need to find a common position on the use and distribution of these materials. Licensing arrangements should not be able to restrict or limit fair use. Preservation efforts for physical format digital publications need close coordination, funding support and will involve approaches to publishers. Any work being undertaken on physical-format digital publications needs to be informed by similar work on online digital publications with a view to integrating both digital formats.

Recommendations

1. That the National Library of Australia and the state libraries cooperate in the development of a national model for a national digital archive.
2. That the National Library of Australia and the state libraries coordinate funding proposals designed to establish the national digital archive.
3. That the National Library of Australia continue to provide the necessary forums and venues needed to ensure the continuation of the process.
4. The National Library continue to develop and maintain contacts with overseas institutions with a view to publicising Australian initiatives and issues in the area of digital preservation, monitoring relevant work being carried out elsewhere, and sharing experience and expertise.
5. The National Library share this information with the Library community via the PADI WWW site and the NATSTATLIBS discussion list.
6. State libraries share any relevant information they have on international developments by the same means.
7. That each state library accept responsibility for active collection of their own state's output of physical-format digital publishing.
8. That the legal deposit libraries formulate a set of guidelines aimed at ensuring that as much of Australia's physical electronic publishing heritage as possible is collected. In some cases this may be by sampling.
9. That the National Library of Australia and the state libraries support the designation of the National Film

and Sound Archive as a national legal deposit repository for physical-format digital publishing.

10. That the National Library of Australia and the state libraries cooperate in the drafting of a statement on the use of legal deposit physical-format digital publications in libraries.
11. That state libraries in those states with more than one deposit library review policies for the deposit of physical-format digital publications with a view to simplification.
12. That the National Library of Australia and the state libraries explore the development of a joint-use standard licence for situations where libraries must enter a licensing arrangement for the use of physical-format digital publications.
13. That the National Library of Australia and the state libraries accept the principle of preserving what they can in the best way they can at the present time.
14. That the National Library of Australia and the state libraries investigate their research needs as decided at the National Consultative Meeting in October 1997, identifying what is currently known, what gaps and barriers exist, looking for relevant research work already underway, and looking for potential partners for research and for research funding.
15. That this activity be coordinated by a national working group consisting of representatives from the preservation services sections of the National Library of Australia and all state libraries, with other people enlisted to help as necessary from other areas of these libraries or from other organisations.
16. That the National Library of Australia and state libraries contribute to a fund to support a modest but focused research effort aimed at addressing the highest priority research needs.
17. That the National Library of Australia and state libraries formally ask publishers and software providers to discuss practical ways they could assist the preservation effort by means such as the level of information provided with

publications, the supply of "preservation-friendly" versions, and the maximum use of backwards and forwards compatibility standards. This assistance would be requested in the context of bona fide respect for publishers' commercial interests.

18. That institutions contribute data, at least at the minimum level prescribed for physical format electronic publications, to the NBD in order to provide a source of copy cataloguing and holdings information for these resources.
19. That the ABN field Actions Note (NTA) and at least subfields a and 5 (preservation action and NUC symbol of institution) be used to record information on intent to permanently retain and/or reformat for continued access.

For a number of years electronic publishing has been providing both opportunities and challenges to writers and publishers as they attempt to take advantage of this new medium to express and communicate ideas. It has also provided libraries with an unparalleled opportunity for increasing access to library materials, as well as challenges in collecting and preserving digital publications.

Physical-format digital publications are part of the broader category of digital publications. Many of the recommendations in this paper relating to physical-format digital publications will also apply to online digital publications. Much work on managing and preserving online digital publications is being carried out in parallel with the work described here.

Physical-format digital publications need to be reflected in the nation's documentary heritage collections. Libraries which have accepted responsibility for preserving Australia's published output will need to play a major role, as neither publishers nor other organisations are likely to be in a position to take on a long term preservation responsibility. However, long term accessibility will require ongoing cooperation between libraries, publishers and others to overcome the significant technical, legal and economic challenges.

In attempting to work out the implications of electronic publishing for libraries, a number of key events and initiatives have taken place over the last few years. In 1995, the National Preservation Office organised the Capturing the Rainbow conference which examined a range of issues associated with multimedia preservation. One of its main outcomes was the development of a set of principles for the preservation of and long-term access to Australian digital objects. These principles were accepted by conference participants, archivists, librarians, publishers and several relevant peak body organisations, forming the basis for future action.

In 1996 the National Library of Australia released a discussion paper entitled National Strategy for Provision of Access to Australian Electronic Publications. The purpose of the paper was to initiate debate on the many issues raised by electronic publishing, both physical format electronic publishing and online publishing. A major emphasis of the discussion paper was that of guaranteeing current and permanent access. Specifically, the paper addressed legal deposit, access conditions including copyright and fair dealing, resource discovery, development of technical and descriptive standards, and the organisation of virtual resources. Comments were invited and were received from a wide range of individuals and organisations. These comments were positive and indicated to the National Library that it should continue to progress these issues at a national level.

The National Library was convinced that solutions to many of the difficulties inherent in handling and preserving Australian electronic publications could only be achieved through collaborative action by libraries, with deposit libraries playing an important role. However, the precise nature and form of that collaboration remained unclear, and one of the objectives of the discussion paper was to raise this issue. Among its conclusions, the *National Strategy* paper noted that libraries would need to forge new relationships and understandings with publishers of electronic publications.

It was therefore a major development when forty publishers and deposit library representatives met in Canberra on 27 and 28 October 1997 at the First National Consultative Meeting on the Management of Australian Physical-Format Digital Publications. The purpose of the meeting was to seek agreement on key principles and an understanding of responsibilities related to the provision of long-term access to digital publications in physical form, and the meeting concluded with the formulation of an action plan designed to put in place agreed strategies to further these objectives. While the emphasis of this meeting was on digital publications in physical formats, further workshops in 1998 will focus on online and hybrid digital information.

This paper, 'Management and Preservation of Physical-Format Digital Publications: A National Library Position Paper on the Role of Australian Legal Deposit Libraries', is an outcome of the National Consultative Meeting. It attempts to define a National Library of Australia position on roles and responsibilities for the management of Australian physical-format digital publications. Specific issues addressed are national coverage and collecting, including legal deposit issues, access and copyright, preservation and control. This initial draft is for consideration, comment and discussion by the Council of Australian State Libraries (CASL). Throughout the paper, a short summary of the current position is followed by identified issues requiring resolution, and recommendations aimed at moving the process forward.

It is expected that this position paper can then be used as the basis for further liaison with publishers. At present, information on the Australian physical-format digital publishing scene is lacking. There is evidence that it involves an extensive range of parties far wider than traditional print publishers. Self-publishers are becoming more common, and for this reason it is increasingly difficult to determine what is being published. A study of the physical-format digital publishing industry to identify publishers of this material has been proposed, and a brief for a consultancy is being developed by the State Library of Victoria.

Ensuring Long-Term Access : Principles anc Issues

The aim of the National Library of Australia is to work with others to find practical, cost effective ways of ensuring the same level of preservation guarantee for this category of publication as for any other.

The National Library seeks to preserve long term accessibility to all the electronic publications it collects. However, there are technical and resource constraints which mean that, even if legal barriers can be overcome, it must set priorities for action. Libraries should take a leading role in identifying the specific technical stumbling blocks to preservation, and in seeking ways to deal with them. It is necessary to invest some effort in practical investigations that can inform decision making. Because the National and state libraries have a shared interest in preserving this kind of publication, these investigations and the decision making should be undertaken cooperatively.

As well as identifying research needs, libraries need to find resources to carry out the research, and partners to supply the required technical expertise. Even if technical and legal problems can be overcome, preservation is likely to be resource intensive in the foreseeable future.

Libraries will need to know the scale of costs they are likely to be asked to commit to, but they are also likely to need additional resources to meet their preservation responsibilities for these publications while maintaining responsibility for existing-and growing-collections in other formats. Whatever work is undertaken should take account of the degree of integration that can be achieved between physical-format digital and online digital publications. The National Library's preferred strategy is one that integrates both digital formats. Libraries need to consider options and articulate their interests so that decisions and commitments can be made that lead to a national model.

Recommendations

- That the National Library of Australia and the state libraries cooperate in the development of a national model for a national digital archive.
- That the National Library of Australia and the state libraries coordinate funding proposals designed to establish the national digital archive.
- That the National Library of Australia continue to provide the necessary forums and venues needed to ensure the continuation of the process.

International Developments in the Management and Preservation of Physical-Format Digital Publications

The National Library has been actively developing procedures to manage the physical-format publications in its collections. Activities focused first on storage and security of the collections then moved on to research in a range of associated preservation problems. In addition, the Library's PANDORA project for archiving Australian online publications includes a prototype metadata repository which will accommodate metadata on physical format publications.

The National Library is in contact with a number of overseas institutions, expressly to monitor developments that might inform our own initiatives in Australia, across the full range of digital archiving and preservation issues and also share our own experience and expertise.

To date, reports from institutions have concentrated on the provision of suitable storage and security but there are few practical examples of institutions addressing the greater preservation problems of rapid hardware and software obsolescence.

A number of European institutions, particularly in the Netherlands, Norway, and the United Kingdom, have made a start. Building on earlier work, most effort is now being concentrated on the NEDLIB project which has been funded to start in January 1998.

The NEDLIB project consortium is headed by the National Library of the Netherlands (Koninklijke Bibliotheek) and includes eight other European national libraries, a national archive and three main publishers. The main goal is to find ways to ensure that both online and offline digital publications of the present can be used now and in the future.

The British National Preservation Office has proposed research into technology preservation, technology emulation and information migration, but this work has not yet been commissioned.

Canada and the United States have not yielded as much practical research as might have been expected despite important papers that have been published on electronic preservation issues by groups such as the Commission on Preservation and Access and the Research Libraries Group. In these countries it appears that the major priorities for libraries are the digitisation of, and provision of online access to, endangered printed materials, and the preservation of online digital material such as electronic journals. The Library of Congress is studying the media deterioration of CDs but is apparently not yet examining the systems and software obsolescence problems.

Recommendations

- The National Library continue to develop and maintain contacts with overseas institutions with a view to publicising Australian initiatives and issues in the area of digital preservation, monitoring relevant work being carried out elsewhere, and sharing experience and expertise.
- The National Library share this information with the Library community via the PADI WWW site and the NATSTATLIBS discussion list.
- State libraries share any relevant information they have on international developments by the same means.

National Coverage, Legal Deposit and Collecting of Physical-Format Digital Publications

Current Situation:

- At present the collecting of physical-format digital publications by libraries in Australia is uncoordinated, and national coverage in collecting is far from complete. A survey conducted by the National Library in 1997 found that only 35% of Australian physical format digital publications were being collected and recorded on the National Bibliographic Database (ABN), an unacceptably low coverage figure for deposit libraries concerned with the collection of national heritage material.
- Legal deposit of this component of the nation's publishing output is essential to ensure its comprehensive collection. While some states have in place appropriate legal deposit provisions, there is no legal deposit legislation for

physical-format digital publications at the national level. There is no designated national repository for films and sound recordings which are increasingly being produced as physical-format digital publications. In the absence of legal deposit legislation at the national level, the National Library has established a voluntary deposit scheme for physical-format digital publications. This is an interim measure only, and the Library does not regard voluntary deposit as a satisfactory alternative to legal deposit legislation.

Issues:

- To improve the collecting situation for physical-format digital publications, a cooperative approach among legal deposit libraries and other collecting institutions is essential. Collecting policies for this material need to be articulated, agreed and published. Cataloguing onto the national bibliographic database would benefit resource discovery and data sharing.
- A coordinated national approach by libraries to the collecting of physical-format digital publications is required, to ensure that all categories of this material are represented in collections, and that early examples of these publications do not vanish.
- There is a need to establish a national repository for films and sound recordings, including film and sound material in physical-format digital form. The National Film and Sound Archive would be an obvious choice as a legal deposit repository for Australia's heritage in this area.
- There is a need for libraries to reach agreement on the conditions for the use and distribution of legally deposited, and voluntarily deposited, physical-format digital publications. Such a document would address library concerns for access as well as copyright owner concerns on protection of their intellectual property. This agreement would form the basis for discussions with publishers.
- There may be advantages in reducing the complexity of demands on depositors. Where there is more than one

depository library at state level, it may be desirable to designate a particular library as the single point of deposit for physical format electronic material. A simple uniform deposit regime of one copy to the national depository institution, and one copy to the relevant library at the state level would be simpler and less confusing to depositors, and the deposit of two copies in two different libraries provides a safeguard for the survival of material in case of disaster.

Recommendations:

- That each state library accept responsibility for active collection of their own state's output of physical-format digital publishing.
- That the legal deposit libraries formulate a set of guidelines aimed at ensuring that as much of Australia's physical electronic publishing heritage as possible is collected. In some cases this may be by sampling.
- That the National Library of Australia and the state libraries support the designation of the National Film and Sound Archive as a national legal deposit repository for physical-format digital publishing.
- That the National Library of Australia and the state libraries cooperate in the drafting of a statement on the use of legal deposit physical-format digital publications in libraries.
- That state libraries in those states with more than one deposit library review policies for the deposit of physical-format digital publications with a view to simplification.

Access to Physical-Format Digital Publications

Current Situation:

- The National Library of Australia believes that information should be accessible regardless of format. The Library considers the fair dealing and library provisions of the Copyright Act to be as applicable in the digital environment as they are in the print world.
- The National Library of Australia, together with other Australian libraries, is committed to complying with all

applicable laws concerned with intellectual property. This commitment includes the full exercise of rights accorded to the Library and its users in the Copyright Act under the fair dealing and library copying provisions which are essential to the functioning of all libraries. The National Library takes all necessary precautions to ensure that Library staff and users are made aware of the requirements of the Copyright Act, but can accept no responsibility for infringement of copyright by its users.

- Many of the physical format electronic products purchased by the Library are received with licences which place restrictions on the users and permitted uses of the product. In particular, printing, downloading, copying and inter-library loan functions may be restricted or disallowed. The Library holds that these restrictions should not be allowed to override the fair dealing and library provisions of the Copyright act.

Issues:

- Where licensing agreements must be entered into by libraries, development of a standard form incorporating library requirements is desirable. The present practice of individual libraries negotiating with publishers over terms and conditions of use for physical format electronic publications is costly and time consuming. A common approach by the legal deposit libraries of Australia would also give them more bargaining power.

Recommendations:

- That the National Library of Australia and the state libraries explore the development of a joint-use standard licence for situations where libraries must enter a licensing arrangement for the use of physical-format digital publications.

PRESERVATION

Current Situation: The National Library has been receiving Australian physical format digital publications since 1983. Until recently, preservation efforts have focused largely on storage and security of these collections. Since the appointment of an electronic preservation officer, a more active programme of testing preservation options has been instituted. There are two critical characteristics that demand an active preservation response: the instability of the media and changes in technology. These characteristics also affect online publications. Many of the distinctions between publishing formats blur in a digital environment, creating the challenge of recognising where similar responses can be used, and where differences need to shape the response.

Issues: There are many issues needing to be resolved in providing a reasonable guarantee of ongoing accessibility. The major issues appear to be:

- *Finding appropriate preservation pathways.* At present it is still not feasible to do more than transfer publications from less stable to more stable carriers. However, to ensure ongoing accessibility, research work is needed on a variety of other options including migration to new hardware and software environments with minimal losses, new software that emulates the operating environment of superseded publications, maintenance of the required hardware and software once it has been superseded, or a combination of these. Research work is needed on all of these options, and on any others that emerge which have the potential to contribute to the available preservation pathways. Libraries also need to maintain current awareness of other relevant activities and to apply information as it becomes available, to assist evolving decisions about the most appropriate pathways to pursue.
- *Facilitating forwards migration beyond current software dependencies.* At present migration appears to be the best solution, supported by other options for selected items. However, widespread migration is still constrained by problems such as inconsistent transfer and recording of information about collection items; physical and legal restrictions on copying; poor use of standards that would support backwards and forwards interoperability, even where they exist; and the practical difficulties of re-writing some programmes to work in a different environment.

Recommendations:

- That the National Library of Australia and the state libraries accept the principle of preserving what they can in the best way they can at the present time.
- That the National Library of Australia and the state libraries investigate their research needs as decided at the National Consultative Meeting in October 1997, identifying what is currently known, what gaps and barriers exist, looking for relevant research work already underway, and looking for potential partners for research and for research funding.
- That this activity be coordinated by a national working group consisting of representatives from the preservation services sections of the National Library of Australia and all state libraries, with other people enlisted to help as necessary from other areas of these libraries or from other organisations.
- That the National Library of Australia and state libraries contribute to a fund to support a modest but focused research effort aimed at addressing the highest priority research needs.
- That the National Library of Australia and state libraries formally ask publishers and software providers to discuss practical ways they could assist the preservation effort by means such as the level of information provided with publications, the supply of "preservation-friendly" versions, and the maximum use of backwards and forwards compatibility standards. This assistance would be requested in the context of bona fide respect for publishers' commercial interests.

Cataloguing Physical-Format Digital Publications

Current Situation:

- On a national level, many libraries are cataloguing CD-ROMs and other physical format electronic publications. The National Library provides access to physical format electronic publications in the same way as it does for print and other types of material in its collections. Catalogue records are created on the National

Bibliographic Database (NBD) to provide both a source for copy cataloguing data and location information to these resources. These records are then added to the Library's catalogue.

- The National Library generally receives CD ROMs and other physical format electronic publications either as individual publications or as material accompanying print publications. Cataloguing of individual publications follow AACR2, rules for the description of computer files; while print publications with accompanying CD ROMs or other physical-format digital publications are primarily described in terms of the print material, with system requirements and related information included in note fields.
- In cataloguing physical format electronic publications, the standards followed in creating data for the NBD are the ABN recommended standards for computer files. These standards support a range of cataloguing levels, with required elements described for both a minimum standard record and a high level record. This provides a degree of flexibility in the amount of information included in such catalogue records.
- These ABN standards prescribe mandatory fields, for both minimum and high level records. Apart from a small number of coded data fields, they are: Title, Imprint, Collation and System Requirements. The General Material Designation (GMD) is also mandatory and [computer file] is used for all electronic materials. For other fields specific to cataloguing physical format electronic publications see the Appendix at the end of this document.
- Cataloguing standards used in descriptive data creation specifically for electronic publications are:

AACR2 rev.

ABN Data Preparation Manual. Part 2: Description and Integrated Tags

ABN Cataloguing Manual

ALA Guidelines for Bibliographic Description of Interactive Multimedia

Other useful bibliographical tools are:

Olson, Nancy B. *Cataloguing Computer Files.*

ISBD(ER) international standard bibliographic description for electronic resources: revised from the ISBD(CF): international standard bibliographic description for computer files, recommended by the ISBD(CF) Review Group.

Issues:

- Good quality, timely cataloguing of physical format electronic publications is essential for library operations such as acquisition by others, and preservation.
- A survey of the current situation with regard to the cataloguing of this material indicates that rates of cataloguing onto the National Bibliographic Database may be low. A higher rate of reporting to the NBD would benefit both resource discovery and data sharing.

Recommendations:

- That institutions contribute data, at least at the minimum level prescribed for physical format electronic publications, to the NDB in order to provide a source of copy cataloguing and holdings information for these resources.
- That the ABN field Actions Note (NTA) and at least subfields a and 5 (preservation action and NUC symbol of institution) be used to record information on intent to permanently retain and/or reformat for continued access.

MIGRATION TRIALS: MIGRATING PUBLICATIONS ON FLOPPY DISK TO CD-R

The collections of the National Library of Australia contain many publications on computer disks which require innovative preservation responses. Unless they are managed carefully, media instability and technological obsolescence will limit the potential for ongoing accessibility.

CD-ROMs are still a current and popular technology with relatively stable media, so attention has first been focused on the floppy disks in the collection. Copying and migration of information on computer disks is likely to be the most useful preservation method currently available. To examine how we might implement these strategies a series of trials will be conducted. The results of the first trial are described below.

Aim

The overall aim of this project was to migrate information from published Australian floppy disks to CD-R (recordable compact disc), to investigate the usefulness of this migration pathway.

It became clear that this was more an exercise in copying data from one medium to another, which is only a part of the process of migration, rather than complete migration across technologies. This has a valid purpose, considering the average life of a floppy disk is estimated at less than ten years. However it does not adequately address the problems of changing operating systems or associated software dependencies. Further research is needed to establish reliable preservation pathways that will work longer term.

Method

1. *Identifying and Locating Disks :* Searching the NLA ILMS (Integrated Library Management System) was chosen as the most useful way of identifying and locating disks in the general collections. (The search terms and results are presented in Note).

This produced a total of 1,539 records and appears to have captured a majority of items. Many of these records, however were for overseas publications, including over 400 records for material mounted on the ADONIS system.

The only serials located in this search were those where the primary material was a computer file. Print serials with accompanying disks were not located.

2. *Selecting Representative Sample for Trial :* To determine the various complications that may be encountered in transferring publications to CD-R, a representative sample had to be chosen for testing. A survey was carried out of all Australian material that may be considered for long-term access, located in the general collection.

From the 405 surveyed titles found to contain computer disks, 66 containing floppy disks were chosen as a representative sample for a migration trial. The publications were chosen to represent a number of variables:

- operating system (e.g. DOS, Mac OS),
- hardware requirements (e.g. processor speed),
- software requirements (e.g. Word 1.1, Word 6 etc.),
- disk size (5 1/4", 3 1/2"),
- number of disks per title (some titles contained multiple disks),
- age (up to 12 years old),
- proportion of publication on floppy disk (whole publication, supplementary material, set-up software for CD-ROM).

3. *The Copying Process :* The copying process devised in conjunction with the Information Technology Branch and the operators of the CD-R writing equipment in NLA (the Photographics section at the time of the trial), was to transfer the data from the original floppy disks to a network drive, download the data to the hard drive of the CD-R host PC, and then write to CD-R. The entire process (with the exception of file comparison) was carried out with hardware and software currently available in the Library.

Of the 66 items trialed:

- 22 items (all PC) were functional before and after copying to CD-R.
- 5 items (all Mac) were functional before, but not after, copying to CD-R.
- 23 items were found to be untestable (and unusable) at the first step, as the Library was unable to locate the necessary hardware or operating software
- 1 item was found to be untestable (and unusable) at the first step because the sliding disk cover had been fouled by a security tag
- 1 item was found at the 3rd step (file scanning) to have accumulated so many errors that it could not be read.

(This also affected another item, but a backup disk had been supplied which was still readable.)

- 12 items were found at the 4th step not have the required software to function properly. These were written to the CD-R, although they could not be fully tested afterwards. However, file comparison results, and tests with similar software to that required, suggested that these items had copied faithfully
- 1 item was found at the 4th step to be blank.

Other problems detected included incorrect path names in supplied disk instructions, and material of such an obscure technical nature that it was difficult to tell whether copying had successfully maintained functionality or not.

A detailed description of the copying process follows.

i. Select appropriate hardware and operating systems, e.g. PC or Mac, with correct size of floppy disk drive.

As noted above, a significant number of older items failed at this step, as the Library has not been able to maintain the necessary range of support facilities for all material entering the collections-in some cases they had never been available.

ii. Virus check of original floppy disks

Using the latest version of scanning software in the Library, no viruses were found.

iii. Physical disk scan to look for media deterioration of original floppy disks

PC based material was checked with Scandisk, Mac material was checked with Nortons Utilities Disk Doctor. Consistent backup file errors on older Mac disks may have reflected a change in the Mac operating system rather than a high level of disk errors.

iv. Install and run from floppy disks

At this stage of testing further significant failures were discovered: one disk being found to be blank, and 12 disks did not have the full range of required software or hardware for full functionality.

v. Copy contents of floppy disks to a network drive

This was successful for all 40 items tested.

vi. Run comparison software to check for differences between original and copy

This was successful for all PC items. Software for this step for Mac material could not be located so they were not tested.

vii. Set as "Read Only" on network drive

This was mainly to see if the files could continue to function as required in a "read only" state, as they would be on the CD-R.

viii. Install and run from network drive

Four items, hard coded to work only from an A: drive, had to be copied back from the network drive to a floppy disk to run; one of these even required renaming of the floppy disk, before it would run.

ix. Unset "Read Only"

x. Organise titles in appropriate file structure using appropriate naming convention

Files were organised into a directory structure according to the ISO 9660 standard. The naming convention would not accept the original file names from the publications, because of illegal characters or extended names (especially with Mac files).

Following a suggestion on file naming from the National Archives of Canada, it was decided to use a "call number" system for naming and arranging files on the CD-R.

xi. Create and attach documents with appropriate details such as installation instructions

A general file was created in ASCII text to describe what is on the CD-R, how files are arranged, and where detailed instructions can be found for each item.

Individual ASCII text "read.me" documents were created for each item, containing:

- call number
- hardware required
- software required
- notes to assist installation

- file name
- number of files
- storage size (in MB)
- original format and number of disks
- title
- publisher
- existence of accompanying materials
- content description (e.g. text, database, software)
- date the original was published (or copyrighted)
- whether there has been a print version of electronic contents located
- any copyright statement from the publisher

In future the text files should also document the date and new format of each migration.

xii. Write to CD-R

This part of the procedure (copying from the network drive to a local PC, automated checking of file names, and writing the CD-R) took approximately 45 minutes, during which roughly 1,900 files, containing 164 MB, were handled.

xiii Run comparison software to check for differences between original and CD-R copy

Comparison checking suggested that PC material had been copied without loss or changes from the original. Mac material could not be tested due to lack of comparison software.

xiv. Install and run from CD-R

The PC files did not appear to have any problems when they were installed and run from the CD-R, but the Mac files did not work.

Technical Problem Solving

Further investigation has shown that Mac files need to be written to a CD-R using the HFS file system, which will require different CD writing software. This suggests that it may be simplest to copy Mac and PC files onto separate CD-Rs.

Time Requirements: It was very difficult to estimate processing times in the trial, as so many steps required investigation, consultation and trial and error. However, as an indication, steps a-h required an average of 40 minutes per item tested; later steps are estimated to require an average of 35 minutes per item when being processed in a large batch (the set up time for some steps being significant whether a small or large number of items is involved). These are very rough estimates and do not take account of problems that often seem to arise, which can take many hours or days to solve, and in some cases may be insoluble. Further action required:

i. Continue tests for Macintosh materials

The migration trial conducted to date was not successful for Macintosh disks. We need to do more work to establish procedures and resources that will work for this important class of material, even if it means adopting parallel procedures.

ii. Assess priorities among "unpreservable" items and explore options

We need to assess whether any of the material we are currently unable to access is a high priority for preservation action, requiring migration or emulation. For any items identified, we will need to investigate and trial the available options.

iii. Outline preservation guidelines for selection and subsequent procedures

Once we have a better understanding of what we can hope to preserve, we will need to develop guidelines for preservation selection or preservation priorities, to complement the acquisition guidelines already in use.

iv. Define metadata and record keeping procedures

It has become apparent that more information than is held in catalogue records is needed for successful preservation management of this material.

The Library is planning to include the extra metadata and information required in the PANDORA database which is being created primarily for online publications. Using the same database for all electronic collection materials will help simplify the management of metadata. Decisions still need to be made on how, where, and when this metadata entry is best done.

v. Upgrade the facilities for preservation management

In the short term the main need is to acquire file comparison software for PC and Mac (when located) that is required to check the effectiveness of copying.

vi. Establish ongoing copying procedures for floppy disks

For the kinds of material successfully handled in the trial, copying to CD-R should be undertaken as a routine operation. It will be most efficient to batch the intake of floppies for copying each year, copying all the Mac files to one disk and the PC files to another, (subject to result of further testing of procedures for Mac files).

vii. Define access and use procedures

Storage and access arrangements for the newly created CD-Rs need to be finalised. Storage is expected to include backup provisions; controlled access arrangements are not expected to be significantly different from current practice, although it will be necessary to take account of the changed access format.

viii. Continue trials on other forms of migration

Many questions about migration will remain unanswered until further testing is undertaken to examine the feasibility of conversion between operating systems, and other, more demanding, software dependencies, to maintain accessibility. Even if some data elements can be successfully transferred, the effect on the look and feel of the publication will need to be assessed.

ix. Report the results of this trial

It is important for this basic applied research to be seen in the context of cooperative action on preservation of physical format electronic publications. We need to maintain and develop dialogue with other key players.

Conclusion

The testing has produced useful results. Not all the material in the sample was successfully migrated, but this was expected. We now have a better idea of the issues involved, and of the hardware, software and copying processes required to use and maintain the collection.

5

Statement of Principles for the Preservation

Introduction

As the twentieth century draws to a close, an ever-increasing quantity of information is created, stored, disseminated and accessed in digital form. Digital objects include data stored in digital form and accessed using electronic equipment. For example, databases, images, sound, video, text-based documents and recordkeeping systems may be digital objects. Access is often dependent on a specific combination of equipment and electronic methods of manipulation or display (software). Some digital objects are accessible only by acquiring a physical item such as a tape or CD-ROM while others are accessible through electronic networks.

The organisations charged with the responsibility of preserving and making available Australia's cultural and intellectual heritage will need to develop a range of strategies to ensure the preservation of and access to various categories of digital objects. Custodial and non-custodial arrangements will need to be considered both from a preservation and an access perspective. Preserving access to digital objects will need to be planned prior to creation if possible and considered throughout the life of the object. Points at which preserving access needs to be considered include:

- systems design;
- information creation;
- creation and capture of metadata and other essential contextual information;

- identification/appraisal/selection/collection of objects by libraries, archives and museums;
- intellectual control and provision of access facilities to the objects by libraries, archives and museums;
- management, maintenance and migration of the objects over time; and
- ongoing assessment of the continuing significance and value of the objects for future retention and access.

Notwithstanding the different strategies that will be necessary for different categories of digital objects at different stages in their lifespan, seven principles have been identified that underpin all strategies. Please note that all seven of these principles are interdependent and that no one principle is more important than any other principle. Individual principles should not be considered in isolation from the other six principles. They apply to all categories of digital objects, both in single item form and in aggregations. The principles are a logical consequence of the policy statements endorsed by the Australian Cultural Ministers Council in its National Conservation and Preservation Policy for Movable Cultural Heritage (1995). Policy statements numbers 4 and 5 are particularly relevant. They are quoted below for reference.

National Policy Statement 4

The Commonwealth, State, Territory and Local Governments recognise the need to conserve and preserve Australia's movable cultural heritage.

The explanatory note under this statement makes it clear that movable cultural heritage includes digital objects.

National Policy Statement 5

The Commonwealth, State, Territory and Local Governments recognise the important right of the Australian people to have a reasonable and an equitable opportunity of access to their movable cultural heritage, subject to cultural restrictions or sensitivities.

These principles for Preservation of and Long-Term Access to Australian Digital Objects do not attempt to describe strategies. Their purpose is to provide a basis upon which all preservation strategies for significant digital objects will be founded. No attempt is made to indicate how decisions regarding 'significance' will be determined. For the purposes of this document, an Australian digital object is defined as one which has been created by a person of Australian birth or residing within Australia or which has a significant proportion dealing with a subject of social, political, cultural, scientific or economic significance and relevance to Australia.

Additional information on preserving access to information in digital form can be found on Preserving Access to Digital Information (PADI) site.

PRINCIPLES

Overriding Statement

In an electronic environment the following principles must be applied to ensure continuing access to all categories of significant digital objects:

Principle 1: Cooperation

The cooperation of all with a role in the generation, use, management, distribution and preservation of digital objects is essential. *Continuing access to digital objects will be dependent on the cooperation of information creators, information system designers, manufacturers, publishers/distributors and information custodians and providers.*

Principle 2: Role of Creator

Creators of digital objects have the initial and in some cases a continuing role in preserving access to them. *Unless creators take initial steps to facilitate ongoing access to their material, access may be lost or the ability of another body to take responsibility for preserving access may be severely inhibited.*

Principle 3: Distributed Responsibility

The location, selection, identification/cataloguing and retention of digital objects will be best achieved through the coordinated distribution of responsibilities. *A national network of archives, collecting organisations and other information providers operating through formal agreements in which responsibilities are well-defined will best serve to preserve access to significant digital objects.*

Principle 4: Appraisal

Access to digital objects should be preserved only for as long as they are judged to have continuing value and significance. *It is neither practical nor desirable to maintain access to all digital objects indefinitely. In applying professional judgement to appraising items, consideration should be given to balancing costs and benefits, including the likely needs and interests of future generations.*

Principle 5: Rights

Rights of creators, owners, providers, users and subjects of digital objects must be balanced and protected. *The preservation of significant digital objects should not be jeopardised by censorship of form or content. Rights of access and the right to receive benefits arising from the digital object need to be carefully balanced and protected.*

Principle 6: Strategies

The adoption of best practices and standards is essential. *Strategies to preserve access to digital objects must consider the integrity and functionality of these digital objects. Standard metadata elements should be used to ensure access to the information. Continuing research and dissemination of findings is essential. Strategies to preserve access to digital objects will need to be periodically reviewed and modified to reflect current best practice.*

Principle 7: Role of Government

Appropriate Commonwealth and State government regulatory, legislative and policy regimes are essential. *The continuing and equitable access to digital objects must be supported by appropriate regimes, including legal deposit legislation.*

6

Archiving, Preservation and Tomorrow's Digital Heritage

Introduction

Tomorrow's digital heritage is very largely a product of our own era. The fact that we use such a term as "digital heritage" suggests two important things: that there are parts of it we want to keep, and that we recognise it is fragile and at risk. The purpose of this paper is to look at recent progress in keeping our digital heritage accessible.

The development of traditional library preservation has involved a number of steps: recognising problems needing attention, developing responses, sharing information and establishing orthodoxies from both conceptual and heuristic investigation. Innovation has been fostered by factors such as: economic pressures, changing attitudes to the ethics of intervention, changing expectations about what is meant by "preserving" or "conserving", and the appearance of enabling technologies. We are now seeing similar serious work and forces for innovation in preserving access to different kinds of digital collections. The National Library of Australia is one of many players looking for feasible ways to maintain access to our digital heritage. Just as it is important to participate in finding solutions to our own needs, we think it is also important to discover and critically consider the work and ideas emanating from around the world, and to share these with others in the Australian library community.

It was with this perspective that the National Library created the PADI website in collaboration with a number of other Australian institutions, and assumed responsibility for its maintenance and development. We need to understand what is happening in the area of digital preservation and PADI is our window to the world.

We would like to regularly review progress in digital preservation, especially as it relates to the Australian library sector, based on our view through the PADI window. We would like to identify the main issues being addressed, the main groups who are involved, and the main directions being explored. We will focus on some areas that look to be most promising, or where there has been most activity that we are aware of.

These include: the development of models for collaboration; models for archiving; and approaches which may assist in preservation, such as persistent identifiers and metadata schemes to support the long-term management of digital objects. We will also discuss the current attention to formats that may facilitate preservation, and the development of strategies for dealing with hardware and software dependencies. In looking at all of these we find ourselves emphasising some recurring threads: the need for testing of concepts and theories as concretely and specifically as possible, the continuing difficulties of dealing with complex multimedia publications, and the importance of encouraging communication.

We are still in the early stages of developing ways of maintaining access to digital material. There is still a great and legitimate concern about our ability even to put workable archiving arrangements in place to provide the first steps in ensuring long term accessibility. It is not at all surprising that most effort has focused on this part of the process, although as one reviewer put it: "... [the processes] which address long term preservation itself receive little attention, even though over the long term they will consume far more resources and management time. This is as if digital preservation were an iceberg, and the cultural world is concentrating uniquely on the visible parts, ignoring the much bigger problems below the water line.... This focus to immediate 'above the water line' issues is understandable: it addresses immediate issues, and these early practices are essential first steps towards long term preservation. However, it is important that longer term issues are also addressed."

Sharing Ideas: Models for International Collaboration

At the broadest level, many institutions have common interests, and initiatives for international consultation and cooperation have been welcomed.

In 1998, the National Library of Australia established an international digital collaboration group with eight other national libraries and three consortia, all known to be active in digital preservation. We have used this collaboration to consult and share ideas on a number of the issues referred to in this paper. Despite the tension between finding time to consult and time to progress institutional programmes, this and other cooperative initiatives have been adopted enthusiastically.

Models for National and Regional Archiving Collaborations

In its seminal report issued in 1996, the (US) Taskforce on Archiving of Digital Information recommended the establishment of a national system of certified digital archives. These archives would be collectively responsible for maintaining long-term accessibility. The report argued that the most effective and affordable strategy in a time of immense change would be a distributed system for collecting, protecting and preserving digital information. Such a strategy would assign responsibility to "those who presumably care most about and have the greatest understanding of the value of particular digital information objects."

We are seeing a range of organisational models evolving in different countries, and as noted in more recent reports, a variety of players are poised to play a role in digital preservation, including legal deposit libraries, data centres, digitisers, universities, research institutions and publishers.

In the USA, the Research Libraries Group (RLG) and the Digital Library Federation (DLF) have set up a joint taskforce to look at policy and practice for long-term retention of digital material. The group includes an impressive array of expertise and a worthwhile brief: to "gather and analyse existing digital preservation policies and practice descriptions for the following classes of electronic materials: institutional records in digital form (i.e. electronic records); locally digitised materials (institutional projects); and electronic publications." It will "create one or more digital preservation policy frameworks that adequately address the material types and relevant institutional contexts ...(and) will make the policy framework(s) widely available..." The task force is due to report in March 2000.

In Canada, a national archiving model is yet to emerge, but the National Library of Canada (NLC) has proposed several possible cooperative arrangements, in a policy document issued in October 1998. The options included: a distributed model possibly including multiple copies of publications stored at different locations; a distributed access but centralised preservation model in which the NLC might store electronic hard copies of publications also stored by other parties on remote servers; or a centralised model in which the NLC would work with other federal agencies to create a central repository for electronic information.

The Canadian Initiative on Digital Libraries (CIDL) consortium may also play a part. With a membership of more than fifty Canadian libraries in the academic, public and special sectors, CIDL aims to "promote, coordinate and facilitate the development of Canadian digital collections and services in order to optimise national interoperability and long-term access to Canadian digital library resources." Part of its brief is to look at the issue of assigning roles and responsibilities for long-term archiving of digital material.

The European Commission has been a very active supporter of regional collaboration in Europe. Among many interesting projects supporting access to digital heritage is the NEDLIB project, a collaborative project involving eight European national libraries, one national archive, two IT development companies and three major publishers, coordinated by the National Library of the Netherlands. The project "aims to construct the basic infrastructure upon which a networked European deposit library can be built" in order to ensure ongoing access to electronic publications.

In the UK, a number of models have been successfully adopted for different types of digital material. The Arts and Humanities Data Service (AHDS) is a centrally managed but geographically distributed service which has assumed a significant role in preserving access to digital resources in the arts and humanities field for the higher education sector. It plays an active role in educating the scholarly community about matters such as the impact of decisions made at the point of a digital object's creation on its long-term accessibility. AHDS also actively identifies and promotes the use of standards to facilitate future access.

The Natural Environment Research Council data centres are also based on a physically distributed model in which materials are housed at locations where there is expertise to manage them. Perhaps reflecting the success of this approach, a recent UK study, funded through the higher education sector's Joint Information Systems Committee, recommended that a body should be established to coordinate archiving of digital materials in the UK but that the job of maintaining the archives should be contracted out to specialist agencies with the appropriate expertise. It was proposed that the coordinating body might be formed as an extension of the National Preservation Office (NPO), currently supported by the British Library with additional financial support from the Public Record Office, The Consortium of University Research Libraries, and five major UK libraries.

In Australia we have been developing a national collection of electronic publications built on shared responsibility for archiving by the National and State libraries. This is still evolving: while a number of State libraries (Victoria and South Australia) have decided to be part of the PANDORA architecture developed by the National Library, some other State libraries (in particular Tasmania and New South Wales) are pursuing their own systems.

We particularly value the evolution of this loose national network and its anticipated gradual extension to other significant stakeholders such as university libraries and major publishers with an interest in archiving. We value the opportunity to develop a national model, but we also value the chance to work with a diversity of approaches. The archiving of electronic theses being pursued by university libraries through the Australian Digital Theses Project is an excellent illustration of the way a national archiving and preservation model is likely to develop: as a patchwork of action by players with particular business needs and interests.

Models for Archiving

As well as the collaborative arrangements which have been established, we have seen a range of archiving models under development. These models are emerging both internationally and through a number of national and local level projects. There is no consensus yet on the "best" archiving model, but this is not surprising given the diversity of user communities with archiving needs. We may never have a single archiving model except at the broadest level.

Internationally, increasing attention is being given to the Reference Model for an Open Archival Information System (OAIS) being developed by the Consultative Committee for Space Data Systems as a new ISO standard. This model provides terms of reference, conceptual data models, and functional models for open archives that can interoperate. It defines the nature of "information packages" in terms of both the content and what is needed to understand, access and manage the content. The model also aims to describe the processes required for archiving to be successful. Clearly this is a very helpful model, of interest to everyone concerned with archiving digital information.

A number of archiving projects, including the NEDLIB and CEDARS projects, are trying to follow the OAIS model closely. Others, such as our PANDORA project, are using its concepts to inform the architecture they are developing. This approach sees the Reference Model more as a checklist of requirements to be addressed than as a definite road map for the archive and all its structures and processes.

At the national and regional levels a number of archiving projects are hammering out frameworks and implementation models reflecting their own needs. Probably all archiving endeavours dealing with digital library information can still be considered experimental to some degree: most are still under development, operating at low volumes or dealing with a subset of expected problems.

Of immense importance in the development of archiving models is the 3-year CEDARS project, being undertaken under the overall direction of the (UK) Consortium of University Research Libraries (CURL), and with funding from JISC, which aims to address the "strategic, methodological and practical issues and will provide guidance for libraries in best practice for digital preservation." The archive architecture developed by the CEDARS project is an implementation of the OAIS model for a distributed digital archive of library resources.

As already mentioned, the NEDLIB project has also adopted the OAIS model as a framework on which to build its archiving model for deposit libraries. It has added a Preservation Module that includes provision for both emulation approaches and digital migrations resulting in changed content.

Both the British Library and the National Library of Australia have been actively developing specifications for digital management systems that will include archiving as one of several key functions.

The British Library (BL) released a Briefing Document in July 1999, providing information on the approach they are taking with their Digital Library Programme. This approach has been to purchase a digital library system (DLS) as technical infrastructure to serve as the basis of the UK national digital archive, enabling the BL "to store, preserve and provide access to the UK digital published output". One requirement is that the overall functional design should conform to the outline model of the OAIS Reference Model. Another is that is must facilitate interoperability with other similar developments in the UK and elsewhere, in particular CEDARS, NEDLIB, AHDS, and the National Library of Australia's Digital Services Project (DSP). The NLA's DSP grew out of our PANDORA proof-of-concept archive for Australian online publications, and the need to improve our management of a range of other digital and non-digital collections. It aims to exploit the opportunity presented by digital technology to integrate at least some levels of discovery, access and management of all of the Library's collections.

The DSP has evolved into a metadata repository and powerful search facility, for which tenders were let in late 1999, and a digital collection management system, for which tenders are currently being evaluated. While taking account of all the archiving models known to us, the DSP specification has developed out of our own particular requirements to manage the processes of archiving, access provision and long-term management.

It has developed as a robust model partly because we have been actively involved in archiving digital publications for some years, and partly because we have invested heavily in a strong and evolving policy framework on which our archiving activity has been built. PANDORA remains selective in its collecting approach, and aims to ensure that what is collected is made accessible and remains accessible. The selective approach makes it possible to apply bibliographic control to the archived files, and to check the effectiveness of the archiving processes applied to each file.

The Swedish Kulturarw project takes quite a different approach. While it also aims to test methods of collecting, preserving and providing access to online electronic documents within its own national domain, it attempts to download everything, rather than undertake a detailed selection process. This approach offers the prospect of more completely automated collecting processes, and a more comprehensive archive of national online publishing activity, if the archive's accessibility objectives can also be achieved. The Finnish EVA project has adopted similar methods for acquiring a national collection of online publications.

The NLC's Canadian Electronic Publications Pilot Project (EPPP), commenced in 1994, aimed "to identify and understand all the challenges associated with acquiring, cataloguing, preserving and providing access to Canadian electronic publications." A small number of Canadian electronic journals and other representative publications freely available on the Internet were used for the pilot project.

The EPPP was used to develop an archiving model that provides the basis of current routine operations at the NLC. The Electronic Collection, initiated in 1997, by mid-1999 had developed a comprehensive collection of government publications and a significant if comparatively small number of publications issued by commercial publishers. There are many other major libraries just beginning to actively investigate digital archiving including the National Diet Library in Japan and the Swiss National Library.

Of course, archiving of digital data is not new, nor is it the exclusive domain of libraries and projects dealing with "published" information. As already implied by the fact that the OAIS Reference Model is being developed by the space data community, there are many communities dealing with the need to preserve many different kinds of data.

The Arts and Humanities Data Service, already mentioned in the context of national and regional collaborations, encompasses a number of service providers specialising in particular kinds of data, such as archaeology and mapping data, text, visual arts data, and performing arts data. These service providers are required to develop archiving programmes appropriate to their collections and their user communities, within the overarching policy framework set by AHDS.

We have much to learn from the way such data archiving communities deal with their problems. However, in keeping with the spirit of learning from diversity, our task is always to recognise what is really relevant only to a particular set of archiving needs, and what may be more generally applicable.

APPROACHES TO ASSIST IN PRESERVING ACCESS

Persistent Identifiers

As a component of many of these archiving models, and in wider discussion, there has been interest in a range of approaches designed to facilitate long-term access.

One such focus has been to find ways of identifying digital objects available on the Internet, so that they remain findable. Although URLs serve to identify resources and describe their location on the World Wide Web, they are notoriously unreliable as they must change whenever a digital resource moves to a new location. Recent attempts to develop more persistent identifiers are driven by the need to provide reliable ongoing access regardless of location on the Internet. The Uniform Resource Identifier (URI) architecture aims to be a comprehensive and persistent resource discovery system for the Internet. This architecture consists of: Uniform Resource Names (URNs) – standard, persistent and unique identifiers for digital resources on the Internet; URLs for locations; and Uniform Resource Characteristics (URCs) – standardised metadata about the resource. Finally, for a user to be able to link to the URL of a digital resource from the URN, a resolver service is required.

A standard URI-architecture has not been realised. While the Uniform Resource Names Working Group of the Internet Engineering Task Force has been developing standards for the URN, a number of unique identifier systems have already been implemented by different groups. These include The Handle System, the Digital Object Identifier (DOI) initiative and the Persistent URL (PURL).

A meeting of the Conference of Directors of National Libraries in 1998 agreed to set up a Persistent Identifiers Task Force, chaired by Winston Tabb of the Library of Congress. The Task Force met in Washington in April 1999, and concluded that while persistent identifiers (PIs) are critical to preserving access to digital information, no completely satisfactory system has emerged that all parties could undertake to use. Diverse needs and approaches mean that a plurality of identifier systems is likely to evolve (and is evolving), so their interoperability is crucial.

At the NLA, we have recognised that we are using something like *de facto* PIs whenever we name a digital file and undertake to maintain external access to it. Having implemented a number of file naming conventions for different digital collections over recent years, we have decided to look at how these naming systems might serve as PIs. We will examine their potential benefits, associated costs and ability to assist with archiving and preservation.

At the same time as we are using our existing collections as a testbed, the State Library of Tasmania has been funded to develop a PI system for digital resources for the Tasmanian government sector. We expect these and other archiving projects to take us towards a workable PI system, or network of systems, in Australia over the next few years.

Preservation Metadata

Another approach to ensuring long-term accessibility has been the development of structured ways of describing the preservation management requirements of digital resources. This preservation metadata may be used to store technical information that supports preservation decisions and action, to document preservation action taken such as migration or emulation, to record the effects of preservation strategies, to ensure the authenticity of digital resources over time, and to note information about collection management and the management of rights. In contrast to descriptive metadata schemas (e.g. MARC, Dublin Core), which are used in the discovery and identification of digital objects, preservation metadata largely falls into the category of administrative metadata, assisting in the management of information.

The development of preservation metadata has been attempted in a number of recent projects. The resource intensive nature of digitisation projects has prompted a number of groups to develop preservation metadata to ensure that the digital content created can be maintained. However, these metadata sets are often inadequate for "born digital" items. Both the CEDARS and NEDLIB projects have been active in developing metadata sets to manage collections.

At the National Library of Australia, work in this area has been prompted by the need to define what information we will need in order to manage long-term preservation of our digital resources. We believe we will only be able to manage our growing archive of digital files, in a great range of formats, through the intelligent use of metadata. It is impossible to determine unequivocally what we will need to know in order to manage digital preservation in the future, so our metadata elements necessarily reflects assumptions about our future requirements. We also recognise that different types of digital materials, and different archiving systems, will need different metadata support. We have tried to specify the information we need from a system in order to support the decisions we will have to make, rather than attempt to prescribe what data should be entered at particular stages and by whom. This is a metadata-output model that we believe should be applicable to many implementations that may decide to record this information in a variety of ways.

Standards

Generally speaking, there has been a move away from relying solely on standards to solve digital preservation problems. It has been recognised that the diversity of needs, the pressure for change which limits market support for long-term standards, and the difficulty in predicting future changes in technologies, all mean that we are likely to continue to see a plethora of standards of short-term applicability. Although the development of standards has been critical to interoperability and to automating processes, standards are likely to play a role in facilitating preservation rather than being a complete solution.

A major focus in recent years has been the use of the standard structured information formats: SGML and its simplified form, XML. The potential for sorting collection items into categories of similar materials for batch preservation action is attractive, as is the encapsulation effect of mark-up languages that separates the content from the structure and formatting. While this is a big step forward – and XML promises to be applicable to many different format types – marking up documents to comply with standards is highly resource intensive. It is also inevitable that libraries will continue to deal with digital objects that are not fully compliant with standards.

Essence

Finally, preservation will be helped by attempts to define the "essence" that must be preserved, and procedures for authenticating its survival over time. This is a complex issue in which developments are likely to emerge as we encounter the realities of the preservation strategies we choose to use and their effects on the objects we are seeking to preserve. Important conceptual work has recently been carried out on developing a canonical reference point for each digital object, so that later versions can be compared with the "essence" that someone has decided should be preserved. It will be interesting to see how this develops, given the resources required, and the compromises in object integrity likely to be a part of any preservation strategy.

Further Archiving Issues

Further archiving issues which we have identified as presenting particular challenges include:

- collecting, managing and providing access to dynamic, software-driven objects like databases. While these types of objects present challenges for long-term management, we have found it difficult to even bring them into an archive.
- the scalability of our archiving models. This issue was identified in a European Commission sponsored study 12 months ago and it remains a concern. Projects such as PANDORA, NEDLIB and others will be crucial in providing us with information on the issues in managing the increasing numbers of items and large amounts of data expected to come into collections over the long term.
- the development of relationships between archiving institutions and publishers, principally over intellectual property concerns. It is understandable that there are unresolved tensions in a period of such profound change. There is a widely held and emerging perspective that these tensions can be worked through by keeping the interests of all stakeholders in mind and looking for arrangements that maximise mutual benefits.
- the need for resources to undertake even relatively simple things like identifying digital items that have entered collections and assessing their current accessibility. For many libraries even these first steps are hard to achieve.

Formats for Preservation

We have seen an ongoing interest in developing formats that will be preservable. Most of these attempts involve some kind of encapsulation, or grouping together, of a digital object and anything else needed to provide access to it. Encapsulation can be achieved by using physical or logical structures called 'containers' or 'wrappers' to provide a relationship between all information components, such as the digital object and supporting information including unique identifiers, metadata, and software specifications. Encapsulation may also encompass the software itself required to read the object. The "package" may be composed of analogue and digital components. An example of an analogue component would be human readable instructions, such as writing on the outer case of a physical format carrier, describing how to use the carrier and interpret the outermost layer of the digital component, most likely the wrapper, which will in turn provide the information required to use the rest of the digital information contained. An alternative to storing all the supporting information with the object is to include a clear pointer to a single, reliable storage area for that information.

Obviously, the encapsulation concept is used in many CD-ROM publications that come with their own operating software and instructions for use. However, preservation interest in encapsulation is based on encapsulating enough information and/or software to allow the digital object to be useable across changes in operating systems over time.

This concept underlies the OAIS Reference Model which employs the concepts of "information packages" (IPs) that are composed of "content information" and "preservation description information" contained by "packaging information". The content information, in turn, includes the actual digital object and the "representation information" needed to interpret it. The preservation description information portion includes information about provenance and context, reference information (such as unique identifiers) and a wrapper which protects the object against undocumented alteration.

Encapsulation has also been explored in a range of other projects and papers. The Universal Preservation Format project has focused on developing a "self-describing" platform-independent format which includes, within its metadata, all the technical specifications required to build and rebuild appropriate media browsers to access contained materials throughout time. Another proposed model describes the encapsulation of hardware, software and data in the form of a "digital tablet". The Digital Rosetta Stone concept relies on keeping a 'meta-knowledge archive' of how to interpret media formats and file formats to support data recovery and document reconstruction processes. For efficiency, it is proposed that this representation information be stored separately from the encapsulation.

Very long-lasting media, in conjunction with encapsulation or secured metadata, have been suggested as a way of allowing documents to remain useable for very long periods of time. This model underlies both the HD-Rosetta product developed by Norsam Technologies under license from the Los Alamos National Laboratory in the US, and the 'digital tablet' (*vide supra*).

These approaches all hold some potential, but are more likely to be helpful in informing other approaches than in being widely adopted themselves. For example, while some may prove to be prohibitively expensive for widespread adoption, they do help us think more about ways of associating content with the tools needed to understand and use it, and recognise that media instability will continue to be an issue wherever we try to store digital information for long periods.

Dealing with Hardware and Software Dependencies

While media deterioration causes some concern, it is the prospect of relentless changes in information technologies that threaten to render digital materials rapidly inaccessible – "held hostage to their own encoding". In recent years a range of approaches to overcoming technological obsolescence has been proposed and debated, and this debate has continued over the past year. In January 1999, the (US) Council on Library and Information Resources (CLIR) published a report by Jeff Rothenberg of the Rand Corporation, which discussed various proposed solutions to long-term digital preservation and elaborated an emulation strategy proposed by himself and others in recent years.

Emulation refers to the process of mimicking in software a piece of hardware or software so that other processes act as if the original equipment or function is still available in its original form. The emulation strategy described by Rothenberg entails emulating obsolete systems so that the digital object's original software can be run. In contrast to migration, in which the original object is successively transferred to new systems, once the data is archived with appropriate metadata and software this emulation model requires no action apart from media refreshing and transfer until access is desired, at which time an appropriate emulator is either found or developed.

Although emulation is a proven technique in current computer systems, there is widespread agreement that its feasibility and benefits are still to be proven for preserving access to large numbers of complex digital objects. Practical studies are planned as part of a collaborative effort involving the CEDARS project team and researchers at the University of Michigan with funding through the Joint NSF/JISC International Digital Libraries Initiative. Their project aims to 'develop and test a suite of emulation tools, evaluate the costs and benefits of emulation as a preservation strategy for complex multimedia documents and objects, and develop models for collection management decisions about how much effort and resources to invest in exact replication within preservation activity... (It) will assess options for preserving the original functionality and 'look and feel' of digital objects and develop preliminary guidelines for the use of different preservation strategies (conversion, migration and emulation).'

The National Library of the Netherlands will also undertake a project to test the emulation strategy for long-term preservation. This project, to be carried out in collaboration with Jeff Rothenberg, will test the viability of using hardware emulation as a means of preserving digital publications in a deposit library. The testbed environment of the Deposit System for Electronic Publications (DSEP) developed in the NEDLIB project, using sample material provided by NEDLIB-sponsoring publishers, will be used to carry out experiments for this project. Both these projects will be crucial in discovering the potential of this largely untested approach to digital preservation.

The recent paper by Rothenberg added heat to the long-running debate between proponents of emulation and migration strategies. Rothenberg attacked the migration strategy as requiring "continual heroic effort" that would, in any case, fail to maintain document integrity. Rothenberg's approach, and the emulation strategy, in turn received criticism from a number of sources, including David Bearman, who warned of the "potentially dangerous wishful thinking" which would result in unquestioning reliance on the ability of emulators to later access digital material and asserted that "Rothenberg is fundamentally trying to preserve the wrong thing by preserving information systems functionality rather than records". Bearman does, however, see common ground in the specification of metadata which is needed to support all digital preservation strategies.

Although emulation has received much attention, migration still looks like the strategy of first choice. In the US, the Digital Library Federation recently published a detailed case study of migration in a specific environment: a social science data archive. The report goes well beyond conceptualising to analyse concrete experience in a controlled but real business environment. The data being migrated is largely homogenous, and yet the report reveals many difficulties, and many useful lessons. In particular, it emphasises the importance of maintaining the documentation necessary to understand the data.

One approach which continues to receive bad press is technology preservation – the maintenance of machines and software in the hope that they will continue to provide access to the digital objects that used them. While this looks no less futile in the long term than it ever did, we need to admit that it remains the key bridging strategy for most of us, whether it is simply trying to hold onto old machines that still work, or maintaining software archives to run the digital objects in our collections.

Finally, the recovery or rescue of digital information from media or formats that have become inaccessible has received some attention. The best review can be found in one of the seven very interesting and useful JISC/NPO studies on the preservation of electronic materials published between 1997 and 1999. This paper discusses a number of problems and scenarios, and reports on programmes to rebuild computers, to build simulators and emulators, and data recovery required as a result of disasters or poor management of technological change. Although most data can be recovered given sufficient resources, the time and money required are such that a strong case needs to be developed to show that the data is worth the cost of recovery. (It also means that "data archaeology" is an expensive and unreliable substitute for more anticipatory preservation activity.)

It is not yet clear whether there will be a single preservation strategy which emerges as being best for all types of digital library material. Given the diverse collections for which libraries are responsible, it appears most likely that combinations of strategies will be used in the foreseeable future. At the National Library of Australia, for example, we know we need:

- some data recovery for the large number of old and poorly documented floppy disks that are currently inaccessible: we are experimenting with some data recovery software to establish guidelines and procedures for this;
- media transfer and refreshing for the data we can access that is currently on unstable carriers;
- some technology preservation, including maintenance of software and even some hardware;
- migration strategies to produce versions for current access using contemporary platforms, while attempting to maintain archival copies of versions of files in their native format. This will enable them to be operated using maintained obsolete systems if available, or accessed by emulators if available. It should also enable them to used as the starting point for re-migration if the ongoing migration stream breaks down for some reason.

We will also need to develop and refine our current investigations of matters such as the implications of new versions of HTML for digital preservation, the conversion of complex files formats to alternative storage formats that might be more easily migrated, and our development of a preservation plan for each type of file format. We are aware that whatever strategies we use, we will need excellent technical and management systems, and excellent metadata to support them.

Making Progress

We are at an interesting stage in the development of solutions to the evolving challenge of digital preservation and it will be exciting to watch where these developments lead. There are, however, some issues that are either receiving a low level of attention, or are poorly documented. These include:

- cost effective ways of predicting deterioration rates of physical carriers;
- useable indicators of technology change that should guide or trigger preservation action;
- decision models for selecting which preservation strategies are most applicable for particular kinds of complex digital information;
- ways of testing our ability to preserve.

Information Sharing and Communication

There is a large and growing "literature" (if that is the right word to use), and numerous active communication channels. From this field we have chosen one small example.

One of the most prominent collaborations in the field over the past few years has occurred in the higher education and research sectors in the UK. The eLib programme has provided both funds and vision for the investigation of digital preservation issues. The programme funds the CEDARS project as a practical way of exploring many of the issues raised in the seven supporting studies on preservation already referred to.

That the studies were guided by a specially formed Digital Archiving Working Group, comprising representatives from the British Library, the National Preservation Office (NPO), the Publishers' Association, universities, data archives, and the Public Record Office (PRO), is indicative of a high level of collaboration focused on systematic research and information sharing.

The seven studies are of interest in themselves, but their value was considerably enhanced this year by the publication of a synthesis of the studies. The booklet reflects the value (and many of the shortcomings) of the studies, and has useful information on cost modelling and on some organisational and decision issues. Further indicating its collaborative nature, it was launched at a seminar organised by the NPO, the Library and Information Commission, the Museums and Galleries Commission and the PRO.

PADI and Information Sharing

Finally, we would like to say more about PADI, our primary vehicle for documenting and sharing information on this critically important subject. In response to a growing recognition of the need to safeguard digital heritage, the National Library of Australia set up its PADI web site in 1997. The Library has since developed this site into a comprehensive subject gateway to resources dealing with a wide range of aspects of digital preservation. The PADI resource plays a role in educating users about the subject areas accessible through the gateway. While users have the option of proceeding directly to a search, a high level of support is available to assist users through the provision of explanatory text. Digital preservation topics dealt with on the PADI site are as diverse as: persistent identification of networked material, the implementation of legal deposit for electronic publications, migration of digital information and preserving access to physical format digital material.

Powerful search capabilities are supported by the assignment of metadata, based on the AGLS and Dublin Core, to linked resources. A thesaurus of digital preservation terms has been developed to provide subject metadata enabling precise retrieval of resources from the PADI database. Certain types of resources may selectively be retrieved: for example, policies, strategies and guidelines, information about digital preservation projects, or articles may be independently selected. Cooperation has played a crucial role in the PADI initiative which has been carried out in partnership with Australian and international experts. A news and online forum area provides an opportunity for all who are interested in preserving access to digital material to send and receive news about digital preservation and to participate in discussion of digital preservation issues. Users are encouraged to suggest resources for the PADI database using a simple online form. In these ways, PADI provides a focus for information sharing and cooperation supporting digital preservation activities both in Australia and worldwide.

A BALANCING ACT: PICTUREAUSTRALIA

The focus of PictureAustralia is on access. It provides a single World Wide Web gateway to the distributed digitised pictorial collections of the image providers participating

[PICTUREAUSTRALIA]. The inaugural participants were the State Libraries of New South Wales, Tasmania and Victoria, the National Library and the Australian War Memorial.

Principles for Access

The participants have agreed on the following points for access:

- PictureAustralia must provide free access;
- PictureAustralia should have a single memorable Web location;
- PictureAustralia must be accessible to all Australians, independent of their location (acknowledging that not everyone will have access to the Web);
- Images may be sourced from libraries, museums, archives, galleries, universities, historical societies and other agencies. Offers of private collections will be encouraged to seek a home at an agency;
- The coverage of the images is essentially expressed as a relationship to Australia. Content or creator is Australian, but the original items and their digital surrogates may reside anywhere in the world.

Distributed Responsibilities

In PictureAustralia, activities associated with management and preservation of collections remain with the image providers. This allows those collections of digitised images to be repurposed in many ways, and indeed, each image provider already hosted its own Web site for its own images before joining PictureAustralia. However, this is not a criterion for participation.

A New Opportunity

Agencies embarking on new digitisation work are utilising the opportunity of PictureAustralia's existence to establish their image digitisation and metadata creation processes in such a way that the results are available to different gateways with a minimum of additional effort. Each agency may therefore provide their images and metadata to their own institutional gateway, to PictureAustralia, and to an educational service provider such as the national Australian Museums and Galleries OnLine network, AMOL. University libraries are an example of an agency who want to provide images to a number of services. As they have some experience in digitising full-text and making it available, they can now digitise under-utilised collections of images which were created as part of faculty research and exist in a range of formats including architectural slides and glass plates. Many universities also have their own museums and galleries or art collections which would have increased use if made available via the Web, particularly for Australians in regional and remote areas.

CROSS-SECTORAL ADVANTAGES

Its hybrid architecture allows PictureAustralia to be a vehicle that brings attention to the collection of each participating image provider. In fact, this type of architecture is similar to that deployed by AMOL (a central metadata repository with links to distributed collections). The difference is that PictureAustralia has endeavoured to be far-reaching cross-sectorally, because the participants believe that the issues for enhancing access are the same, no matter who we are or what we take care of. The National Library also provides an international gateway to information about Preserving Access to Digital Information, known as PADI [PADI]. And since Phase I of the project which developed PictureAustralia, the inaugural image providers have been joined by the Fryer Library at the University of Queensland, and the National Archives of Australia.

SELECTIVE DIGITISATION

Although some of the participating agencies have been providing digital surrogates of their images for some time, digitisation is conducted on a selective basis. That is, while many of the images in the participants' collections are described, they do not all have associated digitised images. At the National Library for example, we digitise routinely as we acquire new materials. We only selectively retrospectively digitise our existing collection of pictorial items, according to demand for activities such as online exhibitions. However, making the descriptions available allows for 'digitisation on demand' to be invoked. This is explained in full in the National Library's recently released digitisation policy [NLADIG].

DIGITISATION AND CONSERVATION

At a recent international library conference, digitisation was not to be an activity which ensures preservation, rather it is considered necessary to deliver access. There is a secondary benefit of conservation of the original item due to the minimisation of the need to access the original item after digitisation. It is possible to take this one step further, by choosing digitisation and description processes which are standards-based. And this will also have a flow-on effect of facilitating migration to new software as it is made available, without having to resort to the original again for redigitisation in the future.

The conference example used was newspapers on microform. The British Library, the Library of Congress, and scholars involved in the Early English Imprints Project have agreed that the availability and performance of scanning and optical character recognition software is sufficient to digitise the microform copy of newspapers for increased access. Standards are a key to this activity. PictureAustralia only required a resource discovery standard to be applied because other metadata to support management and preservation of images are kept by the image providers in other schemas. For example, the National Library has made a preservation metadata schema for digital collections available for comment while monitoring international activities at the same time [Preservation].

THE IMPORTANCE OF STANDARDS

In PictureAustralia, we have applied a process of taking descriptive data from a variety of legacy formats, albeit very rich formats, and converting it to a single structured schema suitable for resource discovery, the Dublin Core. It is then possible to convert this standard schema to a newer enhanced schema in the future. Similarly the JPEG (Joint Photographic Expert Group) format, which was independently chosen by all the participating image providers as the preferred standard for image rendition, should be easy to migrate from because it is a universally recognised standard. In that sense, digitisation is ensuring access in the longer term.

ACCESS FACILITATES ...

The JPEG standard also allows the image providers to create more than one rendition of each image, a thumbnail version, a medium resolution version for larger display, and sometimes a watermarked version. Even the thumbnail-sized version, if of a very high resolution, allows a person to become 'enamoured of the work'. Remote users do not have to access the original to derive the same benefits from our collections as users on-the-spot. To see more examples of national digitisation projects aiming for this goal, please visit the National Library's Web pages dedicated to information sharing in this area [PROJECTS].

THE ROLE OF PRESERVATION AND THE LIBRARY OF THE FUTURE

What is the role of preservation in the library of the future? Will digital technology overcome all of our preservation problems or will we still need to actively manage the accessibility of information? What do we need to do to prepare for the future?

Let me begin by saying that I do not know the answers to these questions. In a time of rapid change it is hard to predict what the library of the future will look like, let alone what preservation issues and solutions it will enjoy. However, we can make some educated guesses.

As a preservation manager, making educated guesses about the future is part of what I am paid to do in order that we can prepare for it in a sensible manner. Therefore I have frequent cause to think about these questions as I try to prepare my colleagues and my institution-and most emphatically myself-for what we will need to be doing in five, ten or twenty years' time.

From this you will gather that this paper is intended to be a small exercise in future guessing, to see if we can pick up some clues as to how we can prepare for the preservation responsibilities that lie ahead of us.

THE EXISTING ROLE OF PRESERVATION IN LIBRARIES

I define preservation, at least in a library context, as the processes of keeping collections and the information they contain available for use for as long as they are needed. Such a definition begs many questions, of course, such as: available for what kind of use? And: needed by whom? However, I believe this is a good enough working definition to take with us on this exercise.

Preservation has played an important role in libraries. Because of the "things" that libraries have collected, preservation has developed with a strong focus on preserving physical material: understanding why materials deteriorate and what we can do about it.

a. *The Threats Preservation is Used to Dealing With:* Our collections are made up of materials that are naturally subject to deterioration, caused or influenced by many things, including:

- the materials themselves-acidic papers, poor quality binding materials, unstable media such as cellulose nitrate and cellulose acetate photographic films, PVC-based audio tapes
- the environmental conditions we store them in-the heat, moisture, light, pollutants they are exposed to
- mould, insects, mice, and other pests that live on them or in them
- the abuses, or just plain uses, of users and staff
- sudden disasters such as floods, water leaks, fire, building collapse, vandalism, acts of terrorism, war

We all know that preservation is about protecting our collections from such threats, or salvaging and repairing them to compensate for their impact.

Of course, our view of preservation, and our sense of priorities, are both influenced by our working context including the kind of collections for which we are responsible, and the kind of threats that are most pressing. For example, in Canberra, where the National Library of Australia is situated, the climate is generally dry and often cool; the air is clean; we have few insect pests that worry us; we are most unlikely to suffer major floods or earthquakes. We have good buildings with reasonable air conditioning systems and reliable electricity supplies. We generally have access to well-trained and well-paid staff. Our traditional preservation priorities tend to focus on dealing with brittle papers, repairing library materials damaged in being used, ensuring the building systems work on the few days of high humidity we experience, and preventing disasters like water leaks and fires.

I know that my preservation priorities would be different if I worked in a different environment, such as one with mould, insects and other pests as constant threats, with high levels of humidity and heat and polluted air, with unreliable building systems or energy supplies, with very few trained staff and inadequate resources to stop damage happening or to repair items when damage occurs.

Whatever our experience and our situation, however, we can recognise that the business of preservation has been to deal with threats of damage or loss.

b. *Preservation Responses:* One would have to say that at the theoretical level at least, the preservation profession has developed good responses to many of these threats. For reasons of limited resources, libraries are often unable to apply them, but we generally know what to do.

We have a range of good strategies for preventing damage. We know that reducing temperature and humidity levels will slow down deterioration, and that we need to filter out air pollutants and control exposure to light and UV. We know how to store, package, and handle collections, and how to train staff and users to do what they can to protect library materials and minimise the impact of use. We are aware that we need pest control programmes and disaster plans. We have even developed national and international campaigns to eliminate the use of unstable materials such as highly acidic papers in publishing and cellulose acetate film in record photography. We have developed good microfilming techniques and standards that allow us to make reliable and long-lasting copies of unstable material or items in high demand.

When our preventive measures fail, the conservators have developed some very effective treatment strategies that can respond to most kinds of damage for most kinds of materials. We have access to a wide repertoire of approaches that draw on long-standing traditions of maintaining and repairing collections developed over many centuries in many parts of the world. We also make use of a great deal of scientific knowledge and technical development that has become available over the past 30 to 40 years as professional conservators and conservation scientists have looked for better ways of protecting and stabilising and repairing documentary materials.

Alongside the practice of preservation, we have developed mature approaches to managing our preservation programmes. We are used to identifying needs, setting priorities, planning and managing projects, bidding for resources, developing skills, allocating responsibilities, evaluating progress, adjusting plans, learning from mistakes and celebrating successes.

Given the right resources, preservation has become one of the mature, functioning areas of libraries, able to draw on a great deal of shared knowledge and some standard ways of approaching problems. There is a sense that we know what needs to be done: we just need the resources and support to get on and do it.

CHANGES IN THE PRESERVATION CONTEXT

However, libraries are changing in quite profound ways. The information they have access to is changing, how they do business is changing, and the demands and expectations of their users are changing. Many of the assumptions upon which library preservation has been based seem to have been shaken.

I want to focus on two quite obvious and related changes: the impact of digital technology, and where collaboration might lead. There are many other changes happening in our library and information world as well, but these two areas seem to have particularly interesting and challenging implications for the preservation role, and for the questions of whether we will continue to need such a function, and what it might have to attend to.

a. *Digital Technology:* The introduction of digital technology is old news: libraries have been dealing with it as a collection issue for at least 20 years. Many of the changes wrought by it are obvious and widely discussed. We are seeing vast amounts of information of varying value published in digital formats, and many libraries are investing heavily in creating digital versions of analogue collection material.

I want to consider the preservation implications of digital technology in libraries, both in terms of managing digital information coming into our collections, and in terms of using digital imaging techniques as a preservation tool that might help us to manage our existing analogue collections.

b. *Collaboration:* Greatly enhanced prospects for collaboration between libraries is just one of the doors opened by digital technology. This is going to be driven by the demands of users for access to information wherever it originates, but it will also be driven by libraries themselves, as they look for opportunities to reduce their costs while improving the services they can provide. Collaboration will also be driven by a survival instinct, as libraries find themselves competing with other providers in an information market place. By working together, libraries will be able to leverage off each other to offer extremely powerful services, based on great expertise in finding, defining, managing and delivering information that people want. On the surface, this may not appear to have much to do with preservation, but I believe it will have a profound impact on what we do and how we do it.

While I am going to discuss them separately, I believe we will feel the impact of these changes working together over the next decade or so.

PRESERVATION AND DIGITAL INFORMATION

On the surface, digital technology appears to offer few preservation problems. Bits and bytes are easy to copy, so there should be no problems in developing an unending chain of copies into the future, and having copies all over the world in case of disaster. However, we already know that the reality is not so simple and that there are very significant technical and management problems. The two main factors leading to inaccessibility of digital information: changing technology platforms and media instability, are relentless, with the potential to render digital information useless. This becomes a critical preservation problem for libraries, because libraries unable to give access to information have no future.

In the past we have understandably, but wrongly, tended to see preservation as what happens after everything else has been sorted out, towards the end of the natural life-cycle of documents, books, photographs and so on. With digital information we cannot afford to build preservation programmes on such an assumption: the inaccessibility factors operate on such a short time span that the problem becomes pressing as well as critical.

This means that preservation functions will have to be much more focused on digital collections than they have been so far. Libraries that have a custodial function will need to bring preservation perspectives to bear on the ways they manage digital information from the beginning.

PRESERVATION RESPONSES

What will we need to do to preserve access to digital information?

One thing we know we have to do is to bring digital information into a safe place where we can manage it and have time to make good decisions about its long-term preservation. The world of changing websites, unstable floppy disks and individual computer systems is not a place where any particular digital resource is secure for very long.

Margaret Phillips, my colleague from the National Library of Australia, will cover much of the territory to do with these highly necessary, preservation-enabling archiving steps for online publications in her paper tomorrow, 'Managing Chaos in the Cyberworld'.

Long-term preservation of digital information across generations of technological change is a daunting challenge. At this stage we still do not know for certain how we will achieve it. There is much research going on at a conceptual level, and some practical experiments underway. There is also a lively debate between proponents of different approaches.

As well as an interest in developing standards (which should ease but not solve the preservation problem), and new formats that might not be affected by either technological change or the forces of media deterioration (which seem to be noble but doomed hopes), most attention is being given to two approaches: migration (in which files are copied to new operating systems and converted so they can be accessed in each new technical environment), and emulation (in which files are maintained in their original formats and accessed using emulation software that recreates their original operating environment). At the National Library of Australia we believe we will have to use both approaches, as some resources will migrate to new standards without problems while others will require special software to access them from their original format. Internationally, there is not much interest in maintaining museums of technology, although we know that we will have to keep some hardware and software in order to maintain accessibility while we are adopting other approaches. For good reasons there is also little faith placed in data recovery as a preservation strategy, although we are using it to good effect on individual items where it is crucial to recover something of the data, even if there is some loss of formatting and other functionality.

The National Library of Australia is very interested in these debates at a conceptual level, and in trying to participate in and contribute to them. But as well as progressing the theoretical debate, we are also committed to making progress with practical things that will be useful for now as well as for the future. We need to take this action so that we don't lose the chance to save what we can now, and so we can influence the discussion in directions that might address our needs. Even when solutions emerge, we will need to decide what is applicable to our situation. To do this we need to be well-informed and aware of what our needs really are, in order to recognise what will work for us and what is actually the solution to someone else's problem.

Those practical things include:

- building the technical infrastructure and procedures for archiving

- establishing mechanisms for recording the metadata we will need so we can manage preservation
- developing persistent naming conventions for digital resources so they remain visible and findable
- moving digital resources from less stable carriers like floppy disks to more stable carriers like CD (knowing that we will have to move from CD within a few years as well)
- identifying formats that we should be able to migrate easily and formats that will cause problems
- setting up registers of existing emulation software that we may need to use
- identifying when we need to take action so that we don't lose access to the digital resources in our collections.

We believe these should all assist us in building pathways from current archiving to long-term preservation.

As we search for these pathways we can see some positive trends emerging that should give us encouragement:

- there is a growing awareness that digital preservation is a critical issue, calling for measures that go beyond immediate archiving
- there are a number of very good projects underway attempting to develop workable approaches and best-practice archiving models. One internationally prominent example is the Reference Model for an Open Archival Information System (OAIS) being developed by the Consultative Committee for Space Data Systems as a new ISO standard. The OAIS provides terminology, conceptual data models, and functional models for open archives that can interoperate. It defines the nature of "information packages" in terms of both their content and what is needed to understand, access and manage the content. The model also tries to describe the processes required for archiving to be successful. This approach is very helpful, and a number of archiving projects are attempting to follow it closely. There are other projects underway, including the National Library of Australia's PANDORA project, that take account of OAIS principles

but have charted a more independent course. It is not yet clear whether the OAIS Reference Model will be more usefully viewed as a street directory to be followed exactly, or as a checklist of requirements to be achieved.

- Many digital archiving issues are coming under some kind of control. The position is very promising with software to harvest information from the Internet efficiently and accurately; there are good tools developing for describing digital resources; and storage systems that move data around, perform back-ups and error-checking, and serve files when requested in accordance with a raft of access criteria
- We have seen progress on standards for formats, producing great improvements in interoperability
- There is a real interest in developing tools for emulation of various formats and in making them available
- There is a substantial international effort in researching many aspects of these problems, largely collaborative in nature by institutions and individuals committed to sharing information. The National Library of Australia maintains a special internationally supported subject gateway called PADI (Preserving Access to Digital Information) as an important part of this information sharing.

Despite these positive trends there are also some negative influences tending to push workable answers further away:

- Libraries are moving to service short-term information-access goals. They have to do this to survive. There is a danger of long-term maintenance issues being put aside, (although in some cases this will be entirely appropriate)
- The volume of digital material is growing geometrically, beyond the capacity of our tools, expertise, management structures, and even just numbers of available people to deal with them
- Unsurprisingly (because it is exactly what we have expected), new formats are entering the market and therefore our collecting landscape, that we do not even

know how to collect, let alone manage for long-term access

- Intellectual property rights issues are becoming increasingly complex. For preservation purposes these may be relatively straightforward, but we know that preservation will involve copying in some form or other, so even preservation encounters some fundamental ownership rights. As digital publications become more and more a virtual product of layers of software and data from various sources, getting permission for even the most simple preservation copying processes may become an impediment
- We are also going to find it increasingly difficult to carve up our preservation responsibilities along clear lines. In what may turn out to seem a very 20 century way of looking at the world, we hope to negotiate archiving and preservation responsibilities along the lines of political boundaries. In Australia we look to each of the State libraries to take responsibility for the publishing output of their State; internationally, we say we will take responsibility for the Australian things. And yet Web-based information makes those concepts increasingly difficult to apply: how do we decide the responsibility for sites and publications that are made up of bits and pieces residing on other sites all over the world?
- The research effort that I have already referred to as a very positive trend, has made progress, but often its most obvious output is to show up the difficulties with other people's proposed long-term strategies. To date, there is little sense that the problems of long-term preservation are being reduced by the research.

These trends lead me think that the preservation problems applying to digital information will not be easily solved, but will remain a very significant challenge to libraries for a long time to come. With great optimism, an Australian colleague recently said that the injection of some millions of dollars and dedicated research might make it possible to develop software tools that would solve the preservation problem automatically: a system that would accept digital information resources in one format and automatically convert them to different formats, again and again, without loss. Such tools are some way in the future; even if and when they do appear, they will have to operate in a context of human-driven decisions about what needs to be preserved. It also seems likely that technology will change significantly enough over time to make such tools themselves obsolete.

WHAT ARE WE TO DO WITH OUR ANALOGUE COLLECTIONS?

Digital technology is probably not going to reduce the size of our analogue collections in the foreseeable future. While the number of publications existing only in digital form will continue to grow, it also looks likely that libraries, or at least some libraries, will continue to collect growing collections of papers, books, journals, photographs, maps, paintings, films, videos, and all the other non-digital things that go into our collections. Even if these collections did not grow at all, we have our existing large collections of these very physical materials to manage.

We have not found any viable large-scale panaceas for the underlying problem of deterioration: the best we can do is to retard its progress and ameliorate its effects.

I need to go back to my earlier description of preservation as a mature, functioning part of libraries. This somewhat complacent comment hides a truth that our analogue collections and our management of them will remain problematical for a long time to come.

As with digital preservation, there are some trends, generally positive, that are worth noting:

- Over the past 30 years various mass deacidification processes for paper collections have looked promising, and a number are in experimental or production use in various countries. Development has often has been constrained by the resources required to do the job safely and well. Overall, mass deacidification has had a reasonably unhappy history, and there are still no processes that have won universal support and acceptance. Because of the substantial investments required, it seems likely that mass deacidification will remain a peripheral possibility for many libraries in our region for some time to come, but it also seems likely to play an important role for our collections in the future, if the resources can be found to pay for it. On the other hand, mass deacidification is no magic bullet-it will not reverse damage that has already happened, and it will require repeated application to intrinsically unstable materials like newsprint

- Perhaps the most promising factor in the long-term preservation of our paper-based collections is the switch to alkaline papermaking that has happened in many countries-for reasons completely unassociated with preservation! As environmental concerns have driven paper manufacturers to change their bleaching and effluent control practices, it has become more economical to change from acidic to alkaline processes. Again, we do not expect this change to solve all our preservation problems but it may mean the worst brittle paper problems are limited to material published between the middle of the 19 and the end of the 20 centuries, and to material such as newspapers. Of course, this is a large enough task, but it looks more achievable than dealing with an unending intake of material on increasingly unstable papers.
- In recent decades there has been a growing acceptance of reformatting as an appropriate preservation tool. It is worth considering the likely contribution of these techniques to preservation in the foreseeable future.

MICROFILMING AND DIGITAL IMAGING

I have already mentioned the positive role of preservation microfilming. Given the expected long life of the materials, microfilming is often referred to as a proven preservation technique. In recent years we have seen improvements in standards, and the widespread filming of materials such as newspapers that have an uncertain future in their original format. With high standards, microfilming can produce copies that divert the pressure of use from fragile originals; if sufficiently well made, those copies can also eventually replace unstable originals that become unusable.

However, it is easier to talk about preservation standards for microfilming than it is to achieve them. I have seen many microfilming projects that failed to deliver preservation goals, for a variety of reasons, including:

- damage caused to the originals in filming
- pages missed in the filming
- illegible film images that could not be used
- the use of unstable base materials like cellulose acetate that become brittle
- the use of camera masters for reference or printing: when they were scratched there was nothing suitable for generating new service copies
- blemishes developing in film because it was not processed or stored properly
- inadvertent filming of material for which there was already suitable microfilm in existence.

In other words, the apparently 'easy preservation option' of the past 30 years demands substantial inputs, significant planning, and a lot of control if it is to achieve its preservation potential.

Apart from those not-insignificant considerations, the main concern that has emerged with microfilming as a preservation strategy in recent years is the reluctance of users to use microfilm. In a service-oriented, client-driven world, this is a powerful difficulty.

The alternative that has encouraged users to speak up and declare their dissatisfaction with microfilm is, of course, digital imaging. From an access point of view, digitisation is streets ahead-and we all know it. Many of us have clung to the idea that we can have the best of all worlds by using microfilm to create a reliable preservation copy that can be safely put away, and digitising to create an acceptable access copy we can make available to users. This was the basic principle behind our largest digital imaging project to date, the Australian Cooperative Digitisation Project 1840-1845, conducted over the past 5 years by the National Library of Australia, the State Library of New South Wales, and the University of Sydney Libraries. After digitising something like 60,000 microfilm images of mid-19 century Australian serials, we are still uncertain about the viability of this approach.

Microfilming gave us a reliable preservation copy, but it added very substantially to the costs of the project. We also know we will seek to maintain the digital files permanently, so it seems reasonable to ask whether we really need the microfilm copy. We will not know the answer to such a question for some time, at least until we have managed to develop and test the infrastructure and procedures for managing digital files long-term. At least until then we will probably be pleased to have the microfilm.

Does digital imaging itself offer us any preservation answers for the future of our physical, analogue collections? This is a complex question. We need to look for an answer in the preservation pluses and minuses that digitisation can produce.

Digitisation can offer some preservation benefits, but as with microfilming, it is entirely possible for digitisation to happen in ways that give us absolutely no preservation benefits. There are two main ways in which digital imaging seems to offer potential preservation benefits: in providing preservation replacement copies for unstable originals, and in providing access surrogates that relieve the pressure of access from valuable or fragile originals.

In both cases, the benefit depends on achieving suitable image quality (which must be good enough to satisfy most demands for use, now and into the future), and on understanding and acting upon the responsibility to maintain the digital files in an accessible state long-term. These two conditions both require informed, conscious decisions that are reflected in well-controlled specifications, quality control management, and considerable investment of resources.

Digitisation's ability to reduce use pressures on fragile originals is also uncertain. We need always to ask not just whether it can have that effect, but whether or not it *will*. The answer requires some understanding of user behaviour: Internet availability sometimes leads to increased pressure for access to the original. At the same time, digitisation may present some threats that need to be minimised, such as exposure of vulnerable and valuable originals to high levels of light, heat, and handling; unsympathetic preparation, and unsuitable scanning equipment.

Rather than solving all the preservation problems of our analogue collections, digital imaging appears to offer some benefits but only if we manage it properly to achieve them, and some potential negatives requiring management. Preservation does not come automatically with the digitisation territory, and its net effect is usually to add to the preservation burden when one takes into account the long-term maintenance of both analogue originals and digital copies.

We are convinced that without being firmly managed the technology tends to run ahead of the objectives that should be driving its use. To achieve the positive preservation potential it seems to have, while avoiding the preservation pitfalls, digital imaging must be based on, and surrounded by, very clear and robust policies, procedures, and understandings. As these are put into place, we can expect to see digital imaging playing an increasingly useful-but probably never complete-role in preservation. Digital technology will be a powerful tool but by no means the only one, and by no means a self-driven, self-managed one. Library managers and preservation managers will need to be clever to choose when digitisation is appropriate and cost-effective, and clever to manage it well.

Regardless of its preservation benefits or otherwise, there will undoubtedly be increasing use of digital imaging to enhance access to our collections. It seems likely that there will be a major role for preservation in helping to manage digitisation programmes as part of multi-disciplinary teams required to achieve a range of institutional objectives.

The purpose of this rather lengthy digression on microfilming and digitisation has been to illustrate the view that while there are some encouraging tools, there are no once-and-for-all solutions to the preservation demands of our analogue collections. It looks very much like libraries will have to continue to struggle with their analogue collections and the influences that tend to make them unusable, while also meeting the challenges of preserving digital information in a range of formats. Rather than doing away with the preservation role, this looks like a future with a growing set of preservation needs.

RESOURCE ISSUES

Resources and support issues are so significant for most libraries that the good things preservation can do for collections and accessibility are often constrained. A likely feature of preservation in the library of the future is an ongoing struggle with those resource issues. We will have to do a better job of sharing our expertise and resources. For many libraries access to training to develop the necessary levels of expertise will help, but in many cases there remains the basic problem of resources. We will have to develop better ways of doing things, even in libraries that are well resourced. We will continue to look for improved processes, materials, and approaches. Innovation is being driven in part by the commitment and initiative of people working in the preservation field, but also partly by economic pressures. They are pressures I expect to feel for as long as I am a preservation manager, even in a relatively well-resourced and well-managed institution like the National Library of Australia.

Many libraries are not so well placed. We will need to find better ways of dealing with critical preservation problems where resource shortages are so acute that collections face disaster. This is an international as well as a local responsibility. Extensive cooperative microfilming programmes seem to have achieved much in many regions where the resources for other kinds of preservation action are insufficient. I will be interested to learn how effective they have been in this region, and whether people believe such programmes can continue to be effective in delivering what users want as technology changes.

7

Future Access-Long Term Preservation

Introduction

Information published in printed form in books, journals and newspapers is collected, catalogued and preserved by libraries throughout Australia, so that all Australians can have access to their published heritage. This is guaranteed by legislation, with publishers of printed materials like books, newspapers, journals and maps required to deposit copies of their works in the National Library of Australia and relevant state libraries.

Legal deposit is a special privilege enjoyed by only a small number of libraries in Australia. The existence of legal deposit provisions have allowed these libraries to build up valuable and comprehensive collections of historic Australian published materials which otherwise might have been discarded-perhaps as they lost their immediate appeal or became brittle or damaged.

Currently, no similar obligation exists for electronic materials. The long term availability to Australians of the full range of their published heritage will be at risk if electronic information is not collected comprehensively and maintained similarly to printed information. The National Library is committed to preserving selected electronic publications of lasting cultural value for access by the Australian community now and in the future, and has commenced a project which is investigating procedures for ensuring this. With electronic publishing in its infancy, the time is right to commence an 'archive' of electronic publications which will document these historic developments for future generations.

ELECTRONIC LEGAL PUBLISHING AND ITS PROSPECTS FOR SURVIVAL

The legal profession in Australia has taken up the cause of electronic publishing with enthusiasm. More and more law related material is being made available in electronic format-either in 'hardcopy' like CD-ROM or floppy disc or online via the Internet or other networked service. The range of materials available is very large-from primary legal materials to commentaries and discussions-and the rate of growth shows no sign of slowing down. While some information more or less duplicates material already in print, some of it is only produced in electronic format. Three titles, which illustrate some of the characteristics of electronic information are discussed in the Appendix.

Electronic materials have certain characteristics that mean their survival prospects are far less assured than those of print media. For instance, early versions of CDROM formats came with statements that they'd last 'forever'. Even if this was true, there is no guarantee that the information contained in them would be accessible into the future. Firstly one would also need to maintain a CDROM player 'forever'. Considering that very few people have 78 rpm drives on their record players, (if they have a record player at all), how likely is it that they would have the correct equipment for their CDROM in 30 or 40 years time? Has anyone tried to access the information on a 5 1/4 inch floppy disc recently?

Even if they could, it is even less likely that they would have the software to read and interpret the digital signals encoded on the disc. At this stage, software obsolescence is running at about twice the rate of hardware obsolescence. At best a meaningless jumble of digital signals would be produced.

It is probably fair to say that if no active steps are taken to ensure access into the future, materials being produced in electronic format today will not be available to the next generation. Publications where the information content has commercial value; are heavily used; and generate sufficient income for the publishers, are likely to be updated or 'migrated' as technology changes so that new 'editions' are always available. For freely available or public domain materials, this is less likely since the ongoing cost of maintaining material may outstrip any resources available to do it.

Even if a publication is updated, there is a question as to who maintains the previous 'editions'. Aunty Abha's Electronic Publishing makes the point that: *With legal research, it is sometimes necessary to know what the law was a few months or years ago. Subscribers to Aunty Abha's CD-ROMs can keep all back copies for historical use..* If technology changes, any back copies may end up being useless unless they also are migrated to a new format.

The more likely prospect for many publications, however, is that each successive version overwrites the previous, or else the previous version is discarded when a new version is issued.

One solution to the problem of historic availability of information is to archive selected materials in a dedicated repository, while updating the information on an ongoing basis and migrating it as technology demands. This is the solution adopted by the National Library of Australia as part of its Pandora (Preserving and Accessing Networked Documentary Resources of Australia) project.

PRINT VS ELECTRONIC INFORMATION

To ensure their long-term preservation and access, a different set of procedures need to be put in place for electronic materials compared to those used for print. There are some important differences that need considering.

Lack of Legal Deposit Provisions

The *Copyright Act of 1968* is currently under review, including its legal deposit provisions. At this stage, any project to archive electronic information with the aim of providing long-term access can only be with the permission of all owners of the information being captured.

Since 1994, the Library has adopted the approach of contacting Australian publishers of hardcopy electronic materials to seek the voluntary deposit of CDROMs and similar media. Many electronic publishers have already responded and publications covering a wide range of topics have been deposited. Deposit does not preclude the possibility of purchase of additional copies where high levels of use are anticipated.

The concept of deposit is harder to define with online electronic publications, and by their networked nature they can be made available to many users at any one time. Rather than ask for a copy of online material to be deposited, the Library is seeking the agreement of online publishers for permission to capture into the Library's own electronic archive a copy of the material as it exists on the Internet.

Fair Dealing and Provision of Access

Provision of access to print materials by libraries is well defined, with copying and fair dealing provisions reasonably straightforward. The same cannot be said for the electronic environment.

The Library realises that most 'hardcopy' electronic publications are expensive to produce and is careful to make sure it does not affect the commercial interests of the producers. The Library has drawn up a set of conditions to govern the use of deposited electronic publications in the Library and to prevent unauthorized copying. Access is generally limited to one user at a time within the Library building.

At present, there is little online commercial publishing on the Internet in Australia, and the Library has not yet attempted to archive commercial materials. We recognise, however, that commercial interests need to be considered and will attempt to establish archiving agreements with commercial publishers with this in mind. Possible options include the withholding of archived information for a set period, or the restriction of access to approved clients only. These models have been successfully implemented overseas. For some materials which are freely available or in the public domain this will be less of a problem. Some organisations-e.g. AustLII, make it clear that they are happy to have their material made readily available.

AustLII aims to put on the Net 'public legal information': primary legal materials (legislation and decisions of courts and tribunals); and secondary materials that are (or ought to be) in the public domain or able to be licensed for free. AustLII's public policy agenda is to convince governments, courts, law reform bodies and other publicly-funded organisations to make legal materials they control available free via the Internet.

AustLII is one of many organisations aiming to ensure that some part of cyberspace is public space, where no one is denied use of resources because of financial considerations. Its aim is to create a public law library on the Internet. (http://www.austlii.edu.au/austlii/faq.html-FAQ 7.6)

At this stage, all publishers of online materials selected for preservation by the National Library of Australia have willingly given approval for their material to be archived. No major commercial publisher has yet been approached, but we are hopeful that we will be able to reach mutually acceptable agreements with them too.

Value Added Information

Electronic publications are not the same as printed materials, even if the actual information contained in them is identical. They almost always have some important 'added value' features-such as online links to similar documents; keyword searching; or browsing facilities. Anyone used to regularly using electronic information would find it very tedious to go back to a print based system (would we want to swap an online library catalogue for a card catalogue?) Not only is it important to preserve the information, it is also important to preserve those value added features.

Hypertext links are a feature of publishing definitely not found in the print media. Some online titles consist almost entirely of links to other documents, which themselves are not necessarily published by the owner of the original title. Problems of copyright and of identifying ownership can become quite complex very quickly. If all the actual linked documents were included, then the size of one single title could become encyclopedic.

Life Expectancy

It is known that the printed word and even microfilm have the potential to last and still be accessible for hundreds of years. There are international standards for paper quality, for processing and storage of microfilm, and for many other factors that affect longevity. But how long are electronic materials going to last? And how long will one be able to access them?

Online electronic materials have no physical format to preserve. They can be removed from the Internet or overwritten almost instantaneously at any time. For material identified as nationally significant, there is an urgency to capture it close to its time of creation to ensure it survives for the future.

Potential lifetimes of some modern media-initially quoted in hundred's of years-are now thought to be rather optimistic. However, rather than being constrained by the actual physical survival of the object itself, there are other factors which are much more important when considering the useful life of electronic information.

Useful Life

With paper and even photographic materials, it is usually the physical object that fails first-paper becomes brittle, photographic images fade or get scratched or otherwise damaged. As long as the physical object lasts, however, it can still be used-even if only to be copied one last time onto a more stable medium. In addition, printed materials are eye legible-all a person needs is good eyesight (or a magnifying glass) and he can read anything published in print or microfilm.

It is not so simple with electronic materials. Not only do they need machines (the hardware) to 'read' the digital signals, they need some special coding (the software) to manipulate, interpret and convert the signals into a human intelligible format. Additionally, the value added features such as searching facilities that make electronic information so attractive are also software based. All the software and the hardware needs to be available if the 'look and feel' of the information is to be maintained.

Hardware and software are not universal-they are specific to each format of electronic material and each sort of code used. In fact, with hardcopy electronic materials, the physical object like the CDROM or floppy disc may still be in existence long after the machinery to play it or the software to interpret it have been scrapped or become obsolescent. Generally, two types of software are involved-the software that allows the machine to read the information and the software that interprets the information. It is no use just capturing the basic bit pattern of an electronic document. It has to remain a useable copy of the original document, and needs all the necessary software to ensure it.

How much can We Preserve and Make Accessible 'Forever'?

The relative ease of mounting an online electronic publication means that there is an ever escalating amount of material appearing in that format. There is so much available even now that organisations like the National Library of Australia, which have a role to preserve the printed literary output of Australia, are not able to apply the same collecting procedures to online electronic materials as they would to their print equivalents.

At present, the costs and staff time involved in acquiring and making available this material are much greater than for its print equivalent, and it is hard to see how this will be reduced, at least in the short term. As a result, there is a need to be much more selective. Although the volume of material in hardcopy format is probably not so great-partly because of the significant production costs involved-selectivity is likely to again be necessary. Updates and cumulations can rapidly increase the amount of material to be preserved.

With much online electronic information, the software needed to interpret it is easily identified. However, software coding for CDROM format is often proprietary, and may be embedded in the object itself. Password or other protection can also create problems of access. If hardcopy format electronic materials are to be archived, then full details of all their operating and interpretive software have to be known.

PHYSICAL FORMAT VS. ONLINE ELECTRONIC FORMATS

There are some other differences between the various formats of electronic documents that will affect their long-term preservation.

Permanent Location

A hardcopy electronic object has a physical format and can be identified and located by traditional library based systems. For online electronic materials, there is no physical format. Information can disappear without trace at any time if a publisher ceases to maintain his site. Alternatively, it might become very difficult to find information if he changes his site without leaving a forwarding address. Any hypertext links to his site from other documents will also cease to be active.

This is not a trivial matter where online information is concerned. A National Library of Australia bibliography on online information, compiled in early January 1996 still points to the AustLII site at UTS, which it obviously left some months ago. Fortunately, an online forwarding address is still available at the original site. Out of 54 entries in the Library database, only 37 titles (or 68%) were still at the same location 12 months later-the rest had moved on or disappeared altogether.

There are some systems being developed that will give a measure of permanence or persistence to locations on the Internet-PURL's, URN's, handles etc. It is intended to incorporate a permanent naming system in the Pandora archive.

Stability of Information-Currency, Authenticity

Once a CDROM is mastered, its information content is fixed. However, for online information it is relatively easy for the publisher or other person to change or edit it online. In quoting online electronic information, not only is the date of creation important, but also the date of viewing (or downloading).

One bonus of the relative ease of changing material online is that it gives publishers a flexibility they never had in print. Corrections, updates, reader feedback, reviews can all be included as they come to hand. This means that the concept of the integrity of a single print 'edition' can completely disappear in the online version. This can make the decision as to when or which 'copy' to preserve very problematical

AustLII discusses the concept of authenticity:

How do I know that somebody hasn't broken in and changed the law?

We are probably far more concerned about this than you are! One of our main system administration tasks is the maintenance of a fairly tight hold over security. It is for this reason that our services are split between multiple services, and also why some services are simply not available from the AustLII sites. (http://www.austlii.edu.au/austlii/faq.html FAQ 6.3)

Similar concerns of authenticity will also need to be taken into account in an online archive.

Finding Online Materials-Metadata

One of the problems of searching online for information is to find a way to restrict the amount of materials retrieved through popular search engines like *AltaVista* and *Lycos*. Because of the methodology of their search strategies they pick up everything containing your search terms-the important, the serious and the trivial-as they search the various indexes they use. These indexes can be built from a variety of sources, some from the titles of documents found on the Internet, some from the documents themselves and some from other indexes or directories.

Although there have been considerable improvements in their design, search engines cannot always closely interpret a user request. For example, trying for 'Australian constitution' on *AltaVista* got over 300 000 matches. Matches 1 to 10 were directly relevant. Match 11, however, was the *Institute of Australian Geographers Constitution.* Using the *Aussie Web Wombat,* which is Australian specific, there were only 1400 matches, but match 1 was for the *Constitution of the Lyrup Village Association, South Australia.* The *Australian Constitution* did not appear till match 19. There are emerging international standards like the Dublin Core for recording metadata (sometimes called 'information about information') for Internet documents. use of these should improve the 'hit rate' for documents by using standard searching techniques.

PANDORA (PRESERVING AND ACCESSING NETWORKED DOCUMENTARY RESOURCES)

This project aims to select online electronic titles for preservation by the National Library of Australia and to implement procedures to archive and make it accessible now and into the future. As a sub-project, it is also considering procedures for preserving physical format electronic materials.

For some months, the Library has been assessing online electronic materials and identifying those that have national significance. Some initial work has been done on experimenting with ways of cataloguing, organising and managing them so that they can be made available to potential users. Guidelines have been established for selection for preservation and titles are being selected in accordance with those guidelines. To date, around 120 titles have been selected for preservation and archiving. These titles have survived both the preliminary selection round, and a further in depth analysis against the selection criteria. The in-depth analysis phase has seen attributes like content, reliability, stability, form and format recorded. There is still work to be done to establish conditions and procedures for the long-term access, management and preservation of electronic materials. This includes establishing cataloguing and bibliographic systems that take account of the needs of electronic materials and to formulating conditions for maintaining and managing an online electronic archive within a library environment. Possible data management systems for the electronic archive are currently being researched.

There are many issues to be finalised, involving both intellectual and physical access design. These include:

- negotiating the right to copy for preservation purposes
- consideration of fair compensation for use
- preventing unfair use and reproduction
- maintaining the integrity of the information contained in the documents
- capturing information in an appropriate timeframe
- maintaining an audit trail of information on archiving
- making access as easy and quick as possible, consistent with the factors above
- looking towards migration strategies as current technology ages.

However, considerable progress has already been made, and we are looking forward to continuing to cooperate with the owners of electronic information to make the Pandora archive a valuable resource for Australia.

APPENDIX-SOME EXAMPLES OF ELECTRONIC PUBLICATIONS

There are many examples that could be used to discuss the importance of Australian electronic resources to the law, the variability of their formats, and the difficulties posed for long term preservation and access. The following three have been chosen to demonstrate some of the ideas discussed above.

Australian Legal Research Library on CDROM (Butterworths)

This title (including a component title *Halsbury's Laws of Australia*) has been placed on voluntary deposit in the Library since 1995/6. The Library also purchases copies of the product for use in by readers, since it has been identified as a high use product.

The deposit copies are kept in the closed stack area of the Library and are clearly annotated as 'for use on stand alone PC only'. At this early stage of their life, the information contained in them is still readable, and the physical objects are in good condition. However, as technology changes, the information contained in these CDROMs and associated software will need to be migrated into an appropriate format. Already, DVD or digital video disc format is attracting considerable publicity.

E-Law, the Murdoch University Electronic Journal of Law-ISSN 1321-8247

This journal, covering general law and legal issues, commenced in 1993. At that stage it was a simple text based publication-in simple black typewriter-like characters on a grey background, available by ftp or email. At that time, advanced graphics-based browsers like Netscape *Navigator* and Microsoft *Explorer* were still some time away.

Since Volume 3 No. 1 (May 1996), it has been Internet based with a simple but effective presentation and access to all issues is possible from the title homepage. The earliest issues are still in ASCII text, but there are direct hypertext links to them-no more need for ftp or email.

As an indication of the importance of such a journal to its client group, its *Netwatch* column, by Anne Greenshields should be noted. This started in 1995, and lists with brief annotations information on the Internet related to law. In the latest issue (December 1996) this column runs to nearly 6 printed pages, ranging from *Australian legal sites and developments* to *technology and the law*.-a total of 39 online hypertext links to legal information.

E-Law is being indexed by AGIS, and has also been selected by one overseas site as part of a trial arching project of scholarly journals.

E-Law fits clearly within the Pandora guidelines, and has accepted our invitation to be archived by the National Library of Australia.

The Australasian Legal Information Institute (AustLII)

AustLII is operated by Faculties of Law at the University of Technology, Sydney (UTS) and the University of New South Wales (UNSW), with funding from a variety of government and other sources. As noted earlier (AustLII FAQ 7.6):

AustLII aims to put on the Net 'public legal information': primary legal materials (legislation and decisions of courts and tribunals); and secondary materials that are (or ought to be) in the public domain or able to be licensed for free.

AustLII is an example of a site that has changed its location. Originally at http://austlii.law.uts.edu.au/, a redirect message says *As AustLII grows and resources need to be distributed, we need the flexibility of our own namespace.* This redirect message is still active over twelve months since the change occurred.

Although AustLII saw as its primary audience Australian academic legal researchers, use statistics indicate that *AustLII's users span the whole community, including educational institutions (about 30%), the legal profession and business (25%), community organisations (15%), government (10%), and 20% from overseas.* At this stage, each update of AustLII overwrites pre-existing information. This means that it is provides current, but no archived or historic information. The AustLII site is what in the terms of the Pandora project we have been calling a megasite. This means that it is so large and all embracing that is a library in itself-it currently contains around 500 000 individual documents. At this stage of the Pandora project, we are not considering the total archiving of any mega-sites (partly because we do not have sufficient resources in place to deal with them), although we may selectively archive part of the site. Although in time this decision might change, if some organisation does not take up the responsibility to save the whole site, the information it contains will be lost to future generations.

A WINDOW ON TO THE WORLD

In this paper I will give a brief survey of Australian newspaper publishing history and a description of the National Library's Australian newspaper holdings. I will outline its newspaper collecting policy and some of the national issues and initiatives being undertaken to ensure access to and preservation of Australian newspapers.

I don't think anyone who has read a newspaper from another country could argue with the idea that newspapers are a window on to the world. They give us a glimpse of the affairs of a country in the most direct and immediate way, and in their singular status as a contemporary record of events they show us not only what is happening but what was thought of it at the time – unique primary source material for researchers for several different reasons.

A Brief History

The history of newspaper publishing in Australia has been described as 'varied, spectacular and honourable'. The first newspaper appeared in 1803, with the publication by the military government of the *Sydney Gazette and New South Wales Advertiser*. This was only fifteen years after Governor Phillip's First Fleet landed and established a colony of convicts in the native bush of Sydney Cove. The *Sydney Gazette* carried the optimistic banner 'Thus we hope to prosper', and remained the colony's only newspaper until 1810, when the *Derwent Star* made a brief appearance in Hobart, to be followed in 1814 by the *Van Diemen's Land Gazette*. Throughout the 1800s, many newspapers prospered briefly and disappeared, while the *Sydney Gazette* ceased publishing in 1842. It was calculated in the 1950s that in the preceding 100 years New South Wales had at least 800 newspapers, of which only 163 then remained. Australia's oldest capital city newspaper is the *Sydney Morning Herald*, first published in 1842 and still owned by the Fairfax family, and its oldest country newspaper is the *Maitland Mercury*, from NSW, first published in 1843.

As in other countries, newspaper publishing in Australia simply reflected the tribulations of the country itself, whether natural, economic or political. Factors affecting the closure of newspapers included droughts, floods, financial crises, the end of the gold rush in the Victorian goldfields and a shortage of newsprint during World War II. Political pressure was also brought to bear on the first Australian newspaper publishers by the colonial authorities – in fact, as soon as independent newspapers began to appear. From the 1820s onwards, Governors or Lieutenant Generals of the day attempted to impose governmental control of the press, which was strongly resisted. These actions created a long-standing tradition of the free press in Australia. However, opinions were sometimes divided on what constitutes a free press. The dilemma was neatly summarised by a contemporary observer, showing how little the issues have changed to this day. E.D. Burn, Tasmanian essayist and dramatist, wrote in 1842:

A portion of the local press, remarkable for scurrility and low personality, poured forth its low hebdomadal tirades in loud and savage invectives, and in the hope of wounding in the tenderest point a ribald malignity was indulged ...The *liberty* of the press is a blessing of most inappreciable value; its *licence* is sometimes too contemptible even for restraint. A large portion of the Tasmanian press has long obtained an unenviable celebrity, so much so as to have subjected it to the severe, reiterated and merited castigation both of its Australasian and British contemporaries.

I think it is fair to say that the basic fight for the freedom of the press had its genesis in authoritarian actions by vice-regal rulers, but that on the other hand it also extended into unrestrained invective on the part of the newspapers. Perhaps because of this basic struggle the more successful newspapers began to gain and maintain some influence within their communities in the second half of the 19th century, and it was commonly believed, for example, that newspapers could and did sway parliamentary elections. There is debate as to whether that influence extends to this day, with a view that it very much does in the non-metropolitan centres of Australia like Adelaide and Brisbane.

The course of time has changed both the influence of newspapers and attitudes towards them. At present in Australia it is estimated that newspaper circulation has fallen by approximately 15% over the last five years, while readership of daily newspapers in metropolitan markets is relatively stable at 63% of the total capital city population. (Australia's total population is 18 million). Small circulation growth has come from the introduction of Sunday editions in some capital cities, while the main national business daily, the *Australian financial review* has gone against the trend and increased its circulation. Using a media-defined figure, there are currently estimated to be:

1 national weekly

2 national dailies

3 metropolitan dailies

8 metropolitan weeklies (usually Sundays)

9 regional dailies

38 regional non-dailies

155 suburban newspapers

The largest network of ownership is Rupert Murdoch's News Limited, which owns eleven metropolitan titles.

The National Library's Australian Newspaper Collection

Most of these titles will be found in the collections of the National Library of Australia, as the Library acquires Australian newspaper titles by virtue of the legal deposit provisions of the *Copyright Act 1968.* (The Act does not currently apply to microform or electronic formats.) There are some exclusions – the Library does not acquire suburban newspapers or those of a purely local community interest. These are considered to be the responsibility of the appropriate state or territory library.

The Library completed cataloguing all of its current and non-current Australian newspaper titles on to the National Bibliographic Database in the late 1980s. Up till then, newspaper holdings were listed in a National Library publication entitled *Newspapers in Australian libraries* (1985, now out of print), which probably still stands as the most complete union listing as of that date, but with many bibliographic inaccuracies.

A survey of the Library's holdings indicates that as of July 1999 522 current Australian print newspapers are held, together with 1,558 ceased titles. 147 current titles are also received in microform, while 1,417 non-current titles are held in microform.

Australia is a multicultural society, with a history of immigration from all parts of the world, and our newspaper collection reflects this. Of the current print newspaper collection, just over 18% of the titles held are in languages other than English. We believe this represents an underestimate of the actual proportion, as ethnic language newspapers are often not deposited with the National Library. The ethnic publishing community is one of the more elusive publishing communities with which we engage, and a consistent resource-intensive effort to maintain contact is required. The pattern of ethnic newspaper publishing has varied over the years according to the pattern of new arrivals and the traditions within each community: the Chinese and Vietnamese languages are dominant among newspaper titles currently received, while Italian, Polish and German are all on the decline.

The Library's collecting policy for Australian newspapers was reviewed in 1996 and issued as part of its latest Collection Development Policy, which was published in July of this year. The full text can be found on the Library's Web site and the newspaper collecting policy is reproduced in full in Appendix.

Retention and Preservation Issues

Newspaper collecting within Australia is well covered by the National Library and the state and territory libraries who together hold the most complete record of Australian newspaper publishing. However although Australia's newspaper history is only 200 years old, it is known that many early, small or local newspapers have not survived, or only a handful of issues exist. For example, only four issues of the *English and Chinese Advertiser* are known to have survived. This fascinating newspaper was published in English and Chinese during the early gold rush in Ballarat, Victoria. A survey conducted in the early 1990s identified gaps in 164 newspaper titles published in Australia, mostly dating back to the 1800s, but some as recently as 1956. It was also found that some local newspaper sets were held in university collections but not in the relevant state library. Retention, preservation and access issues are therefore a concern for all the libraries, In early 1992 the Council of Australian State Libraries agreed on a cooperative effort between the state libraries and the National Library to carry out a national newspaper preservation plan (NPLAN).

In the U.S. the United States Newspaper Programme has similar aims, as does the British NEWSPLAN, which focuses on local newspapers. The National Newspaper Plan's stated goal is to preserve all Australian newspapers and to ensure the public has acces to them. A basic principle of the NPLAN is that primary responsibility for retention of newspapers in hardcopy rests with the State or Territory library in the State or Territory of the newspaper's origin. Its objectives areas follows:

- Acquisitions

  To collect hard copies of all newspapers as published

  To identify, locate and collect missing issues

- Bibliographic control

  To record all hard copies and reproductions on the National Bibliographic Database

  To produce a national register of microform masters from the NBD

- Preservation

  To retain as long as feasible at least one hard copy of every newspaper

  To create or purchase an archival standard microfilm master of every newspaper for permanent preservation

  To create a copying master and working copies

Progress with NPLAN

One of NPLAN's objectives was to run a publicity campaign to locate missing or unknown newspapers held in private homes, community organisations, newspaper offices and local authorities. Under the rubric 'Australia's most wanted newspapers' a list of titles was advertised which had large gaps, such as the *Bendigo Advertiser* from Victoria, the *Huon Times* from Tasmania and the *Swan River Guardian* from Western Australia. The idea for the campaign came from the very successful 'Last film search' conducted by the National Film and Sound Archive in the 1980s to locate film stock held in private hands; however it has to be said that the search for missing issues of newspapers was much less successful. While some issues were donated by the public, the majority of the titles sought never turned up, perhaps reflecting the transitory nature of the newspaper both physically and in the public perception.

However, NPLAN did fulfil the function of raising awareness of newspaper preservation issues amongst Australian libraries themselves. Good progress has been made on microfilming of newspapers, both by individual libraries and in cooperative projects. The State Library of New South Wales in Sydney claims that it will have all of its newspaper collection filmed by 2000, while the National Library continues its successful programme of cooperative filming, of which more below.

The National Library's Retention and Preservation Policy

The National Library is committed to the preservation within Australia of the total output of Australian newspapers, and developed its newspaper retention and preservation policy with the national newspaper plan in mind. The full text of the National Library's Policy on the Retention, Preservation and Repatriation of Australian Newspapers is attached at Appendix 2. In keeping with the spirit of NPLAN's principles, the National Library will:

- accept responsibility for the preservation, in hardcopy and surrogate form, of titles that are national in scope, coverage and distribution, as well as newspapers published in the Australian Capital Territory, where the Library is located;

- continue to develop an extensive hardcopy collection of Australian newspapers that have are not yet been microfilmed;
- repatriate hardcopy holdings to allow preservation microfilming to occur (the Library will repatriate to allow a State or Territory library to microfilm a title for which they are primarily responsible, or if the Library's holdings are duplicated by microfilm working copy);
- enter into and partially fund cooperative microfilming projects;
- provide free Cold Store storage for archival standard preservation masters;
- record all newspaper holdings (hardcopy and microform) and preservation intentions on the National Bibliographic Database (NBD).

Repatriation

The repatriation issue was a particular initiative of the state and territory libraries, which in some cases lacked newspaper issues held by the National Library or university libraries. In NPLAN's early days there was some success in achieving the repatriation of particular titles, mainly from university library collections to the State or territory library, but there has been little activity recently. The National Library will repatriate titles if fairly stringent preservation and access conditions can be met, and it has emerged that few libraries have been able to meet these standards.

Cooperative Microfilming Projects

An effective way for the Library to encourage adherence to good preservation standards as well as to advance the preservation effort is to work with other libraries and provide financial support to microfilm newspaper titles. The Cooperative Microfilming Project was established in the mid-1990s with a budget of $20,000-$30,000 a year for the last five or six years. Requests for assistance from Australian libraries are considered on the basis of available funding, forward work plans, and conformity with the Library's criteria. For newspapers the first criterion is age: newspaper backsets more than thirty years old are considered to be at the greatest risk of loss due to the quality of the paper on which it is printed. The highest priority for filming is given to newspapers which are:

- defined by the holding institution as either heavily used, brittle or at risk because of poor storage conditions
- defined by the National Library of Australia as unique or at risk because of the dispersal of the few remaining
- defined by agreement between the holding institution and the National Library of Australia as being of particular importance.

Progress with cooperative microfilming has been slow but satisfactory, underling the importance of a long term approach with reliable funding and administrative support.

Looking into the Future: the Australian Cooperative Digitisation Project

Underpinning the Library's newspaper preservation policy is a commitment to microfilming as the most viable current preservation format for newspapers, and it is committed to promoting the use of Australian and international standards for preservation microfilming. The archival standards applied are listed in Appendix 2.

However, microfilming has always been just one of a number of reformatting options. Digitisation as both a preservation and access strategy is clearly an important area for newspapers, and I will close this paper with a brief account of the Australian Cooperative Digitisation project. This project, led by the University of Sydney Library, was a trial of the digital conversion of several significant nineteenth century Australian books and journals, including 38 newspaper titles. The project partners are University of Sydney Library, the State Library of New South Wales, the National Library of Australia and Monash University Library, suppc ted by ten other institutional and industry groups. The full content-text and images-of a range of journals, newspapers, novels and short stories published in Australia from the period 1840-45 was digitised using OCR technology and is progressively being made available on the Internet. The purpose of this collaborative project is to ensure both increased access to, and preservation of, this material through an integrated process of preservation microfilming, digital scanning, network access and selected full-text enhancement. One of the project's aims is to investigate and develop technical benchmarks for similar digital library projects involving the conversion of retrospective print material. It is an opportunity to develop technical and management experience and skills in such work at both the library and vendor level for the benefit of future projects in Australia. Close contact has been kept with US institutions carrying out similar work, particularly Cornell University's Digital Library project and Yale's Open Book Project. Other projects taking place that have assisted or will assist in the Australian trial include the Library of Congress digital project, the Making of America (Cornell and Michigan Universities) and the UK Elib sponsored project, the Internet Library of Early Journals.

The newspapers of the period 1840-1845 represent a unique record of the settlements, but their physical size presents particular problems in digitisation, especially in the delivery of the images and print reproduction.

Methods Employed

Technical and user specifications for the project were developed by the ACDP partners and the production work of filming and digital conversion was contracted to commercial vendors.

The identification and checking of the original material proved to be rather complex, much more so than anticipated. Identifying complete sets, or filling gaps when parts of titles may be held by different institutions was part of this process and required the input of staff with very highly developed bibliographic skills. It also required the selection of the best copy for the project. A good deal of the material in the time period of this project had already been microfilmed. Consideration was given to the utility of these existing microfilm sets as a source for scanning, particularly in regard to quality and page orientation on the film (the digital image must appear in "portrait" style with the image appearing on the screen as straight up and down). Older microfilm was replaced by technically superior modern film to ensure the highest fidelity was achieved during the digitisation process. While the print material itself was out of copyright, issues such as rights over the master microfilm, and rights over the final digital images needed to be considered. Some initial conservation work was done on the original material. Fundamental to the project was the maintenance of the integrity of the original material. The material is scarce and of cultural significance, so no actions were taken that might have damaged the originals.

Of the 90-odd serial titles listed for the period in the Ferguson *Bibliography of Australia*, there were 11 titles that could not be tracked down anywhere in Australia, and another five titles that were withdrawn from the project because they proved to be impossible to digitise adequately with current techniques–mainly because of the page size and the poor quality text. This left about 74 titles, of which five proved to be unsuitable for scanning from microfilm. These are now being filmed directly from the source using digital cameras. This is an experimental addition to the project, and looks to be quite successful; 2,000 images of the *Geelong Advertiser* have just been produced and the production methods will be compared and assessed.

For the periodicals and newspapers, the basic approach was to create TIFF images at resolutions of 400 dots per inch, converting to PDF format for multi-page delivery. This meant images of pages are obtained, rather than searchable text. The images have been mounted on the Library's website and are retrievable both through the navigational tools on the Project pages and at title level through the NLA catalogue. They will be maintained and developed as part of the National Library's growing collection of digital research materials.

Outcomes So Far

The message of the Australian Cooperative Digitisation Project so far is very simple: it's not easy. Digitisation of large format materials like newspapers continues to be difficult and time-consuming. OCR scanning of this kind of material is very difficult because of the great variety of print fonts and the variable image quality, and digitisation does not solve legibility problems. Another critical technical issue in the development of the specifications is the data file size of the images-the larger the file size the slower it is for the image to be retrieved across the internet, the slower to download, and the more space it will take on disks to which the images have been downloaded.

In investigating these problems the ACDP team consulted with several digital projects working with newspapers, and all (at least for now) rejected using the Internet as the delivery means of images of large format newspapers. The document structure developed for the project can be used for organising and browsing newspaper pages, and similarly for the provision of images on CD-ROM.

This seems the likely option for the newspaper situation, but further investigation is required. Desirable solutions to at least some of the problems are the ability to deliver large quantities of data over the Internet is needed, together with improved software for the manipulation of images to cope with the variability of print formats. In addition, OCR technology does not solve the issue of text searchability.

However the fact remains that it is now possible for researchers anywhere in Australia or the world to call up images of the Sydney Advertiser, the Dispatch or the Sun over the Internet and view every page directly from the screen. That is a great advance on accessibility and certainly on preservation. The ACDP site will be formally launched in Canberra in August or September and a seminar on the project will be held in Sydney in November 1999. Titles are accessible now, at http://www.nla.gov.au/ferg/.

There were 24 titles available when I last checked, it is growing almost daily and you will also find several articles about the project by those involved, amongst whom is my colleague Colin Webb, Preservation Services Manager at the National Library. Anyone interested in knowing more about it is very welcome to contact Colin direct. Work remains to be done on the site, improving the contextual information and the navigational tools, but it is already a valuable research resource. Finally, anyone interested in looking at how the National Library plans to manage these and other digital resources should look at our Digital Services Project site, at http://www.nla.gov.au/dsp/.

Conclusion

I opened this paper by talking about newspapers being windows on to worlds, and it seems fitting to have closed it with an account of another kind of window being opened through the availability of 19th century newspapers on the Internet. While newspaper readership appears to be declining, research demand for newspapers as primary source material is increasing, and the problems for libraries of managing newspaper collections grow with the collections themselves. In Australia the National and State libraries have generally taken a cooperative approach to dealing with the issues of access and preservation, with real progress being made on microfilming and bibliographic control. The technical possibilities of digitisation as a medium for newspaper preservation and access have been explored and will provide a foundation for further work. And although Australia is a relatively small country, with only a 200 year newspaper publishing history, there remains a great deal to be done.

Appendix 1

National Library of Australia's Australian newspaper collecting policy

[Excerpt from *Collection Development Policy*, 1999, pp. 23-24, available at: http://www.nla.gov.au/policy/cdp/]

The Library will collect all Australian newspapers except those that fall into the following categories:

- those intended primarily for advertising purposes and consisting mainly of advertisements, including real estate papers
- newspapers distributed at the suburban and regional levels which consist of generic text that is used for distribution to different communities and towns accompanied by a cover page that localises the newspaper by containing information relevant only to the particular community or town. A sample of the generic text will be collected in each case, but not all the local editions distributed.
- titles containing predominantly information that would be largely of local community interest only in that it

concerns local social, sporting and community events and local services information and advertising.

These categories are considered the responsibility of the relevant State or Territory library and any titles received by the National Library that fall into the categories above will be referred to that library. In deciding whether to collect a specific title, emphasis is placed on content. Newspapers that are a primary source of current news connected with public affairs either regional, national and/or international in scope, including titles published by ethnic groups and political organisations, and those representing special interests, will be collected. If intended for a general audience, they should contain a broad range of news on all subjects and activities, but if intended for a special interest group they should include features and topical news of particular interest to that group.

Generally back issues and retrospective runs of newspapers will only be acquired if they are available in microform. In general, the retrospective acquisition of newspapers in microform will follow the policy for the acquisition of current titles except that additional factors such as length of coverage, cost, historic and geographical significance, and research value will also be taken into consideration. Often the last two factors only become apparent in retrospect. The increasing availability of runs of newspapers in microform as once only acquisitions makes the wider selection of retrospective titles more feasible.

The Library is committed to the preservation within Australia of the total output of Australian newspapers and will cooperate with other institutions through the mechanism of the National Plan for Australian Newspapers (NPLAN) to achieve this. It accepts that it is responsible for preserving national and Australian Capital Territory newspapers in paper and microform formats, and that preservation of local, regional and State newspapers is the responsibility of the appropriate State or Territory library. Where the relevant State library has agreed to retain the hard copy of a newspaper the Library will repatriate or discard its hard copy as long as a microform copy exists.

The Library will also enter into selected cooperative filming projects to preserve unique/rare and other newspaper titles considered of importance.

Appendix 2

National Library of Australia Policy on the Retention, Preservation & Repatriation of Australian Newspapers [available at: [http://www.nla.gov.au/policy/revnpan.html]

1. In late 1990, the National Library initiated a major review of its policies and procedures associated with the acquisition, control and preservation of Australian newspapers. The review was initiated at about the same time as the Council of Australian State Libraries (CASL)-at the time known as the State Libraries Council (SLC) – was discussing the feasibility of developing a national newspaper plan. The plan, subsequently named the National Plan for Australian Newspapers (NPLAN), was announced in early 1992. The Library was involved in the formulation of the

   Plan and its basic principles and aims have influenced to a large degree the Library's revised policies on Australian newspapers, especially in the area of preservation.

2. The basic understanding of the NPLAN is that each State or Territory library is responsible for the collecting, control and preservation of newspapers that originate in their State or Territory. While the NPLAN does not identify a significant role for the National Library, the Library considers that it does have a major part to play in working with the State and Territory libraries to ensure the goals of the NPLAN are realised.

In summary, the Library will:

- accept responsibility for the preservation, in hardcopy and surrogate form, of titles identified in this policy;
- continue to develop an extensive hardcopy collection of Australian newspapers that have are not yet been microfilmed;
- repatriate hardcopy holdings to allow preservation microfilming to occur; enter into and partially fund cooperative microfilming projects;
- provide free Cold Store storage for archival standard preservation masters;

- record all newspaper holdings (hardcopy and microform) and preservation intentions on the National Bibliographic Database (NBD).

Note: In this document the term preservation master is used for first generation master (1st generation); copying master for printing master (2nd generation); and working copy for service copy (3rd generation).

3. In July 1999 the Library issued its Collection Development Policy for Australian printed materials which includes collecting policy for newspapers. The Library's collecting role in this field is much wider than its preservation responsibility under NPLAN and is not influenced by the principles underlying the Plan. The Library will continue to develop an extensive Australian newspaper collection, in both hardcopy and microform, to support current and future research needs.

Retention in Hardcopy

4. A basic principle of the NPLAN is that primary responsibility for retention of newspapers in hardcopy rests with the State or Territory library in the State or Territory of the newspaper's origin. In keeping with the spirit of this principle, the National Library will accept responsibility for the retention in hardcopy of:
   - newspapers that are national in scope, coverage and distribution. (To date, these have been identified as the Australian (national edition), the Australian Financial Review, the National Times, the Nation Review, and the Independent. (This list is not intended to be definitive. Other titles may be added later if judged to fit the criterion. In this event, State and Territory libraries will be advised.)
   - newspapers published in the ACT. Shared responsibility for these will be negotiated with the ACT Reference Library when established.
5. There may be issues or runs of other titles that the Library decides to retain in hardcopy because, for instance, they form part of a private collection or have particular research relevance to the Library. These will

be decided on an individual basis. (Newspapers in this category will be housed in preservation conditions and microfilming for long-term preservation will be negotiated with the library primarily responsible for the title.)

Preservation Action

6. For national and ACT titles, as identified in paragraph 4 above, the Library accepts responsibility for retaining hardcopy for as long as feasible and for preserving information content in surrogate form. The following action will be taken to achieve this:
   - where there are gaps in runs of titles the Library will seek to fill them and where the condition of the Library's hardcopy is poor, copies in better condition will be sought;
   - the best available hardcopy will be housed in preservation conditions to minimise the rate of deterioration. No attempt will be made to reverse chemical deterioration unless a cost effective technology becomes available;
   - where they do not already exist, an archival quality preservation master and a copying master of each title will beproduced and stored in preservation conditions;
   - access to hardcopy will be restricted. For general use, a microfilm working copy will be acquired or created ifone is not already available;
   - where archival standard preservation and copying masters already exist but are not held at the Library, free storage at the NLA's Cold Store will be offered to institutions unable to meet the storage conditions required for preservation masters, as outlined in paragraph 13. Free storage will be contingent on the institution's ability to guarantee that the preservation master meets standards outlined in paragraph 13.
7. To ensure national access to newspapers for which the National Library accepts responsibility all hardcopy and microfilm versions will be recorded on the NBD.

Repatriation of Hardcopy Newspapers in the Library's Collection

8. In support of the goals of the NPLAN, The Library will repatriate to the relevant State or Territory library hardcopy newspapers for which it does not accept prime preservation responsibility. However, in the interest of ensuring long-term preservation and future access to information in the newspapers, repatriation will be subject to certain understandings and agreements as outlined below.
9. The Library is aware that there are risks in relying on microfilming to preserve and ensure future access to the information content of newspapers. For instance, its useful life or usefulness as a preservation surrogate can be compromised by:
   - An unstable film base (such as cellulose acetate) or inappropriate film type (such as diazo for preservation masters);
   - Inappropriate environmental storage conditions;
   - Copying master not produced, threatening the integrity of the preservation master; Incomplete filming, producing film which has, for example, missing pages;
   - Poor quality of the original and/or poor filming, producing images which are faint or illegible;
   - Inappropriate use;
   - Inappropriate storage security.
10. The Library therefore considers the conditions under which hardcopies are housed and the standards used for production and storage of preservation masters are critical considerations in ensuring long-term preservation of the newspaper component of the national heritage.
11. The library will repatriate in the following cases: a request for repatriation is made by a State or Territory library because they intend to microfilm the title in the near future, the Library's holdings of hardcopy newspapers are duplicated by microfilm working copies.

If the paper copy (whether held by the NLA or the relevant State or Territory Library) is in sufficiently good condition to allow the prospect of future re-filming should problems with the microfilm later emerge, the NLA will repatriate its paper copy without undertaking quality control checks on the microfilm service copy; However, if the paper copy is in poor condition, the NLA would negotiate with the relevant State or Territory Library to establish procedures and priorities for undertaking a frame by frame check of the preservation or copying master, with the view to future re-filming if necessary.

12. The following understandings will apply when repatriation occurs:
    - the National Library will meet the costs of repatriation;
    - the receiving library is able to provide equivalent or superior preservation storage for the hardcopy (Seeparagraph 13);
    - where issues of the hardcopy are duplicated, those in the best condition will be retained;
    - the receiving library will record holdings of repatriated hardcopy on ABN;
    - where a title has already been microfilmed, the relevant library accepts responsibility for ensuring the preservation master, wherever located, has been produced according to national archival standards, is housed inappropriate preservation conditions, and is recorded on the National Bibliographic Database (NBD). If the master has not been produced according to national archival standards or has been degraded as a result of inappropriate storage, it is assumed refilming will be scheduled;

When repatriation occurs to enable preservation filming:

- filming will be to current archival standards and a copying master will be produced as well as the preservation master;
- the masters will be stored in appropriate conditions;

- the National Library will have continuing access to a free working copy for on-site use and one will also be made available for use in the library holding the preservation master;
- the existence and location of the preservation and copying masters will be recorded on ABN according to agreed standards. (The National Library will consider assisting with this if necessary.)

When repatriation is agreed to by both parties, the Library will assume that it is based on an acceptance by the receiving library of the understandings outlined above. Repatriation can be initiated by either a State or Territory library or the National Library.

Preservation Standards

13. The preservation standards followed by the National Library are outlined below. It is expected that when a title is repatriated, the minimum preservation conditions and treatment that will be provided by the receiving library will be at least to the same level, regardless of the form of preservation undertaken.

Preservation Storage for Newspapers

Packaging: Heavily used titles are stored in specially designed polypropylene boxes. Low use titles are shrink wrapped.

Storage Equipment: Items are stored horizontally on appropriate sized fixed or mobile library shelving elevated off the floor, not in close proximity to light sources or fire sprinklers.

Storage Environment: Environmental conditions are monitored, and appropriate air conditioning and filtration systems are in place to maintain stable and appropriate levels of temperature, relative humidity, and air quality. Temperature is maintained at the lowest level consistent with human co-habitation. Relative humidity is maintained between 35-45%. Light levels are low, with undetectable levels of ultraviolet radiation. Light are switched off when not in use. A high level of cleanliness is maintained. Precautions are taken to exclude animal and insect pests and active pest control procedures are taken as a necessary part of an integrated pest control system.

Security: Protection is at a high level, with restricted access. All material is identified clearly. A fully implemented disaster preparedness and response plan exists. The NLA building provides a high standard of protection from natural disasters. Fire protection includes a Very Early Smoke Detection Apparatus (VESDA) system. Boxing or shrink wrapping provides added protection against risk of damage from water.

Control of Use: For material available in surrogate form, use of originals is restricted to last resort use under supervision.

Microfilming standards

The latest versions of:

ANSI.IT 9.1

1992 American national standard for imaging media (film)-silver-gelatine type-specifications for stability

ANSI.IT 9.5

1992 American national standard for imaging media (film) ammonia-processed diazo films-specifications for stability

AS 2840

1986 Microfilming of newspapers for archival purposes

ISO 4332

1986 Photography-processed photographic black and white film for archive records-silver gelatine type on poly(ethyleneterephthalate) base-specifications

Preservation Storage for Microfilm

Microfilm masters are stored in the Library's Cold Store. The environmental conditions in the room are normally maintained at a temperature of 8 +1C and a relative humidity of 35 +5%, in which collection material entering or leaving the room is required to acclimatise for 24 hours.

Higher temperature levels are acceptable, but RH levels must be set within this range. Stability in temperature and RH, and air quality including the absences of gaseous contaminants, are considered to be critical. Unstable film and acidic packaging are excluded. Fire protection is provided by a VESDA system and a dry pipe sprinkler system. Access to the area is restricted to key personnel.

Cooperative Microfilming

14. The National Library accepts that it has a responsibility to ensure preservation of the national documentary heritage through national cooperation. An effective way in which it can contribute to the long-term preservation of Australian newspapers is by participating in cooperative projects to microfilm backsets which are more than thirty years old, subject to the criteria outlined in the Library document Policy on participation in Cooperative Microfilming projects with Other Institutions.

Use of National Library Cold Store for Storage of Masters

15. If necessary to ensure appropriate storage, the National Library will store free of charge preservation microfilm masters which are silver halide emulsion on a stable film base (polyester/polyethylene terephthalate, not a cellulose acetate), processed to the archival standards outlined above, in good chemical condition, packaged in appropriate stable containers, and unlikely to require frequent retrieval.

Discard of Hardcopy Newspapers

16. The Library will consider discarding hardcopy newspapers in its collection if its holdings are duplicated in the State or Territory library primarily responsible for preserving the titles concerned, and the holdings of the State or Territory library are in as good or better condition as the Library's holdings.
17. Where a State or Territory library considers it important to preserve a second hardcopy set of a title somewhere in the country, the Library will repatriate to the institution nominated by the relevant State or Territory Library. The Library will not itself maintain duplicate hardcopy sets of State or Territory titles.

8

Digital Conversion of Nineteenth Century Publications

Intellectual Significance : The primary purpose of the project is to enhance literary and historical research on nineteenth-century Australia by providing improved access to, and preservation of, scarce primary material confined to a few major library collections. The period 1840-45 was selected by an advisory group of academics as significant for recording, for the first time, the emergence of a particularly Australian political, social and literary character.

Their advice, to treat the period comprehensively and to cover all the journals that began publication in the period as well as the novels, determined the character of the project and dictated many of the subsequent technical processes. The bibliographical source for material was Ferguson's Bibliography of Australia-the most comprehensive bibliography of nineteenth century Australian material, from which 75 journals and four novels were initially identified as the subject of the project.

Nature of the Original Material : Having taken a comprehensive view of the content we were committed to handling all the physical variations of these publications-not only in size, from quarto to broadsheet-but also the variety within any one title-from foxing and discolouration, to the use of varying fonts and point sizes on the one page. This diversity of sizes and variation of condition presented challenges for image quality, file size and delivery mechanisms.

The selection and assessment process-where each title was verified, located, identified as 'best copy', gaps identified and remedied by access to other copies, and assembled for microfilming presented a different array of challenges requiring detailed bibliographic skills and untold patience. The documentation of the assessment process on a title-by-title basis became a critical management tool for monitoring and controlling workflow.

As the project developed, we learnt just how important this final pre-filming assessment was. It was impossible to achieve satisfactory results by treating all materials the same way. Material had to be assessed more closely than we had expected to identify the likely challenges and quirks of each title. This was similar to normal microfilming practice, but with the discipline imposed by later scanning of the microfilm, this pre-film sorting and description of the material needs to be much more rigorous.

From the outset we were committed to ensuring the physical integrity and conservation of the original material throughout the process. This concern was met in part by the decision in our production model to microfilm first as we were confident, from experience, in the ability of microfilm agencies to handle fragile heritage material in an appropriate manner

Nature of the Digital Content : The technical aspects of the digital images (file size issues, delivery considerations, quality issues) are detailed in the discussion of production issues, below. The pertinent point here is to appreciate that through digital conversion and reformatting the value and potential of this content has also be transformed in fundamental ways.

The decision to take a comprehensive approach immediately highlighted one of the primary benefits of the digitisation of this material-the merging of distributed physical collections into one complete virtual collection. Such an endeavour required both a national viewpoint and an effective collaborative organisation

Project Organisation and Management

ACDP was intrinsically a collaborative project. This presented great benefits as well as challenges for the project partners and vendors involved in the collaboration. The challenges included managing the flow of information, ensuring inclusive decision-making, maintaining adequate documentation, monitoring progress, and adjusting procedures. On the positive side, the collaboration provided a wide pool of expertise, experience, motivation, and diversity of ideas and styles that all added greatly to the project, helping us deal effectively with most issues. These benefits extended well beyond ACDP to other projects.

The vendors (chosen through selective tender) themselves needed to set up the required infrastructure (investing in expensive imported hardware, and undertaking considerable programming and software development) to provide the level of throughput and quality required by the project.. The working relationship between the project partners and the vendors was a key part of the project, though sometimes rocky as we tested and reviewed outputs against our specifications (we went through 10 testing and feedback stages-see Appendix 1). The decision to outsource by contract was fundamental to the project-we wanted to use this opportunity to assist the development of industry skills among contractors in the field, and to facilitate the investment and foster the expertise for use in similar projects in the future. This has been one of the many successes of the project.

APPENDIX 2 LISTS FACTS AND STATS OF ACDP

Project Management Issues : The first production issue was to recognise the complexity of this sequence of steps and objectives, and the need to manage them closely and well. Often the issues that arose in managing workflows and communications seemed the most critical of all.

The exploratory nature of the project, the interdependence of processes, the number of players involved, and the distance between them-all meant there was potential for many risks including confusion, delays, loss of accountability, and important things falling between the cracks. The project management team recognised many of these risks and sought to manage them proactively with a variety of tools and responses, including:

- appointment of a dedicated project coordinator (located at SLNSW)

- preparation of detailed specifications
- establishing a project management structure consisting of a high level Project Management Committee, a more operationally-focused Project Steering Committee, and a Technical Advisory Group
- allocation of operational responsibilities between partners
- agreeing on communication guidelines and mechanisms, including meetings, and regular email and phone contact between meetings
- negotiating communication mechanisms with vendors, including regular meetings, reports, and other feedback opportunities
- negotiating timelines for expected deliverables
- developing tables of titles and what had to happen to them
- batching of work

Project management inputs turned out to be a very large-and largely hidden-investment. We came to recognise the reality of the often-repeated assertion that the organisational and management aspects of digitisation projects-and especially complex collaborative ones-may be more challenging than the technical issues.

Access Issues

This project was devised and designed to serve preservation objectives while greatly improving the accessibility of material that had previously been difficult to access.

Internet access was the rationale behind the project, so the main access issues were to produce file in formats that could be effectively delivered to users over the Internet, and to develop a user interface that would be easy to use.

Formats and Files Sizes : Bandwidth is a major problem for delivering large, high-resolution images over the Internet, and it was inevitable that this would be a challenge for ACDP. Legible images of difficult, small print text necessarily produce large file sizes. And, as the dimensions of the original material increase, file sizes increase geometrically.

We also found that, while images of photographs and painting can remain worthwhile for reference purposes even at low resolutions, text images are useless if they are illegible. Finding ways to deliver legible images at acceptable speeds became a key focus. These issues needed to be resolved at the earliest possible stage so that production work would support, rather than complicate, the eventual storage and access systems. Development of the system architecture, document control structure, image management and retrieval system, and user interface-undertaken by NLA-ensured a consistent approach to services delivered from its website.

Following tests of a range of delivery formats with the project's prime target audience, Adobe's Portable Document Format (PDF) was chosen as the online delivery format for the compressed bitonal TIFF images. A number of images (between 1 and 10) are embedded in each PDF file, providing multi-page files for easier moving between pages. PDF also offered advantages for zooming and for printing, important features given that whatever the format, most pages cannot be viewed on screen as a whole at a legible magnification. The need to download an Adobe viewer was acknowledged as a possible barrier to access, but due to the increasing likelihood that users would already have suitable viewers installed, this was not seen as an impediment.

Possibilities for Searching Text : The great majority of images produced are bit mapped images of text, rather than text that is searchable. Because most of the original serials lack indexes, finding specific content is difficult. This made the project partners interested in the possibilities and potential of using optical character recognition (OCR) software. However, the characteristics of the original material-small and variable typefaces, poor print quality, and complex arrangement of print on the page-meant that available OCR software was ineffective. Interest in using OCR for the serials remains, and further trials are now being conducted with more satisfactory results.

User Interface and Access Points : The user interface allows browsing of titles, and searching by title, year of first publication, and broad subject. Users can also access detailed information on how to use the site, notes on the digitisation of each title, and background papers and reports on the project. Following NLA practice, both MARC bibliographic records and Dublin Core resource discovery metadata are used as points of access from outside the project website. There are direct links to titles from Kinetica; bibliographic information is also included with images in the interface. For each title reproduced by ACDP, catalogue records are created for the original hardcopy version, for the microfilm version, and for the digital file.

Preservation Issues

Preservation considerations were manifested in four ways: attention to protecting the originals from damage during the process, aiming for image quality that would minimise the need for users to access the originals, use of microfilm to provide a long lasting analogue preservation copy, and attention to the archiving of the digital files.

Care of Originals : Although most material was more than 150 years old, it was generally in reasonable condition. Much had been printed on rag paper, and showed little sign of brittleness. There were occasional legibility difficulties, due to poor contrast between faint print and darkened (but not brittle) pages. Apart from some minor repairs to tears, very little conservation work was needed to deal with physical damage. This was in line with developing best practice: tailoring microfilm-preparation conservation work to the minimum required so material can be safely and effectively filmed.

Image Quality and Preservation of Originals : The use of the source material by researchers was relatively low-indeed the academic advisory group commented that this material was under-utilised because of difficulty of access. However the preservation requirements would not be realised if the digital images simply stimulated users to increase their demands on the originals, so image quality in the microfilm and digital versions had to be sufficiently high to meet most research needs.

Use of Microfilm : Use of microfilm as an intermediate source for digital imaging, a master for re-scanning, and a long-term stable storage format was a key feature of this project. At the start of the project, we were convinced of the need to produce microfilm as a reliable preservation copy. We are no longer convinced that digital copies cannot provide a suitable preservation medium, although it remains to be proven over extended periods of time that digital images will be cost-effective preservation masters. One should also not be too starry-eyed about microfilm as a preservation master: it is expensive to store properly, requires some vigilance to detect deterioration, and in most cases provides a less-than-perfect replica of the source. However, it remains true that poorly maintained microfilm is more likely to yield at least some of its information content than poorly maintained digital data.

Archiving the Digital Files : The preservation aspects of the project did not depend primarily on long-term maintenance of the digital files, but given the very large investment in them and the unlikelihood of ever assembling material to repeat the exercise, the project partners paid some attention to that outcome. There was a concern to make the digital images worth preserving. This largely came down to a question of capturing all significant detail. From tests it was established that 400 dots per inch bitonal images would substantially achieve that. Bitonal scanning cannot be accepted as a totally satisfactory replica, and the realities of scanning make it is difficult to define the smallest significant detail that will be captured or not captured. However, the project partners agreed that this approach would produce images that would be worth preserving.

There was also concern to use a file format with a reasonable chance of being preserved. At the time of the project, this was clearly TIFF, (Tagged Image File Format), a non-proprietary standard which should be relatively straightforward to migrate, and with sufficiently widespread use for there to be a critical weight of demand for migration tools. The format also offered good lossless compression, and the ability to re-use the images in a number of derivative formats. It was (and is) widely accepted as the closest thing to a preservation format for digital images.

To provide the kind of active archival management that will be needed requires systems, procedures and commitments. As part of the project, NLA has accepted responsibility for maintaining both microfilm and digital versions of the ACDP output.

Production Issues

The basic production issue was how to achieve the goals of access and preservation objectives cost-effectively.

To gain some sense and appreciate the complex processes involved in production, one need only consider the exhaustive steps that project managers and vendors needed to manage, once specifications and contracts were in place:

- locate material from a range of sources amongst the participating partners and elsewhere, negotiating release of additional material for filming if necessary
- choose copies for inclusion from multiple copies held in various collections and in various conditions
- check and prepare material including any necessary conservation work
- assemble material at a central point and provide specific item and batch notes
- transfer material to the vendor
- microfilm material to specifications and produce duplicates for checking by both vendor and project manager
- vendor quality control checking and documentation
- transfer duplicate film to the project manager along with original material and documentation if needed to support quality assessment of the film
- quality control checking of microfilm by the project manager (at SLNSW)
- accept or reject the film and advise the vendor, returning material for re-work if necessary
- re-work of microfilming, duplication, and quality assessment if necessary
- duplicate the film to produce first-generation preservation master, second-generation duplicating master, and third-generation service copies
- assess suitability of the film (both pre-existing film and that prepared for the project) for scanning
- scan the second generation film if suitable

- enhance the images if necessary
- vendor quality control checking of digital images, and documentation
- name the files, apply specified metadata, and save to CD-R
- transfer the CD-Rs (and if necessary for quality control checking, the microfilm and the original material) to NLA
- quality control checking of digital files by NLA
- accept or reject the digital files and advise the vendor, returning material for re-work if necessary
- re-work of digital scans, image enhancement, metadata, file names, file saves or documentation if necessary
- repatriation of original materials to owners and supply of microfilm service copies
- convert the digital TIFF files to access format for online delivery to users
- mount the access files on server
- possibly apply optical character recognition (OCR) to selected titles, assess, edit and mount on server
- archive and maintain digital copies in all formats selected for long-term maintenance, as well as microfilm preservation and duplication masters (and originals).

Project Management

The development, and review of specification, a process of testing and feedback to vendors, and the requirements for and coordination of dedicated staff resources were among the realities underlying project management

The project invested heavily in developing detailed specifications to cover all production processes, with an emphasis on achieving suitable image quality.

For all the work put into specifications, vendors frequently complained of difficulties in complying with them to achieve the results we wanted. (This may have been because the specifications were wrong, or because they had been misunderstood, or because they demanded solutions the vendor was unable or unwilling to use, or the project could not afford) By the end of the project we accepted that our initial specifications may have been too focused on how results were to be achieved. We concluded that for large projects, it would be better-pragmatically-to have an overall framework of objectives and 'bottom lines' negotiated with vendors, supplemented by detailed specifications for small batches of material.

Testing and Feedback: One of the project management tools we valued most was a feedback approach-tests, reports, communication of experiences between vendors and project managers ("this worked, this seemed not to work"), and subsequent decisions about the need to adjust procedures. Such an approach was intrinsic to the project management philosophy of ACDP, and is critical in such a developmental project.

It is possible to see this 'feedback' approach at work throughout the project: the whole production experience can be seen as a series of tests, interspersed with production phases. In total we went through 10 testing phases, and while this may seem excessive it was both appropriate and necessary, particularly given the developmental nature of the project.

Decisions on how to respond to feedback were mostly pragmatic. On some issues we adjusted procedures because we could see the necessity to do so; on some we adjusted because we accepted it would be impossible to achieve what we wanted in the circumstances; on some issues we decided not to adjust because we were still convinced we were right; and on some we decided not to adjust because the project had been set up to test certain things and we felt it was too late to abandon them. Our ultimate conclusion is that it is not possible to eliminate these tensions-it is frustrating to delay production for feedback to be analysed, but the feedback is necessary all the same-at best one can hope to strike a good balance. Likewise, it is very unlikely that project specifications will serve without some adjustments and compromises-again, the best one can hope for is to identify the really crucial requirements and try to negotiate robustly, honestly and reasonably to achieve them.

Dedicated Staff Resources : The allocation of dedicated staff resources to the project was tremendously important, as was the commitment, initiative and good humour of all the people involved. However, many of the issues were just too big for the part-time resources allocated, and simply required more input, more sorting out, and more hands-on management than was available. We concluded that life would have been much easier with a full-time coordinator in each of the main operationally-involved libraries (NLA and SLNSW), rather than a part-time coordinator in one institution supported by less-than-part-time staff trying to fit the project into other demands.

We also learned something about the effects of such a large project on the people involved. The ARC grant for the project was approved in late 1995; the final production phase Request For Tender was issued in February 1997; digital capture was completed in March 1999; file mounting was completed in early 2000. This timetable far exceeded anyone's expectations, and imposed its own difficulties as a number of people moved on to other things before the project was completed. (Of approximately 35 people with significant involvement in the project, only the three members of the Steering Committee maintained their active role from start to finish.) Maintaining continuity through such a lengthy and complex exercise required a strong project plan and documentation and continuing institutional support. Smaller projects that could be completed within a shorter timeframe would have many advantages in comparison.

Image Quality Production Issues

Many production issues centred on image quality and how to achieve it. In particular we needed to explore how high quality microfilm images would convert to ensure high quality digital images.

Management of image quality in production basically occurred on two fronts: the production processes, and quality control.

Microfilming, Scanning and Image Enhancement

Most production challenges arose from the interaction of microfilming, scanning and image enhancement, and the often conflicting demands of image quality on the one hand, and production throughput on the other. The thrust of technology and project management has been to find a workable compromise that maximises both image quality and throughput.

Two of the project partners and the project vendor were able to draw on extensive experience with preservation microfilming. Apart from a few errors, the microfilming processes of the project went well, producing high quality film that would meet all relevant standards.

However, automated scanning processes demonstrated that more consistent image placement, skew, and masking of edge and gutter shadows were needed. More consistent image contrast is also an issue, though contrast variations are intrinsic to the material being filmed and largely beyond the control of the camera operator.

We eventually asked the vendors to do test scans to work out the best means of maximising legibility and throughput.

Detecting the edges of images was a key requirement for the film scanner and for post-scanning processing software. Skew and gutter shadows were found to complicate this, especially if text came close to the edges of the page or close to shadows that sometimes appear in microfilm images. Both image quality and throughput were affected by this.

A suite of software was used for image enhancement. These tools fit best into a production model where they can be automatically applied to all images with a minimum of human decisions. This brought its own problems, as it was hard to determine at production levels just how much enhancement was a good thing, and how much was too much. De-speckling, for example, can actually reduce legibility by eliminating parts of letters.

We reached a threshold point for image enhancement dilemmas on a number of titles that included very faint, broken-up print, or very discoloured paper, or very obtrusive bleed-through, occurring inconsistently through a volume, and sometimes even across a single page. We also found that automatic de-skew and cropping could remove text that encroached on margins on badly skewed pages. Customising enhancements for parts of volumes or even parts of pages, drastically reduces output levels. If this is not built into the pricing structure and budgets for the project, it tends to create more pressing deadlines elsewhere in the project, so the ultimate effect is felt far beyond the individual images that may have been initially involved.

In some cases we were led to ask how much difficulty was too much for the material to be worth scanning. A small amount of material was rejected from the project on this basis. At the individual page level, however, we sometimes found we had to accept quite marginal legibility when all reasonable options had been exhausted. In these cases we have included a message referring to the difficulties of the original.

Use of greyscale at lower resolution levels was one of the options tested. This gave a more legible result than high-resolution bitonals for some poor contrast material, but produced no improvement at all in some cases, and came at the cost of very large file sizes, so it was generally not used.

Overall, the project pushed the microfilming end as far as it could go for some material; to make improvements the only remaining leverage rested with scanning and image enhancement. There is some give and take between filming, scanning and post-scan enhancements, demanding conscious decisions about what manipulations and enhancements will work most cost-effectively at what stage.

These trade-offs, and the complications that one process can cause for later steps, give a powerful advantage to arrangements which make the same firm, and possibly the same operators, responsible for the entire chain of processes.

Assessing Existing Microfilm for Scanning

While the project originally sought to make maximum use of pre-existing microfilm, very little suitable film was found to exist and most material was scanned from microfilm created specially for the project. However, assessment of existing microfilm for scanning purposes remains a key concern of the project partners.

How does one decide if existing film is suitable for scanning? While it is not very helpful, the answer is really that it depends on what image quality is required at the end. It requires decisions about the minimum level of legibility and aesthetics that will be acceptable, and the resources one is willing and able to make available to achieve that minimum or something better. It also requires a deep level of interaction between project managers and vendors to articulate, test, refine and establish what is achievable. Only then can one decide whether "the best we can get" will be worth the cost and effort.

Quality Control and Image Quality

In line with our "feedback" philosophy, quality control was a key production issue. Vendors were required to thoroughly check all deliverables, and the project managers also set up quality checking arrangements for microfilm (at SLNSW) and for digital images and files (at NLA).

There has been widespread discussion of tools for quality checking of digital images. While there is undoubted value in improving these tools, we were convinced that the main quality checking requirements could be met pragmatically with simple tools and approaches-the main requirement is that the images be assessed. Our assessment fell into two categories:

- use of software to check file formats, file names and header information, resolution, compression type, and number of files. This was applied to 100% of files.
- subjective visual inspection-looking at the images on-screen and in print-outs, for legibility, polarity, skew, orientation, image cleanness, and matching file names.

Although we were aware of other approaches that attempt to measure image quality objectively, we were satisfied that our subjective inspections told us what we needed to know, and provided an adequate and agreed basis for negotiation with our vendors. This was done on a basis of random sampling at various rates, although for many titles we did check all images.

The use of technical targets, familiar from preservation microfilming practice, proved to be problematical. We decided to incorporate some targets that could be compared across film and digital scans, but we recognise that they were not well used and that microfilm targets would have served as well.

File Format and File size-production Aspects: Most file format issues were already decided outside the production process, but they did have some impacts:

Maintaining something like deliverable file sizes did constrain the vendors' options for solving image quality problems.

File naming became a production issue at various stages. The project decided to use "intelligent" file and directory names, built around ISSN numbers and incorporating dates, issue numbers, and page numbers. This was intended to make the files easier to track and easier to name; however, vendors found the naming convention complicated and prone to errors. An alternative "dumb" running number system may have been easier to apply. The National Library is currently exploring models for persistent names that can be applied to digital files required for ongoing public access. Its findings will influence naming conventions for future projects in which it is involved.

One advantage of the TIFF format is that metadata tags can be added to the digital object. The project specifications required the vendor to add certain information to the TIFF headers. This had some major production implications as vendors had to develop programmes to add the information automatically. (There was also some discussion of the value of the information, given that most users, and indeed most project managers, did not have access to a viewer that would allow them to access or evaluate the header information.)

Evaluation of Production

Technical Viability: The project often felt like it was on the edge of technical viability, trying to do things for which the technology was not yet available. And yet, the results suggest that most of what was wanted was achieved. The main technical issues remaining are:

- capturing sufficiently legible images from marginally legible originals-perhaps we need to explore alternatives such as direct scanning for some materials
- better tools for dealing with contrast problems
- techniques for dealing with broadsheet newspapers, probably including more effective compression approaches
- bandwidth improvements that will allow improved delivery speeds for large image files

- improvements in OCR technology to handle difficult historic print materials
- better tools for scanning from existing microfilm, to cope with the impact of skewed, inconsistently placed images. This remains an important goal, given the very large amount of microfilm that has been produced in the past and for which there would be value in more user-friendly access
- preservation techniques for digital files and technical infrastructure to manage them.

In almost all cases the technology already exists to address these issues.

Preservation Viability: The preservation viability of projects like ACDP is still to be proven. They provide at least a short-term preservation benefit as an alternative access medium to microfilm. However, the net effect is likely to be a considerably increased preservation requirement, to deal with the digital images as well as the print copy. However, the access benefits are such that similar projects will continue, their outputs becoming part of digital collections for which preservation programmes are increasingly responsible.

At the other end of the process-ensuring material is not damaged in the digitisation process-the ACDP arrangements worked extremely well. The combination of a conscious and articulated commitment to protect the originals, well planned workflow arrangements, and carefully selected and conscientious vendors, produced ambitious results with no noticeable damage.

Commercial Viability: The commercial viability of the ACDP arrangements is harder to evaluate. The costs of digitisation are high, and the market in Australia remains small. From a purely commercial point of view it is unlikely that ACDP is repeatable. Its demand on resources from the project partners (and probably the vendors also) far exceeded expectations. Many processes that were expected to be easy to automate turned out still to require a large manual input. For the kind of difficult material processed in ACDP, a 'production' business model is probably quite different from the model that could be applied to less difficult material. We may need to devise hybrid models involving different balances of outsourcing and inhouse work where there are processes that are not commercially viable or over which we want to have a high degree of control.

On the other hand, it also must be recognised that ACDP was throughout its life experimental. There were large set-up costs and management inputs required at almost all stages. So long as future projects can make use of the many lessons learned from ACDP, and build directly on its foundations, the economic viability should improve considerably.

Conclusion

While in many ways the ACDP seems, particularly in hindsight, an ambitious-perhaps overly-ambitious-endeavour it has provided us with hard-learnt experience which is already being applied in other digital programmes. This project has assisted the National Library in assessing and furthering parts of its major Digital Services Project initiative and has provided the basis for further work. The State Library of NSW has initiated several digital projects, including the Banks and Flinders projects. The Library at Sydney University has established the Scholarly ElectronicText and Image Service (SETIS) which is developing several electronic text projects following the processing of the ACDP novels, and now hosts a large fulltext Australian literature database.

As importantly, the project has also provided us with conceptual understandings of digital library processes and structures as well as matters such as institutional infrastructure, organisational implications, new relationships with clients, the benefits and processes of collaboration, and-of course-concerns regarding costs and funding.

Digital conversion is not the seamless, simple process often portrayed by some digital library proponents. While the ACDP was funded to handle a set body of content, the trade-offs regarding cost-effectiveness and cost-benefits of digitisation requires some hardheaded and informed decision-making. The close management and scrutiny of the processes that has taken place throughout the ACDP has better equipped us for these tasks. In the end, however, it is the content that validates the process, and the voices of the 1840s-'fully represented in the periodical press'-are now transformed and freely accessible to give us an insight and understanding of their time and place.

ELECTRONIC ALCHEMY

Take the curious and arcane titles of the newspapers and periodicals published so prolifically in colonial Australia of the 1840's, combine them with the electronic technology of the late twentieth century and you will have a kind of modern alchemy at work. In an exciting new cooperative project initiated by the University of Sydney Library, the full content-text and images-of journals, newspapers, novels and short stories published in Australia during the years 1840-1845 is in the process of being digitised for delivery to users through the Internet. This project, though focusing on a particular body of material published in a few short years in the 1840's, is a significant step forward in the efforts currently being taken by librarians and academics to use the opportunities provided by the new technology to achieve enhanced access to the accumulated riches of the social, cultural and political heritage of Australia buried in the musty pages of rare and fragile publications held in only a handful of institutional libraries.

In the libraries and archives of the world, much is being made of the capability, both actual and potential, for information to be delivered electronically to a personal work station in the home or office. Budget-strapped libraries, hard-pressed to keep up with the explosion in world publishing, have been keen to realise what may be called a technology dividend, the substantial savings which might be accrued in the efficiency of the delivery of information and in the overheads traditionally associated with acquiring, controlling, housing and preserving materials such as books, documents, journals and periodicals and a range of other print and paper-based products.

Libraries, which as cultural institutions, represent tradition and continuity and perhaps, in the minds of some, a certain kind of otherworldliness, now see themselves positioned to achieve a miraculous transformation. Instead of bricks and mortar and the stretching kilometres of densely packed shelves, the library can now recreate itself to exist and flourish in the vast realms of cyberspace. The library, once real and actual, is capable of changing its identity to achieve instead a state of virtual reality. For many, this is a compelling idea, promising as it does a concept of access and accessibility never previously realised despite the tradition of democratic access which was (and remains) one of the fundamental planks of modern librarianship.

But if the promise of technology is great, the present reality is that libraries remain to a substantial degree the captives of their conservative past, the custodians of vast acreages of books, the repositories of what is sometimes called the collective memory of the world. Or put into a national perspective, books and associated forms of record embody and represent the history and culture of a country and of the growth and development of its people. If, prospectively, information may be efficiently managed and delivered for use by means of new technology, what of the legacy of the past which is precisely what it is claimed to be, the record of human development and experience, the memory of the world, of each country and of each and every region and local community?

In Australia, it is exciting to report that four major libraries of record, the National Library of Australia, the State Library of New South Wales, Fisher Library in the University of Sydney and Monash University Library in Melbourne, working in association with an Academic Advisory Group, have secured a substantial funding allocation from the Australian Research Council to implement the Australian Cooperative Digitisation Project, 1840-45. Although on an individual basis a number of libraries have developed digitisation strategies of their own, this project is a major first step in Australia by librarians and academics working in partnership and using computer technology to tackle the problem of the management, care and use of the huge retrospective holdings of printed materials which make up Australia's publishing history. This current project provides for the digital conversion of a selected body of nineteenth century Australian material, principally the proliferation of journal and newspaper titles published in the various Australian colonies in the years 1840 to 1845. Although in the early stages of implementation, the project already offers an indication of what might be possible on a larger scale, depending of course on the availability of resources.

It is of interest that the origins of this project lie in the efforts over several years of Dr Neil Radford, Librarian of the University of Sydney, to raise the awareness of his professional colleagues to the importance of preserving for future use the fragile paper-based materials which remain the basic stock in trade of most libraries. Although Radford's concerns were shared by a few, principally leading preservation experts such as Dr Jan Lyall of the National Preservation Office in the National Library in Canberra and Alan Howell, Manager of the Preservation Branch in Sydney's State Library of New South Wales, he recognised that for most of his colleagues in the various university libraries, preservation of 'old books' seemed somewhat quaint, old-fashioned and unexciting. The issue certainly ranked low in the priorities of many of his colleagues.

Against the more obvious appeal of the trialling of centrally mounted data bases, investigations of electronic publishing and the seductive lure of '...gadgets, flashing lights and whizz-bang technology', Radford felt pessimistic about the chances of mounting a strong case for the infrastructure funding which would enable a major preservation issue to be addressed. Quite quickly, however, the preservation cause was able to take advantage of exciting changes occurring in the same field internationally. At a conference on preservation microfilming presented in Adelaide in 1994 by Australia's National Preservation Office, Ross Coleman, Sydney University Library Collection Development Librarian, and others had been alerted to the work of the Cornell Digital Library at Cornell University Library in the United States and recognised immediately its application in Australia to deal with the issues of both preservation and access which Radford and his colleagues had been pushing for several years. More importantly, perhaps, was the fact that the Cornell project and another at Yale (the Open Book Project) had secured the support of prestigious national funding bodies in the U.S.-the National Endowment for the Humanities and the Commission for Preservation and Access-and that this offered an encouraging precedent for Australia. The focus of the two American projects was clear: to test the relationship between microfilm and digital imagery in order to, in the one operational process, create microfilm for preservation and digital images for access purposes. As Radford has observed, here was the opportunity to turn old books into a shiny new electronic product and to attract the necessary dollars from funding bodies.

Another powerful factor working in favour of the substantial funding of an Australian digitisation project was the growing commitment by the community of Australian libraries to cooperative action to enhance the overall effectiveness of the Australian library system to deliver services to the nation. Led in part by the National Library (particularly by its Deputy Director-General Eric Wainwright who has provided a high level of intellectual leadership), but with the strong support of both state and academic libraries, a broad consensus had been reached which recognised the cumulative value as a national resource of individual library collections around Australia.

The concept of the Distributed National Collection led in turn to broad agreement on an ambitious series of cooperative initiatives developed at the Towards Federation 2001 Libraries Summit hosted by the National Library of Australia in 1992. In was in this larger environment that Neil Radford and other like-minded colleagues could at last see a window of opportunity through which Australian libraries could utilise the new technology to broach the large task of repackaging older print collections both to meet preservation objectives and to serve the needs of academic and other researchers. Other factors encouraging optimism were the range of government initiatives of national importance including Open Learning and the Commonwealth Government's Creative Nation statement which embraced the new technology as a means to enhance access by Australians to a broad range of cultural and educational programmes and to the materials held in institutional collections all over the country.

But where to begin and how to focus a project which might deliver a real benefit to the Australian community? With the benefit of advice provided by a panel of academic experts led by Elizabeth Webby, Professor of Australian Literature in the University of Sydney, the project narrowed its options from potentially the entire range of eighteenth and nineteenth century titles listed in Ferguson's Bibliography of Australia to a select body of newspaper and periodical publications issued in the several Australian colonies in the years 1840-1845. As Webby puts it, this was a period of 'emergent nationalism', following the end of convict transportation to New South Wales and preceding the influx of the gold-rush migrations of the 1850's. The 1840's was a period when a real explosion began in local publishing A wider geographic dispersal of publishing began to produce a greater variety of locally written material in publications designed to meet the needs of different audiences. Although a considerable range and variety of material emerged both in colonial capitals and regional centres such as Geelong and Maitland, Webby makes the point that for a project of this kind, the output is manageable while the material itself has a distinctive voice and character which helps to give historic definition to the 1840's as an important period of transition. Webby emphasises two key elements of the early years of the decade: the beginnings of diversifcation in publishing with the appearance of journals devoted to topics as varied as science, sport, temperance as well as the first papers specifically directed to a working class audience.

Culturally, it is also important to recognise that the 1840's saw the first significant appearance in print of a distinctively Australian fiction, stimulated in part by the demand for local writing encouraged by the serial press. With this link, it makes sense therefore to include the texts of the handful of novels which achieved publication in the years between 1841 and 1845 and which offered a distinctively Australian setting for the stories they told. Webby stresses that one of the major benefits of this project will be to make accessible to a much wider audience a range of materials which because of its rarity and fragility has been available only to the few. She suggests that the project has the potential to create a whole new audience: cultural historians; social historians, economic historians; family historians as well as to schools: 'There is still so much work to be done on this period and the wealth and variety of the published record has barely been tapped'.

If access is about to be transformed, the project is also important in other ways. Colin Webb, Manager, Information Preservation at the National Library places emphasis on the conservation and preservation advantages. As a conservator constantly challenged by the fragility of paper-based materials and what he describes as '... *the ever-present need to reconcile the conflict between preservation and use...*', Webb welcomes the opportunities which this project presents to reformat materials, initially through microfilming, but then, through digitisation, to deliver access to an image which is significantly superior both to microfilm and in some cases even to the original itself. Colin Webb is excited about the opportunities which this project presents for conservators to move beyond microfilming as a reformatting medium. He notes that digitisation does things which microfilming does not do very effectively: mistakes can be corrected; images can be enhanced and replicated endlessly without any loss of quality; and although the initial costs of digitisation are high, Webb points out that the subsequent costs of duplication and electronic delivery to users are very low indeed. While the long-term archival stability of the digitised image cannot be guaranteed, Webb argues that this project is also worthwhile as the means to experiment with a very exciting and powerful technology. The benefits of accessibility are obvious and immediate and he is optimistic that a solution will be found to meet the long-term needs of archival retention using data migration methods.

The responsibility for the coordination of the project rests with Ross Coleman from his base at Sydney University. Coleman brings a high level of enthusiasm to his task and, like other members of the team, is excited to be involved in the breaking of new ground. He is conscious too of the responsibility which he carries to deliver a good return on the investment of close to half a million dollars which is the total cost of the project. Coleman is especially pleased to be part of a project which represents the best elements of cooperation between libraries and of partnership between librarians, academics and conservators.

He sees the project as a special kind of opportunity: 'It's both a test and an opportunity' he says, 'a chance to work with the technology, to deliver a greatly improved level of access to rare materials and to provide the quality benchmarking which will assist with the development of future projects'. He is proud also that with this project, Australia is engaging very creatively with the new technology: 'Australia is up there with the best and most innovative overseas projects of a similar kind. Our experience will be valuable not only here in this country but will be of benefit internationally.'

From the confines of library basements to the cutting edge, the persistence of Neil Radford and his colleagues in promoting a stronger sense of professional obligation to the 'old books' of the past is about to be vindicated. This cooperative project brings an exciting new dimension to Australian librarianship, scholarship and to those who work behind the scenes to ensure the survival of those fragile materials which are the stuff and voice of history.

THE FERGUSON PROJECT

John Alexander Ferguson noted, in the introduction to volume 3 of his *Bibliography of Australia*, that "one strange feature of this period is the extraordinary number of 'ghost' books, that is, books to which a reference has been made in some other publication but which cannot be found today in any library or collection."

I wish I could present a claim to you that by some mysterious alchemy we had made these rarest of the rare re-appear, but I cannot. Instead, I do want to tell you about a slightly less ambitious, but more achievable, project that should help us look after *and* improve access to some of the genuinely rare, but extant, materials documenting nineteenth century Australia.

I need to make it clear from the outset that I am drawing heavily on two reports by the project coordinator, Ross Coleman of the University of Sydney Library, who is currently overseas. I have substantially modified Ross's papers, so I suppose I am responsible for any comments you might find contentious. I also want to thank Margaret Dent, who has kindly agreed to present this paper on my behalf.

In talking about the Ferguson project it would be easy to get into a lot of technical detail-at the present time, this feels like the most interesting and challenging part of the project, because it is what we are immersed in-but papers full of technical detail can be eye-glazingly boring, and there is probably virtue in talking about the concepts rather than the detail. It is unfair to suggest this, but I'm sure that Alan Ventress, who is also involved in the project, would be willing to discuss the details if you have any questions. The way I want to approach this is to give you some background, and describe the project, and then talk about where we are up to and our experiences so far.

THE PROJECT

The Ferguson in the project title refers to the same Ferguson's *Bibliography of Australia* that I just mentioned, of course-the most comprehensive listing of titles published in Australia prior to 1900. It is important to remember that we are talking about a concept, a list of publications, rather than a single collection. This fact provides one of the fundamental reasons for the project, and many of our challenges.

Preservation is a concern with a lot of this material. Much of it is in surprisingly good condition, but much of it is poor, mainly because of use. A lot of it is rare, existing in only one or a few copies. The main response to the preservation problem over the years has been to do some repair work, worry about how the material is housed, and restrict access.

In recent years-let's say the past 25 years anyway-there has been growing interest in what we call reformatting-probably just a fancy name for copying-as a way of addressing both preservation and accessibility problems. Reformatting doesn't deal with either of them perfectly-it hardly solves the access problem, as anyone who stares at a microfilm reader or a computer screen all day will testify; and it doesn't amount to a complete preservation strategy, either-but reformatting to a high standard, taking pains to make the copy as user-friendly as possible, does offer some improvements in access to material that otherwise might have been withheld from use; and it does protect fragile or rare originals from the loving over-attention of users.

The Ferguson materials have long looked like a choice candidate for reformatting, and over the years there have been a number of proposals to microfilm all or part of them as a way of building an accessible and comprehensive virtual collection out of the bits and pieces scattered over many institutions. These proposals have always failed because the expected low demand for microfilm did not seem to justify the size and cost of such a project. So, what happened to make a difference? The answer is complex, but it has a lot to do with the possibilities offered by digital imaging-capturing digital copies that can be stored, manipulated, and delivered using computers and related equipment. This promise was enough to encourage people from a number of institutions to try to design a feasible proposal for a limited, developmental-even experimental-project that could attract funding. This project, which in our loose way we call the Ferguson Project, but which is officially called the Australian Cooperative Digitisation Project 1840-1845, is the result.

Its purpose is to provide large-scale digital reformatting of serials and fiction published in the period. I now want to tell you a little about the project-who is involved, what we are trying to achieve, and how we are trying to achieve it, with some of the benefits that it should bring to managing, preserving and providing access to this rare 19th century material.

Some words from the project submission to the Australian Research Council may help give you a feeling for the vision behind it:

> *This project will create a unique research infrastructure in Australian studies through the digital conversion of Australian serials and fiction of the seminal period 1840-45. It will ensure access to, and preservation of, this material by a process of microfilming, scanning and networking. The first project of its kind in Australia, it will introduce international best practice, act as a technical benchmark, and provide a new level of resource sharing.*

The success of the submission was a recognition that digital collections of otherwise rare source material could be important research infrastructure for academic use.

The project is a truly collaborative effort. There are four core partners-the University of Sydney Library, the State Library of NSW, the National Library of Australia, and Monash University Library, each of whom is making a large contribution in terms of time, expertise, and cash. Each of the project partners brings particular experience and interests to the project, and all will benefit by acquiring technical and management skills. Common concerns for all participants include selecting content, preparing material, design, technical production and conversion, user focus issues and detailed management of the project.

The project is substantially funded by the Australian Research Council, which provided a research infrastructure grant for 1996, in response to a submission which included statements of support from the four partners, two other State libraries, four other University libraries, and from bodies such as the National Preservation Office, the National Centre for Australian Studies, the Macquarie Dictionary, and a multimedia firm. The project has academic and technical advisers from nine institutions, including Cornell and Yale University libraries in the US. Collectively, this represents an extensive pool of support and expertise committed to making the venture a success. It is worth emphasising that as an ARC infrastructure project, the needs of the scholarly community in terms of content and useability are given a very high priority-getting the user focus right is fundamental.

What should be included in the project was refined through several discussions with a focus group of scholars in nineteenth century Australian studies. It was important to define a fairly narrow time period to be covered, so that a realistic proposal could be developed. There was early consensus that the target period should be 1840-1845, a time which saw the emergence of an Australian colonial culture and identity, marked by an upsurge in local publication. The scholarly reference group were also emphatic on the need to do this as a block exercise-to do all titles in the period rather than be selective.

The decision to concentrate on serials followed testing of a small sample of books from the Mitchell Library, which highlighted a number of physical problems. The focus group recognised serial literature as an important untapped primary source, which had also been identified as a priority area for action by the National Library and the Council of Australian State Libraries.

The Ferguson *Bibliography* lists seventy-five serial titles as having commenced in the period 1840-45. (Only six of these continued publication after 1855, the general cut-off date for the project.)

A small component of published fiction was added to the project, building on the interest of the National Centre for

Australian Studies at Monash in developing fully-searchable text of nineteenth century fiction. Only four works of fiction were identified from the period.

We know from experience that any reformatting project attracts compromises, because it is almost impossible to foresee all the dilemmas that will arise. This makes it particularly important to build up a sound conceptual framework to guide project managers towards the client-focused objectives of the project-if you don't have this, it is just too easy to end up a long way from the aims you set out to serve. I want to talk about that conceptual framework now.

THE HYBRID APPROACH

The technical concept is based upon what we and others have described as a "hybrid" approach to reformatting-a process of microfilming *and* digitisation to provide long-term preservation *and* digital access at the same time. It is an attractive approach that recognises the needs of present users while trying to ensure the material can be maintained for future use. I have already mentioned the benefits of digitisation in providing simultaneous, almost instant access, anywhere in the world, to images that can be easily searched, copied, printed, zoomed, manipulated-all the things that networks and software let us do with digital data.

The importance of microfilm in the hybrid approach is that it provides a chemically and physically stable storage format, with an anticipated life of around 500 years. It is relatively technology-independent, not requiring computers or special software for access, but is able to be read with the assistance of a lens-something that digital images, with their total dependence on changing technologies, cannot match. Microfilm can be used as a source for duplicating throughout its life. It does not need repeated intervention or refreshing for maintenance, and its storage requirements are well understood. Basically, it is a proven technology with which we have a lot of experience, with established standards and some reliable vendors.

Given the decision that we wanted the benefits of both microfilming and digitisation, there was the question of what should be done first. Put simply there are two models of the hybrid approach. Cornell University Library have developed a model which is to scan first and then produce microfilm from the digital images. This has the advantage of allowing the digital image to be manipulated in order to get the best possible microfilm image. On the other hand, Yale University Library have reversed the approach, filming first, and then scanning from the film. These complementary models have generated important information on standards, comparative costs, and techniques. Anne Kenney and Paul Conway, the coordinators of these projects respectively, are technical advisers to our Ferguson project.

We have chosen to follow the Yale model, and film first. It is an approach that suits the rare and fragile material we are dealing with, and it allows us to take advantage of the extensive experience we have had with preservation microfilming. A number of aspects illustrate the strength of this approach and the options it can open up.

For example: Concern about the physical integrity of the original materials was a motivating factor for the project partners; it was also raised early on as a key issue by the academics advising the project. Access was to be enhanced, but the original material was also to be protected. It is reasonably common for non-preservation oriented projects to virtually destroy the originals in the interests of high speed copying. Projects in the US where brittle originals were discarded after re-formatting, have been criticised as "the latest form of book-burning", where the physical objects become "sacrificial offerings in the name of textual preservation".

These concerns regarding the significance of original materials, highlight a distinction between "replacement" and "surrogacy" in reformatting. Some material may *need* to be reformatted to produce a replacement copy-one that will take the place of the original-a legitimate preservation step if it is simply not feasible to maintain an unstable original forever. But in our project we are looking at conversion not as a replacement, but as a form of surrogacy, to deflect casual use away from the originals and towards an easily accessible copy. The digitisation stage is meant to be a relatively high speed process where digital bitmapped images of each page will be scanned from a duplicate negative microfilm at fairly high resolution (approximately 400 dots per inch). We will produce something like 100,000 uncompressed TIFF digital files, with compressed versions to be also created for networked access.

Like the microfilming, we expect this part of the project to be carried out by commercial vendors, to set technical and quality specifications. Rather than setting up in-house facilities, we wanted to follow this path for such an investigative project, because of the investment required in specialised equipment. It is also in the interests of collecting institutions to have a viable and high standard commercial sector able to provide the production requirements of projects like this one.

Work practices and technical standards are not as well established for digital reformatting as they are for microfilming, so specifications needed to be developed and agreed on early in the project. As I will describe in a moment, that remains a challenge for us.

USER INTERFACE

But it is not just a matter of good microfilming and scanning. How easily the images can be retrieved, read and printed, is critical. I have already said that this is a major focus of the research infrastructure grant, and it is time to turn back to this aspect of the project.

It is important to understand that in all cases other than the four fiction titles, we are making digital *pictures* of the pages, not searchable text. We have always recognised that it would be good to be able to do both. The only impediment has been the state of Optical Character Recognition (or OCR) technology, which has problems with marginally legible material-it is unreliable enough to require intensive proof reading, estimated to multiply the cost of the project by about eight times. Without full text searching, we have to provide other logical ways into the material.

What we are building is a kind of structure of digital data that can be turned into recognisable images. Structures like this need architectural attention, and there are at least three levels of architecture we have to attend to-how the information is put together within the file (what we call the document control structure); the structure of the database, or the collection of files and how they are indexed; and the structure of the tools that will make the images available-the delivery system. Without these, we may as well not bother scanning, as microfilm will be far more user-friendly than poorly structured digital data.

Our database will be set up to allow searching down to the page level-in other words, you will be able to call up a serial title, and any issue within it, and choose a page number to look at. You will also be able to call up all the issues of titles within a date range. The delivery system for providing access to the images uses the World Web Web, using a powerful file server at the National Library. It is possible that we will also be able to provide CD-ROM versions on demand, although at this stage we are focusing on Internet access.

The vision for the project was meant to be fairly open-ended. We aim to provide an electronic collection or corpus of nineteenth century source material produced to defined standards so that researchers can access, search, and download material as they see fit for their particular purposes. It should also be possible to enhance the information by later OCR treatment or other manipulation that would support its research use. This is particularly appropriate for serial literature where different sections (such as prose, letters, poetry, news, articles, advertisements) may be used in many different ways. It also recognises the needs of different types of users such as historians, linguists, literary scholars. All in all, it is quite an ambitious project. The philosophical basis is classic access and preservation. To provide scholars with access, and with opportunities to investigate and even enhance primary source material irrespective of their location. And to provide future scholars and the custodians of these resources with sound and stable means of preservation, not for the next five or ten years, but for many hundreds of years.

We believe the hybrid approach offers all these possibilities.

WHERE ARE WE NOW?

The funding for the project was announced in late 1995, and we began work in earnest early this year. Where are we now, and what experiences have we had? I suppose the first thing to say is that the project has had all the challenges we envisaged at the start, and a whole lot more besides, and we are still at a testing stage.

Microfilming and scanning the four works of fiction were completed early in the piece so that they could be worked on separately while the technical issues for the journals and newspapers could be addressed. Work on optical character recognition to produce searchable ASCII text is proceeding, despite some difficulties with the software.

Mounting these fiction files will require a different database structure from the rest of the project because we plan to make both the ASCII form of the page and the image available for viewing at the same time, so that users can find the text they want and see how the page looked.

In common with most experimental digitisation projects every step, every aspect, seems to have taken longer than we expected. Despite the excellent background we have in cooperative microfilming projects, we have found it difficult to deal with the distance between Canberra and Sydney when there are complex decisions to be made. Much of the work of these months has been tied up in checking holdings and selecting "best copies" for use in the project. Just identifying holdings, and gaps in holdings, at each site has been a major task, even with the range of bibliographic tools available. It was difficult to establish criteria for deciding which copy to film.

All of this has been complicated by the very things that make rare serials such a delight to work with-annotations that may or may not be significant; erratic numbering of issues and pagination; frequent and subtle changes of title. In many cases, what the NLA holds matches the State Library's holdings-almost. Except that we have issues 20 to 35, they have issues 1 to 25; our are in good condition for the first 10 issues, theirs for the last 15; ours include annotations that look like they might have been made by John Dunmore Lang, on pages where the printing ink is faint, whereas theirs have no annotations, but they do have a handwritten index tipped into the front; ours are falling out of their bindings, while theirs are tightly bound and would be hard to film. And so on for many of the

75 titles. For all that, we did manage to come up with a definitive list of what should be filmed-or perhaps it was two definitive lists?

The other major focus of this part of the project has been developing technical specifications. They have been needed for the microfilming, for the digitisation, and for the document, database and delivery structures that I mentioned earlier. And they needed to be comprehensive and reliable before calling tenders and letting contracts could go ahead. We set up a Technical Advisory Group to help us work through the whole process conceptually to arrive at these specifications. And we have recently realised that we don't know enough to be confident that a specification for the whole project will work.

For our broad database architecture and document control structure, we have decided to build on the National Library's growing expertise in putting together Web server databases of images, with the help of documentation from the Library of Congress and Cornell University Library. We will specify the kind of file structure in which images must be delivered by the scanning contractor so that they can be easily loaded into the database. This kind of structure must be able to handle and describe various kinds of pagination (such as covers, fly leaves, title pages, tables of contents, missing pages, inserts etc.) as well as including information or metadata on technical specifications used and other relevant matters such as source. I will probably be shot by the people involved for saying this, but all of this looks like the easy part of the project.

There are two other technical issues that have made us realise that we need to do more testing. We are troubled by what we might call the image quality/image delivery dilemma, and the image quality/production output dilemma.

The critical technical issue in developing microfilming and scanning specifications has been the file size of the data making up the images. We believe it is possible to produce high quality images of even poor originals, with annotations, and with much of the feel of the original, even from large format pages-but only at the cost of huge file sizes that are expensive and impossibly slow to retrieve across the Internet, and that will exceed the space on most PCs if someone tries to download them. In other words, we would hardly meet our accessibility objectives anyway. File size issues are related to issues of image quality, and data compression. We need to find or develop an optimal scanning specification that will provide most images at the best quality with the minimum file size. This means playing around with image depth (whether we scan bi-tonal or with shades of grey), and with resolution (the number of dots per inch).

Data compression offers some hope of getting useable file sizes without losing image quality, but again it comes with a range of less than perfect options. All of them would require users to download some form of viewer from the Project website, and some of them would involve very significant additional costs to pay for the compression itself. Unfortunately, what looks like the most promising compression option (fractal compression) would add about $1 per image to the cost-or $100,000 to the project.

The second dilemma I mentioned was the image quality/ production output one. Scanning from very challenging originals, or from very challenging microfilm of very challenging originals, leaves almost no margin for error in scan settings-too much and it has picked up the background, making the image illegible; too little and it has missed the text. This means that every image may need to be individually assessed and "massaged". This is a long way from the kind of production outputs that we envisaged for the project. Because of these difficulties, we decided that we needed to do two things we hadn't planned when we started: Firstly, we have decided to introduce a longer testing phase into the project, working in conjunction with a company which has some experience in the area. This should help us iron out some of the unknowns in reconciling image quality, file sizes and network delivery before we proceed to call for quotes for the whole project; and Secondly, we also decided that we should put off digitising the large format newspapers till later in the project, and investigate other means of delivery such as CD-ROM for them.

TESTING PHASE

We have now entered this test phase with a local vendor. It is due to be completed in November. The vendor will work with us on five titles we have chosen to represent the challenges of the larger project. Three will be filmed and scanned from the print originals-these are *The True Catholic: or Tasmanian evangelical miscellany* (Jan 1843-Jun 1843); *The Colonial Observer* (7 Oct 1841-26 Dec 1844) and *The Colonial Literary Journal* (Jun 1844-Mar 1845). Two other titles-*The Colonial Magazine and Commercial Journal* (Jan 1840-Dec 1843) and *The Star* (2 Mar 1844-23 May 1845)-will be scanned from existing microfilm.

In doing this work as a test phase, we are requiring the vendor to also work with us to tighten up our specification for the main project, and to help us refine and test the work flow procedures we need to make it all work smoothly and reliably.

We are hoping to have some images available from the test phase by the end of this year, and to go into production phase for the rest of the project early in 1997, with the project to be completed by mid 97.

When we entered the project we talked about it being a benchmarking exercise in this country. We were probably not aware of the technological limitations that still seem to constrain us. Eventually most of these will be overcome, although in some cases it may take technological developments that will happen after we have finished.

This project will add to the research infrastructure of the nation, and will make a significant improvement in both the access to, and the preservation of, these important 19th century materials. All of these we set out to do. In the process, however, we are also finding that we will have to push back the horizons a little more than we expected.

9

Interoperability for Digital Objects and Repositories

Introduction

For several years the Digital Library Research Group at Cornell University and the Corporation for National Research Initiatives (CNRI) have been engaged in research focused on the design and development of infrastructures for *open architecture, confederated* digital libraries. The goal of this effort is to achieve *interoperability* and *extensibility* of digital library systems through the definition of key digital library services and their open interfaces, allowing flexible interaction of existing services and augmentation of the infrastructure with new services. Some aspects of this research have included the development and deployment of the Dienst software, the Handle System, and the architecture of digital objects and repositories.

In this paper, we describe the joint effort by Cornell and CNRI to prototype a rich and deployable architecture for interoperable digital objects and repositories. This effort has challenged us to move theories of interoperability closer to practice. The Cornell/CNRI collaboration builds on two existing projects focusing on the development of interoperable digital libraries. Details relating to the technology of these projects are described elsewhere. Both projects were strongly influenced by the fundamental abstractions of repositories and digital objects as articulated by Kahn and Wilensky in *A Framework for Distributed Digital Object Services*. Furthermore, both programmes were influenced by the container architecture described in the Warwick Framework, and by the notions of distributed dynamic objects presented by Lagoze and Daniel in their Distributed Active Relationship work. With these common roots, one would expect that the CNRI and Cornell repositories would be at least *theoretically* interoperable. However, the actual test would be the extent to which our independently developed repositories were practically interoperable.

This paper focuses on the definition of interoperability in the joint Cornell/CNRI work and the set of experiments conducted to formally test it. Our motivation for this work is the eventual deployment of formally tested reference implementations of the repository architecture for experimentation and development by fellow digital library researchers. In Section 2, we summarize the digital object and repository approach that was the focus of our interoperability experiments. In Section 3, we describe the set of experiments that progressively tested interoperability at increasing levels of functionality. In Section 4, we discuss general conclusions, and in Section 5, we give a preview of our future work, including our plans to evolve our experimentation to the point of defining a set of formal metrics for measuring interoperability for repositories and digital objects. This is still a work in progress that is expected to undergo additional refinements during its development.

Interoperability—Definitions and Scope

The scope of the work described here is restricted to interoperability for repositories and digital objects. Nevertheless, some of our results can be generalized to other digital library components or services. Any generalizations, however, must be made with an understanding of what we mean by interoperability and what assumptions were made in our approach.

Interoperability is a broad problem domain. It is typically investigated within a specific scope, such as within a particular community (*e.g.*, libraries, commercial entities, scientific communities), within a particular classification of information (*e.g.*, electronic records, technical reports, software), or within a particular information technology area (*e.g.*, relational databases, digital imaging, data visualization). Current research on interoperability in digital library architecture addresses the challenges of creating a general framework for information access and integration across many of the above domains. A common goal of these efforts is to enable different communities, with different types of information and technologies, to achieve a general level of information sharing and, through the process of aggregation and computation, to create new and more powerful types of information.

In the context of the Cornell/CNRI work, interoperability is defined as the ability of digital library components or services to be functionally and logically interchangeable by virtue of their having been implemented in accordance with a set of well-defined, publicly known interfaces. In this model, different services and components can communicate with each other through open interfaces, and clients can interact with them in an equivalent manner. When repositories and digital objects are created in this manner, the overall effect can be a federation of repositories that aggregate content with very different attributes, but that can be treated in the same manner due to their shared interface definitions.

There are many approaches to achieving interoperability. Paepcke, et al.. have categorized many of the prevalent approaches and have provided an informative discussion of the challenges inherent in creating interoperable digital libraries of global scope. Some of the common approaches have included: (1) standardization (*e.g.*, schema definition, data models, protocols), (2) distributed object request architectures (*e.g.*, CORBA), (3) remote procedure calls, (4) mediation (*e.g.*, gateways, wrappers), (5) mobile computing (*e.g.*, Java applets).

Our approach to interoperability can be generally classified as a hybrid that includes several of the above. There are three fundamental principles behind our approach: (1) agreement on common abstractions, (2) definition of open interfaces to services and components that implement the common abstractions, and (3) creation of an extensibility mechanism for introducing new functionality into the architecture without interfering with core interoperability. We found that a distributed object approach and the use of mobile code provided the best foundation to achieve these principles. It could be argued, then, that our model also employs a standards approach in that our implementations are CORBA-based (OMG/IDL and IIOP standards). The fact that we have introduced a level of standardization at the communications and interfacing level does not restrict communities in their ability to select their own underlying data formats and standards for the creation of digital objects.

An Interoperable Architecture for Repositories and Digital Objects

Cornell and CNRI have a strong history of collaboration. As a result, both the Cornell and CNRI repository projects share a set of fundamental goals that include the development of:

1. A digital object model that enables the aggregation of distributed, heterogeneous elements or streams of data to create complex multimedia objects.
2. An extensibility scheme that allows digital objects to be accessed via one or more community-defined interfaces (*e.g.*, book, journal, corporate report, etc.).
3. A general repository framework that provides for the storage and access of these complex digital objects in a networked environment.
4. An open, well-defined protocol to facilitate global federation of repositories and digital objects.
5. A framework for associating extensible rights management schemes with digital objects to protect intellectual content.

As a result of these common goals, the Cornell and CNRI projects had been developing along similar lines. However, we realized that a more robust architecture for interoperability could emerge from a convergence of our two designs. To test our assumptions, we undertook a comprehensive analysis of both implementations and agreed on a collaborative approach that leverages their respective strengths. The architecture that we used as the basis for the experiments described in this paper draws upon both CNRI's DigitalObject and Repository Architecture and Cornell's FEDORA (Flexible and Extensible Digital Object and Repository Architecture). The shared interface definition that describes the components of the architecture is referred to as RAP (Repository Access Protocol).

The architecture described in this paper is one possible framework for interoperable digital libraries. A promising aspect of this work is the integration of an open repository architecture with an extensible digital object model to promote interoperability. Our extensibility scheme provides a powerful means for integrating community-defined behaviours into generic digital objects. The open interfaces defined by RAP enable interoperability while allowing for different underlying system architectures. This approach also makes it easier for other similar architectures to interface with repositories that conform to the Cornell/CNRI specification.

In this interoperability effort, both sites agreed to use the same architectural abstractions. The four principal abstractions in the architecture are: the *Repository*, the *DigitalObject*, the *Disseminator*, and the AccessManager. Access to the functionality offered by these abstractions is expressed through the open interface defined by RAP. To enable our interoperability experiments, the existing Cornell and CNRI repository implementations were modified to conform to the new joint specification. Although both sites used CORBA/IIOP with the Java programming language, each used different Object Request Brokers (ORBs). Furthermore, each implementation was distinct in its underlying system design. We provide a brief description of the joint interoperability architecture here, and refer the reader elsewhere for more detail. The AccessManager, used for rights management, will not be discussed in this paper.

Repositories

Digital libraries should be able to store a variety of traditional types of content—books, journals, corporate reports, software—as well as complex multimedia entities that are mixtures of text, images, full-motion video and data. While each form of content has unique aspects, it is desirable to *manage* this content in a uniform manner. Repository management can be a highly burdensome task when every type of object must be treated differently. To alleviate this problem, a common set of operations has been defined to perform basic repository management functions such as storing, copying, depositing, and archiving disparate forms of data. The *Repository* forms the first layer of functionality in the architecture. It addresses the need for uniformity by treating all forms of content as opaque, uniquely identified structures known as *DigitalObjects*. By opaque, we mean that neither the internal structure nor the semantics of DigitalObjects are exposed. Essentially, from the Repository perspective, DigitalObjects are atomic units, identifiable only by their unique names. These unique names are URNs that are registered in the Handle System. A Repository provides a set of RAP functions to store, access, replicate, move, and delete DigitalObjects.

Digital Objects

Content creators should have significant freedom in joining together various media forms—text, images, full-motion video, data—to create objects that richly convey information. For example, a chemistry book in the traditional sense is constrained by what can be displayed by ink on paper. In the digital sense, this "book" can be a collection of multiple page images, complemented by video streams that demonstrate experiments, and programmes with datasets for use in experimentation. This book may also have other information associated with it that may be owned and administered by external organizations. For example, the chemistry book can have an associated MARC record administered by OCLC.

These complex requirements are addressed by the next layer of functionality, which formulates DigitalObjects as structures for content, and provides the mechanisms for constructing and deconstructing them. The basic building blocks for aggregating content in DigitalObjects are components called *DataStreams* (in FEDORA) or *Elements* (in the CNRI Repository work), which arc (MIME) typed sequences of bytes. We will refer to them as DataStreams throughout the rest of this paper. An individual DataStream may be either *local* or *remote*. If local, the byte stream is physically associated with the DigitalObject. If remote, then the byte stream is logically associated with the DigitalObject, but is actually stored in another DigitalObject. A remote DataStream may also be produced dynamically by another DigitalObject (described below).

Each DigitalObject has a set of native operations, defined by RAP, to structurally access and manipulate content. Among these functions are the abilities to list, access, delete and create new DataStreams. At this structural level, interoperability among DigitalObjects is achieved through the ability to aggregate and manipulate these streams in a generic manner from repository to repository. For example, use of the generic RAP request GetDataStreams. Clients issuing this request will retrieve all of the DataStreams of this DigitalObject, without regard to the underlying (MIME) types of these streams.

Disseminators—Extensible Interfaces to DigitalObjects

The basic set of structural operations described thus far is not sufficient to provide the rich functionality required by actual digital library users. While enabling interchangeability of data, these operations will not convey all of the information and semantics intended by object creators. Users from diverse communities should be able to interact with DigitalObjects in a familiar manner using "real world" metaphors such as books and diaries, or more esoteric objects such as programmes or multimedia presentations. Architecturally, this means endowing DigitalObjects with operations that mimic the semantics of these abstractions. For example, once all the page images of a book are stored in a DigitalObject in one or more DataStreams, these images should be accessible through operations such as "turn the page" or "view the table of contents".

The architecture uses the abstraction of a *Disseminator* to associate these higher-level operations with DigitalObjects. Disseminators are used to extend the behaviour of DigitalObjects, enabling clients to interact with them through semantically rich interfaces. Each Disseminator defines two classes of information. First, it defines a *Disseminator Type* (also known as a *Signature)*, which is a set of operations that extends the functionality of a DigitalObject. Second, it defines a *Servlet*, which is a mechanism for producing the results (disseminations) of these operations. A given DigitalObject can have multiple Disseminators associated with it, in effect providing multiple "views" of the content in the DigitalObject.

The two Disseminators associate both "Book" and "DublinCore" functionality with the DigitalObject. Internally, each Disseminator references an appropriate Signature to assign additional operations to the DigitalObject (*e.g.*, GetPage, GetChapter), and a Servlet to execute these operations. From the client perspective, these architectural details are hidden. Clients simply use generic RAP requests to discover and invoke these Book and DublinCore operations.

Disseminator Types. A Disseminator Type is a set of operations that extends the basic functionality of a DigitalObject. These operations may or *may not* be directly related to the structure of a DigitalObject—they may produce transformations of stored content. In the simple case, a book Disseminator may define operations such as "get the next page" and "get the table of contents." Such operations may disseminate pages as direct transcriptions of content stored in DataStreams. Other operations may be computational in nature. For example, a book Disseminator can provide operations such as "translate text" from French to English, or "create audio presentation" of the first 15 minutes of a book. In fact, operations can be totally dynamic (*e.g.*, "get the current time").

Since new community-specific notions of content will continue to appear, there must be mechanisms for defining and registering new Disseminator Types. Communities can develop their own Disseminator Types (Signatures) by formally defining sets of operations that reflect the desired functionality of particular content abstractions. The codification of a Signature can be stored in a DigitalObject and given a unique name (a URN). Once stored, a Signature can be disseminated from the DigitalObject like any other form of content. Thus, DigitalObjects can be used to make Disseminator Types available in the infrastructure.

Servlets

A Servlet is an executable programme that is capable of performing the set of operations defined for a specific Disseminator Type (identified by the URN of a stored Signature). Since the operations defined by a Disseminator Type may be derivable from a number of structural configurations, there may be multiple Servlets that "implement" a Disseminator Type. For example, a Servlet could be built to execute the operations associated with a book (*e.g.*, "get the next page") using a set of scanned page images. Another Servlet could use an XML marked-up ASCII file. Thus, Disseminator Type *equivalence* is achieved when different Servlets operate on different types of underlying DataStreams to produce equivalent results.

In the same fashion as their associated *Signature*, *Servlets* are stored and registered in the infrastructure in their respective, uniquely named DigitalObjects. This design allows individuals to create new Servlets, store them in repositories, register their URNs (in the Handle System), and make them accessible for use in any other DigitalObjects.

Extensibility

In summary, the key to the architecture's extensibility is the clean separation of the object structure, extensible interfaces (Disseminator Types), and the mechanisms that implement extended functionality. This scheme allows for the addition of new Disseminator Types at the repository infrastructure level. It also enables the evolution of DigitalObject functionality over time. Consider our example of a DigitalObject with a "Book" Disseminator. At a later time, the rights holder of this object could decide that the photographs in this book are of interest in their own right. To enable viewing of these photographs outside the context of the book, the owner of the object can endow the existing DigitalObject with additional functionality.

New interfaces can be added to existing DigitialObjects. In our example, a new Disseminator (*e.g.*, of type PhotoCollection) can be associated with the original DigitalObject. The result is that the DigitalObject has both Book and PhotoCollection interfaces. The new Disseminator would reference a Servlet that allows a user to view the photographic images in the book as if they were part of a photo album. Such a Servlet would implement a "PhotoCollection" Disseminator Type using image detection and extraction techniques to present the images on demand (*i.e.*, in response to a "get next photo" request). In short, DigitalObject behaviour can be extended by (1) identifying or defining a Signature for the desired behaviours, and (2) acquiring or developing an appropriate Servlet for transforming content into the new "view."

Interoperability Experiments

The architecture described in Section 2.0 has three tiers. The first tier is the Repository layer where DigitalObjects are stored and accessed as opaque entities through a set of RAP requests. At the next layer, generic behaviours of the DigitalObject are exposed, allowing clients to access content and manipulate the structure of DigitalObjects through a set of RAP requests. At the third layer of the architecture, Disseminators are used to extend the generic behaviour of DigitalObjects. One or more Disseminator Types can be associated with DigitalObjects, endowing them with operations that have rich, community-specific semantics. Although these extended operations are not part of RAP, clients can discover and invoke them using RAP requests intended to support this extensibility. Thus, the DigitalObject extensibility scheme is generic.

A series of experiments were designed to test the interoperability of the Cornell and CNRI implementations across all three of these architectural layers. The first two tests focused on whether the implementations achieved a state of syntactic and semantic interoperability. Our first test (IT0) focused on whether clients could effectively communicate with both repositories over an IIOP transport layer and whether both repositories could recognize and properly respond to all RAP requests. This test established basic communication and ensured that both implementations conformed to the syntax specified in the RAP interface definition.

Once this basic state of interoperability was established, we proceeded with our second test (IT1) which focused on the semantics and functionality of components at all levels in the architecture. Specifically, we moved beyond the simple interface-level testing to an exploration of whether our Repositories, DigitalObjects, and Disseminators behaved in a consistent and predictable manner. From a client perspective, both implementations were shown to be indistinguishable at all three architectural layers.

Our third test focused exclusively on the extensibility mechanisms in the architecture. We recognized that extensibility can actually compromise interoperability if not properly integrated into the architecture. In this test, we demonstrated that both repositories were able to accommodate new interfaces (Signatures) and mechanisms (Servlets) to extend DigitalObject behaviours.

Specifically, we showed that the Signatures and Servlets used by Disseminators could reside in either repository and that both repositories could locate and execute them on demand. Furthermore, we tested the ease with which clients could add new Disseminator Types to the architecture by depositing new Signatures and Servlets in either repository.

Interoperability Test 0 (IT0): Protocol and Syntactic Interoperability

The first of our tests was intended to provide a very simple validation of our model for repository interoperability. Our goal was to confirm that clients could successfully connect to independently-developed repositories, issue all of the requests defined in the RAP IDL, and receive the proper return types for those requests. Success at this stage gives a limited measure of overall repository interoperability, nevertheless, it establishes that basic communication between the tested Repositories and their DigitalObjects can occur.

To conduct this test both CNRI and Cornell obtained an identical copy of the joint RAP IDL and compiled it using their respective CORBA ORB software (Visigenic for CNRI and OrbixWeb for Cornell). For IT0, we developed minimalist repository implementations that simply received each RAP request and returned a pre-determined test value of the specified type. This enabled us to focus on issues of syntax and ORB compatibility without introducing other implementation issues of logic and semantics. Fully developed repository implementations were used in subsequent tests.

IT0 was designed to isolate three issues: (1) effectiveness and compatibility of IIOP communications across different ORB vendors, (2) recognition of RAP requests, and (3) validity of return types. The tests were successful and we were able to verify that the established RAP interface definition achieves syntactic interoperability across different repository implementations. Also, we confirmed that the IIOP protocol was successful in its role as the common transport protocol between our separate implementations. IT0 established a baseline for our next two tests.

Interoperability Test 1 (IT1): Functional and Semantic Interoperability

Although the first interoperability test focused on whether our repositories could effectively communicate and recognize all RAP requests, it could not test whether requests would be fulfiled in a consistent and meaningful manner. Interoperability for repositories and digital objects is more than an issue of inter-communication of components via well-defined interfaces. The design and utility of these components also plays a role in interoperability. There are many issues of function and semantics that need to be tested before we could deem our repositories truly interoperable. One goal at this stage was to ensure that the Cornell and CNRI Repositories and DigitalObjects are functionally interchangeable from a client perspective, meaning that a client can perform the same tasks in each repository and obtain predictable results. An equally important goal was to show that the DigitalObject design promotes functional interoperability without constraining flexibility in the underlying data types, structures, or extensible behaviours of an object.

In IT1 we used our fully developed repository implementations and focused our testing on actual DigitalObjects. The test consisted of three experiments, described as follows.

Experiment 1.1-DigitalObject Access: In this experiment, our goal was to confirm that DigitalObjects in our two repositories are semantically interoperable at the structural layer of the architecture (as described in Section 2). Accordingly, we focused on the operations that enable access to the underlying DataStreams of DigitalObjects. We did not test any extended behaviours the DigitalObjects may have acquired through associated Disseminators. To run the experiment, we created DigitalObjects in each of our own repositories that were arbitrary configurations of typed data. We published the handles (URNs) of the test objects to each other and proceeded to run a general access test to see if each side could successfully locate and access the objects. We established the functional interoperability of our DigitalObjects by showing that a client could access an arbitrary DigitalObject, discover its contents at run time, and retrieve this content using the RAP structural requests—without any pre-existing knowledge of what the object contained.

Experiment 1.2-DigitalObject Creation: The second experiment focused on the repository and DigitalObject "factory" behaviours, namely the structural RAP requests that allow creation and manipulation of new DigitalObjects. In this test, we created identical DigitalObjects *in each other's* repositories. All objects were accessed and examined to confirm that each repository responded to the creation requests in the same manner. The objects were checked for structural integrity, meaning they all contained the same type and number of DataStreams and Disseminators. They were also tested for referential integrity, meaning that they all maintained the same internal structural relationships (*e.g.*, Disseminators do not reference DataStreams that don't exist). Ultimately, we tested the functional interoperability of the test objects by ensuring that each was capable of producing the same results for all DigitalObject structural requests. In short, we demonstrated that both repositories behaved equivalently and consistently in the creation of new DigitalObjects.

Experiment 1.3-Extensible Access: In our third experiment, we demonstrated that DigitalObjects in different repositories can attain functional equivalence at the extended behaviour layer of the architecture. We were able to show that different DigitalObjects can yield the same disseminations to all clients, regardless of the underlying DataStream types and Servlet implementations. In this test, both Cornell and CNRI worked with two general types of objects, those that disseminated Dublin Core records and those that disseminated simple images. Before creating our respective DigitalObjects we formally defined behaviours that constituted the Signatures for two Disseminator types (DublinCore and Image).

The DublinCore type definition specified the behaviours GetDCMeta to disseminate a full DublinCore record, and GetDCMetaElement to disseminate a particular element of the set. The Image type defined GetImage, GetThumbnail, and

GetDescription to disseminate an image, its thumbnail representation, and a textual description of the image, respectively. Since these Signatures were designed to support our tests, they were not intended to declare the definitive set of methods that could pertain to DublinCore or Image entities. With these simple Disseminator Types, we successfully associated the same extended behaviours with our respective DigitalObjects. Functional equivalence was established by using RAP requests to dynamically discover and invoke the same behaviours on both the Cornell and CNRI DigitalObjects.

Interoperability Test 2 (IT2): Interoperability of Extensibility Mechanisms

The third interoperability test (IT2) builds on the previous two tests (IT1 and IT0) and was motivated by the tenuous relationship that exists between extensibility and interoperability. Solutions for extensibility can sometimes limit interoperability when extended functionality cannot be dynamically integrated into a common architectural base. Our strategy for achieving extensibility *with* interoperability was to develop a scheme for incorporating new behaviours into DigitalObjects in a globally scalable manner.

To review, DigitalObject functionality can be extended using Disseminators. In Section 2, we introduced the Disseminator as a generic component that associates a new interface (a Signature) with a DigitalObject, along with an executable programme (a Servlet) that produces the behaviours defined by the new interface. Signatures and Servlets become available throughout the infrastructure when they are stored in DigitalObjects and their URNs are registered with the naming service (Handle System). The importance of a global naming service is particularly highlighted in this test. The repositories consult with the Handle System to locate these special DigitalObjects to obtain disseminator Signatures and Servlets as needed. This occurs when clients make requests on *other* DigitalObjects whose Disseminators refer to the URNs of registered Signatures and Servlets.

IT2 was specifically designed to test the extent to which this scheme promotes extensibility without compromising interoperability. Our test focused on the *mechanisms* that enable the creation and dynamic acquisition of new Disseminator Types. IT2 consisted of two experiments. This first was designed to test the ability of a repository to dynamically load the Signatures and Servlets necessary to support disseminations of our test DigitalObjects. The second experiment was designed to demonstrate the flexibility with which new disseminator types are dynamically added to the infrastructure.

Experiment 2.1: In our former tests, both CNRI and Cornell implemented their own Servlets and Signatures for the test Disseminators (DublinCore and Image). These Servlets and Signatures were stored in uniquely named DigitalObjects in each respective repository. All of our test DigitalObjects referenced *local* Servlets and Signatures (stored in the same repository as the test DigitalObjects).

In the current test, both CNRI and Cornell created another set of DigitalObjects that referenced *remote* Signatures and Servlets stored in each other's repositories. The CNRI and Cornell repositories with the DigitalObjects used in this test. In each repository, there are two DigitalObjects with DublinCore Disseminators. These objects are all functionally equivalent, but they use different Signatures and Servlets to produce DublinCore disseminations. In the Cornell repository, the first object ($Cornell_1$) references a local DublinCore Signature ($Cornell_{DC}$) and a local DublinCore Servlet ($Cornell_{DC-1}$). A second object ($Cornell_{2)}$ references a remote Signature ($CNRI_{DC)}$ and a remote Servlet ($CNRI_{DC-1}$)stored in the CNRI repository. The CNRI repository contains objects that mirror this scenario.

The goal of the experiment was to test the ability of the repositories to generate interoperable disseminations from all of the test DigitalObjects, regardless of the particular Signature or Servlet implementations. Our test clients requested disseminations from objects $Cornell_1$ and $CNRI_1$ using locally stored Signatures and Servlets. The next step was to test the ability of the repositories to generate disseminations from the DigitalObjects using remotely defined disseminator Signatures and Servlets. Each repository must locate and download a remotely stored Signature and Servlet to fulfil the dissemination requests made by the clients. The result was that all objects produced equivalent disseminations of DublinCore records. This same test was repeated with the Image Disseminator. The ability of each repository to locate, acquire and execute remote Disseminator Type mechanisms is particularly significant. It shows that our independently-developed Signatures and Servlets are interoperable and that both repositories have equivalent mechanisms to locate and use them.

Experiment 2.2: The second part of IT2 was designed to demonstrate the flexibility with which new Disseminator Types are dynamically added to the infrastructure. The ability to conceive of a Disseminator Type, formally define it, and easily implement it is an important aspect of the architecture. In this final test, we first demonstrated that a client could develop new Signatures or Servlets and store them in DigitalObjects in *either* repository. Secondly, we showed that DigitalObjects in either repository can use these new Signatures and Servlets. This test challenged each repository to be able to accept Signatures and Servlets that were created externally, without regard to the particulars of the underlying repository implementation. This test was important because it suggests that, by adhering to set of specifications, third-parties can create self-contained Signatures and Servlets that are compatible with these repositories. Conversely, either repository should be able to store and execute any third-party disseminator Signatures and Servlets that adhere to the defined specifications.

Interoperability Experiments: General Results

Our first series of interoperability experiments were a success, and we were able to demonstrate that the CNRI and Cornell repositories achieved multiple states of interoperability. Specifically, the two implementations were shown to achieve syntactic (protocol) and semantic (functional) interoperability at all levels of the architecture. We also demonstrated that the extensibility mechanisms are themselves interoperable.

In IT0, we established a baseline for interoperability by showing that clients could successfully communicate with both repositories through the well-defined RAP interface. Using IIOP as our transport protocol and OMG/IDL to define the RAP interface, we established a state of syntactical interoperability between the Cornell and CNRI repositories. Both repositories recognized all RAP requests and responded with proper data types. Although our architectural abstractions are general enough to be implemented in other ways, we believe the distributed object approach, enabled by CORBA, provides an appropriate level of abstraction and flexibility for our implementations. At a minimum, interoperable repositories must share some common high level standards for connectivity and interface definition.

Our second test (IT1) established the functional equivalence of the Cornell and CNRI repositories, meaning that clients can perform the same tasks in each repository and consistently obtain equivalent results. Through a series of incremental experiments, we unveiled the significance of the DigitalObject component design in promoting interoperability.

A key attribute of the architecture is the ability to contain heterogeneous data streams and their relationships inside DigitalObjects. Once contained, content is accessed via a set of generic RAP requests that allow clients to access DigitalObjects in the same way from repository to repository without being exposed to the underlying complexities of the object. The model enables the association of extended behaviours with DigitalObjects (such as our example DublinCore and Image behaviours) without compromising the interoperability of the object. In both the Cornell and CNRI repositories, clients can discover and invoke these additional behaviours through RAP requests. We have concluded that our extensibility scheme provides the ability to associate a rich set of behaviours with DigitalObjects without compromising interoperability.

Our third test (IT2) yielded one of the most important results of the interoperability experiments. We confirmed that the extensibility model provides a powerful mechanism for the integration of community-developed standards into the architecture. Third parties can define sets of behaviours that apply to particular types of objects (*e.g.*, books, photos, reports) and then formalize these behaviours in an appropriate Signature. The resultant Signature, known as a Disseminator Type, is then implemented by one or more self-contained Servlets. These Signatures and Servlets can then be used by others to associate new behaviours with DigitalObjects in an interoperable manner.

Although our extensibility scheme is powerful, there are some nuances to the overall design to which repository implementers must adhere. The extensibility implementation requires that Repositories interact with each other using the full functionality defined in RAP. It is therefore absolutely necessary that Repositories be IT0 and IT1 compatible before attempting to satisfy the IT2 level interoperability. For a Repository to achieve this level of interoperability, it has to be able to load, initialize and execute all Signatures and Servlets that are registered within the infrastructure. All Repositories must implement their extensibility mechanisms in accordance with the defined Servlet and Signature specifications.

Interoperability will be compromised if the tools for extending DigitalObject behaviours are difficult to adopt. We have concluded that new Signatures and Servlets can be easily built without having to know about anything of the infrastructure apart from a simple set of interface definitions that apply to Servlets and Signatures. The requirements are well defined, and the use of the Java language provides some simple form of enforcement that should help developers in creating Servlets and Signatures that can operate in all repositories. New Disseminator Types become available in the infrastructure by the mere acts of depositing them in DigitalObjects and registering them with the Handle System with a URN. Once deposited and registered, all properly implemented Repositories can locate them, and dynamically load them to produce disseminations of other DigitalObjects.

Of course, from the perspective of clients accessing DigitalObjects, the extensibility scheme is transparent. The ultimate effect of our architecture is seen when clients are able to communicate with multiple repositories to access DigitalObjects with rich sets of behaviours, without regard to the underlying structures and data types contained within these objects.

Future Work

Interoperability may not be an all or nothing proposition. In one of our next experiments, we will begin to investigate the conditions under which differences can exist in our repositories without jeopardizing interoperability. Our hypothesis, corroborated by our interoperability experiments, is that repositories do not have to be 100% similar in their functionality or behaviour in order to be interoperable. Repositories could be built to achieve certain states (or levels) of interoperability compliance. Our initial tests have outlined three types of interoperability for repositories and digital objects—protocol/syntactic, functional/semantic, and extensibility mechanism interoperability. We believe there may be other levels of interoperability that intersect with these. So, for instance, a repository could be in a state of partial functional compliance if it implements a subset of the functionality specified in RAP. Such an implementation might support the deposit and retrieval of opaque DigitalObjects, without providing any additional operations.

In our upcoming research, we plan to define a set of metrics that could be used to measure levels of interoperability that different repositories have with each other. Such metrics may enable a larger community of repositories and clients to interact with each other. We hope to show that partially compatible repositories can join federations, and that clients can dynamically determine relative compatibility of repositories and how best to interact with each. Although we have not yet formulated specific metrics, we will use the results of our interoperability tests to develop initial categories and benchmarks for measuring interoperability.

We are also planning another set of interoperability tests that will continue to test the limits of our respective repository implementations. These tests will be built around some of our current activities targeted at testing the scalability of Disseminators—particularly Servlets that support complex community-developed Disseminator Types.

We are currently investigating a proposal to accommodate objects that conform to the new Making of America II document type definition (DTD). As part of these investigations, we will also test the portability of complex Servlets that require supplemental libraries or utilities to run in a repository. We will also look at the use of XML DTDs to describe various types and configurations of DataStreams that must be present in a DigitalObject for particular Servlets to execute successfully.

In the upcoming year, we plan to focus heavily on the issues of security and access management. A major theme of this research will also be extensibility and interoperability of security mechanisms for DigitalObjects and Repositories. Both Cornell and CNRI have separate implementations of a prototyped, architectural component known as the AccessManager that will allow the association of third-party access management mechanisms with DigitalObjects and Repositories. We will also investigate security issues brought on by the use of mobile code.

Clips and Pointers

The European Visual Archive (EVA) is a two-year, transnational project that began on 1 December 1998. It is being funded in part by the European Commission via DGXIII, the directorate responsible for telecommunications and the information market. The EVA project is one of 20 selected from a total of over 140 applicants under the INFO2000 programme call for initiatives to exploit Europe's public sector information.

The EVA project is a European Strategic project involving both private and public sectors to stimulate the use of multimedia information content by exploiting resources in public archives. The principal aim is to enhance access to European Heritage through digital preservation of archival collections. In the case of EVA, this means photographs from 1900 to the present being digitised and displayed on the World Wide Web. The universal nature of the photograph makes an ideal subject for an international project. The dream would be for a researcher interested in a particular subject and time span to have ready access via the Internet to images held in many different archives across Europe. Thus, someone researching docklands pre-1914 could locate images in Antwerp and London and compare installations regardless of language or national barriers.

The initial stage of the project is to establish a large enough digital databank of photographs from the archives of two major cities, London and Antwerp, to examine the best methods of digitisation, levels of description, and presentation on a website. A total of 20,000 photographic images will be made available to researchers. The EVA project aims to extend this to other European public archives who then will be able to benefit from the EVA project studies on description standards, image quality, metadata, copyright and pricing policies.

At the end of the project, a working model will be developed so that all European public archives will be able to use the system. This working model will have solutions to language barriers; will use appropriate search and navigation methods; will employ direct charging systems; and, thereby, will introduce a very easily accessible tool for the multimedia industry and all archive users.

The EVA partners are:

- Telepolis Antwerpen (TA) Belgium
- London Metropolitan Archives (LMA) UK
- Stadsarchief Antwerpen (SAA) Belgium
- Nederlands Instituut voor Wetenschnappelijke Informatiediensten (NIWI) Netherlands
- European Commission of Preservation and Access (ECPA) Netherlands
- Lernout and Hanspie Speech Products (L+H) Germany

The project is worth approximately 1 million ECUs, of which the European Commission contributes 50%.

EVA will run in partnership with a number of other information projects including EUAN (the European Union Archive Network) from the INFO2000 programme. Whereas EVA is starting at item-level description of archives, the EUAN project is starting at series-level description of archives. It will be useful to construct an interface between these two projects each of which have similar challenges, both technical and legal, to meet. EVA will work within international standards already established and looks forward to close cooperation with the International Council of Archives (ICA) and regional and national archives in the European Union. The results of the EVA project will be disseminated as widely as possible.

Building Earth's Largest Library: Driving Towards the Future

The purpose of my article, "Building Earth's Largest Library: Driving Towards the Future" was to explore what might happen if we applied the Amazon.com business model to the library world. Amazon built Earth's Biggest Bookstore by allowing their customers to search one huge catalogue listing all of the 4 million books, CDs, and videos they had a reasonable chance of getting, even though Amazon actually only maintains a few hundred thousand of the most popular titles in it's own inventories.

So, suppose we built Earth's Largest Library by allowing our patrons to search a huge catalogue that listed all the books (and other materials) we could get, instead of just those few items that happened to be in our own collections? There are any number of ways you could build such a catalogue, but probably the easiest and most straight-forward approach would be to take the OCLC Worldcat database and combine it with a list of current and forthcoming titles like that found on Amazon. That would give you a catalogue of around 43 million items—certainly enough to qualify as Earth's Largest Library, and enough to satisfy the needs of even your most discriminating patrons. (I know, I know, this catalogue wouldn't include a lot of non-English language material, and it would be heavily focused on the US—but we'd try to address those problems in the next phase.)

Suppose further, that we've gone through that catalogue and, wherever possible, we've "enhanced" our cryptic bibliographic records by adding cover art, jacket copy, tables of contents, indexes, reviews, selections from the text, and anything else that might help our patrons evaluate and select the books they want—just as Amazon has gone through and added all kinds of content, special browsing arrangements, recommendation "engines" and other features to try to make it as easy as possible for their customers to find what they want.

Finally, suppose we made this catalogue available over the Web, so your patrons could logon and search it from anywhere in the world any time of the day or night—just as they can now with the Amazon catalogue. And when your patrons searched the catalogue, they would get back a result set that showed—not who owned the item, or where it was located (most could care less)—but how quickly they could get it (*e.g.*, this title available immediately from at your local branch; this title ships in 24 hours; this title ships in 2-3 days; etc.) When a person found what they were looking for, all they would have to do is "click" to check it out. They could arrange to pick it up at their local library or have it shipped directly to them for a small additional fee.

Of course, all of this would cost a lot of money—Amazon spends around 12.5 million per year to develop and operate its catalogue, Web site and transaction system—but that is only a small percentage of the 465 million per year *Library Journal* estimates libraries are currently spending on automation systems alone. And the question is, how many catalogs and circulation systems do we need? Do we really each need to spend the millions we are spending to maintain separate, and often pretty rudimentary, catalogs and circulation systems at each institution, or wouldn't it be better to pool our funds and develop one really nice catalogue and circulation system that would work for all?

The article goes on to explore the various ramifications such a system might have on library operations: how you might be able to use it to transform the way we do collection development; how libraries might be encouraged to make their collections available for loan; potential new revenue sources it might open up; and so forth—all in much greater detail than I can relate here.

I am very gratified that the article has generated a substantial amount of interest and comment,—enough so that the editor, Barbara Quint, has asked me to do a follow-up piece to try to address the various issues that have been raised. I would welcome comments, suggestions, and even criticisms, from the readers of *D-Lib Magazine* who might have an interest in this subject matter. The only thing I ask is that you please read the article first. It is over 10,000 words in length, and it is almost impossible for me to do the article justice in this forum. Also, I'll need to have any comments by June 1st in order to insure they are incorporated into the upcoming piece. You may email me at or phone me at 1-800-582-1093. Feel free to say whatever you'd like, I welcome any and all comments. Finally, if you would like to explore the subject in more depth, you should know that the Internet Librarian Conference is planning a full track on Building Earth's Largest Library at it meeting in San Diego this November.

Journal of the American Society for Information Science (JASIS)

Guests have access only to tables of contents and abstracts. Registered users of the Interscience site have access to the full text of these issues and to preprints. We are still working on restoring access for ASIS members as "registered users."

Project Runeberg was begun in 1992 to provide online access, free of charge, to old books from Sweden and the Nordic countries in several languages (most are in Swedish). Project Runeberg now lists more than 200 titles, catalogued alphabetically, and more titles are continuing to be added. The project is an open and voluntary initiative to make the texts available.

All Library Directors are invited to this special forum. Martin Dillon and Erik Jul will discuss lessons learned from the past year's seminars. Registration is requested, but the event is free of charge.

- Special Issue: Imaging Visualization and Humanities Research, Call for papers.

Papers are requested for a special issue of *Archives and Museum Informatics*, the cultural heritage information quarterly, a peer-reviewed journal from Kluwer Academic publishers, that explores the application of imaging technologies in humanities research. Papers are invited that report on how imaging technologies were used in a humanities informatics project to further the research goals of the investigator.

Full papers will be accepted for peer review and possible inclusion in this issue until June 30, 1999.

- The Educause Institute Management Programme, 10-22 July 1999, Boulder, Colorado, USA.

The audience for this EDUCAUSE Institute is described as: The EDUCAUSE Institute Management Programme is the foundational programme of the Institute. Established in 1990, the Management Programme has served more than 1,000 professionals in higher education. Attendees of the Management

Programme come from many professional domains and parts of the world. Past graduates have included campus information technologists, librarians, information resources professionals, and functional managers who depend on information technology. The curriculum of the Management Programme has been designed to give participants a sound working knowledge of key management practices and techniques to allow them to lead intelligent and effective change at the departmental or functional level of the campus.

- International Conference on Information Visualisation, 14-16 July 1999, London, England, UK.

The sponsors describe the scope of this conference thus: "There is a growing demand in establishing processes through which data and information can be best captured, archived, shared and explored. Visualisation of data, information and knowledge is at the forefront of these activities that has led to a convergence in the use of computing among various disciplines.

The diversity and complexity of information and its applications has consequently created a domain of erosion of boundaries between information users and information originators. This revolution has in turn created new contexts, needs, and potential for interaction between users and information. Now the core question is, how will humankind tame this boundless potential? "The theme chosen for this conference is "A PROGRESS FROM THEORY TO PRACTICE". Information Visualisation'99 (IV'99) conference aims to focus on the interdisciplinary methods and affiliated research done among various science disciplines, medicine, engineering, media and commerce. This three day event will focus on the research and developments conjured to meet the roaring demand of today's "Information Transfer" through the medium of computing, accentuating on the linkage that shapes academia and industry with the goal of stimulating views and providing a forum where researchers and practitioners can discuss the latest developments linked to Information Visualisation."

SSD is held biennially at various locations throughout the world. The prime application area for the conference is geographic information systems; however, spacial database technology has been developing a wider application such as:

- o 2D or 3D geographic space; GIS, urban planning, geology, meteorology
- o the universe; astronomy
- o the human body; medicine
- o molecular structures; molecular biology
- o VLSI design spaces with electronic circuits
- o 2D images; image retrieval by content
- o 2D images + 1D time: video, multimedia objects
- o high-dimensional feature spaces; similarity search

- The Second Asian Digital Libraries Conference, 8-9 November 1999, University Library of the National Taiwan University, Taipei, Taiwan. *Call for papers. The submission due date is 31 July 1999.*

The *Asian Digital Libraries Conference (ADL)* tries to bring together researchers and developers from academia, industry and government to advance the research of digital libraries in Asia. The conference will be immediately followed by IRAL¡¦99 (Workshop on Information Retrieval with Asian Languages, 1999), to further facilitate interchange between the DL and IR communities.

Papers are being sought on the following topics:

- Collection
  - — Archives
  - — Arts
  - — Geographic Material
  - — Government Information
  - — Humanities
  - — Manuscripts

1. Digitalizataion and Preservation
   - — Archiving
   - — Authoring
   - — Image Processing
   - — Multimedia
   - — OCR
   - — Watermark

2. Information Organization
   — Data Modelling
   — Knowledge Representation
   — Metadata
   — Multimedia
   — SGML, XML, HTML, RDF
   — Thesaurus and Corpus<
3. User Interaction
   — Evaluation
   — Learning and Instruction
   — Presentation
   — User Feedback
   — User Study
   — Visualization
4. Information Retrieval
   — Automatic Indexing and Classification
   — Cross-Language Retrieval
   — Distributed Access
   — Information Extraction
   — Information Filtering
   — Intelligent Agent
5. System and Infrastructure
   — Content Management
   — Data Mining and Knowledge Discovery
   — Naming Scheme
   — Network
   — Security and Access Control
   — System Architecture
6. Cultural and Social Issues
   — Authentication and Authorization
   — Economic Issues
   — Education
   — Legal Issues

— Policy

— Publishing

- Museums, Libraries, and Archives: Summer Institute for Knowledge Sharing, 2-6 August 1999, UCLA, Los Angeles, California, USA.

This summer institute is designed to provide both theories and practical applications in cultural heritage information management and knowledge sharing. Planned are lectures, panel sessions, and workshops which will take place at the new Getty Centre and the University of California, Los Angeles (UCLA) campus.

The course is aimed at professionals in museums, libraries and archives, and will emphasize team approaches to work across departmental and institutional boundaries.

- 26th International Conference on Computer Graphics and Interactive Techniques, 8-13 August 1999, Los Angeles, California, USA.

This five day conference will include presented papers, panels, courses, exhibitions, and a computer animation festival.

Papers are classified under the broad headings of Rendering, Modelling, and Interactive Techniques, and they cover subjects such as efficient lighting; data captures; texturing; hardware; image-based rending; meshes & morphing; virtual reality; interactive techniques; and imaginative rendering.

Panels explore the art and science of image and interface, and address technical, practical, aesthetic, and social challenges. After their presentations, authors and panelists will move on to practical demonstrations.

Three days of courses for professional development are offered for everyone in computer graphics and interactive techniques, from first-job novices to 25-year veterans. The courses include full-day courses, half-day courses, and two-hour tutorials. Full Conference registration allows attendees to select from over 40 SIGGRAPH 99 Courses. In addition, attendees who select the Full Conference registration option receive access to all SIGGRAPH 99 Courses and the Course Notes on CD-ROM. The computer animation festival will present stories and non-narrative works that reflect on the past and illuminate the future, in imagery and animations, film and video, live and interactive performances. The year's outstanding achievements in digital experience appear in the evening and matinée shows of the Electronic Theater and Animation Theatres.

- Strait to the Future, 8th Asia-Pacific Specials, Health, and Law Librarians Conference, 22-26 August 1999, Hobart, Tasmania, Australia.

This conference includes three tracks: the first for special librarians, the second for health librarians, and the third for law librarians. A sample of papers—for just the first day of the conference—in the three tracks include:

- Special libraries:
  - — Outsourcing-giving librarians back to their isolated clients
  - — Using external service companies to improve an information service-a positive view of outsourcing
  - — From farmgate to knowledge gateway
  - — The diffusion of IR research to the practice of librarianship

1. Health libraries:
   - — Clinical Information Access Project (CIAP): A unique resource for all NSW Health Clinicians
   - — The impact of hospital networks on hospital libraries in Melbourne, 1995 to 1999
   - — Comparing the value and impact of information obtained by health practitioners undertaking literature searches with those undertaken by library staff
   - — Strait to Recognition: practical client services benchmarking of hospital libraries in Queensland
2. Law libraries:
   - — The future of the past, the development of Australian legal history
   - — New Zealand legal material on the internet

- One person libraries, islands or innovators?
- Economic rationalisation and its effect on government services

• Society of American Archivists (SAA) 63rd Annual Meeting, 23-29 August 1999, Pittsburgh, Pennsylvania, USA.

This conference is for SAA members. Preconference workshops for the SAA Annual Meeting include:

- Archival Cataloguing as a Component of Description
- The Application of the USMARC Format
- Encoded Archival Description
- Digital Imaging Technology
- Understanding Archives
- Oral History: From Planning to Preservation
- The Reformatting Challenge: Management Issues
- Preservation Planning: Surveying, Selection and Holdings Maintenance
- Probing Appraisal Practice: Contending with Methods, Mayhem and Madness
- Writing Your Disaster Preparedness and Recovery Plan
- Administration of Photographic Collections
- Basic Electronic Records
- Advanced Electronic Records

• SCOPE 1, Information vs Meaning, 30 September-1 October 1999, Vienna, Austria.

For two days, international experts in technology, design, economics and science will convene at the Vienna Hilton Hotel to present current research trends and innovative cutting-edge projects in the field of information technology.

The main emphasis of scope1: information vs. meaning will be on recent developments in information technology and their impact on the way knowledge is handled and managed. Leading experts from fields such as computer science, physics, interface design and artificial intelligence will present inventive solutions and strategies which will profoundly change access to and use of knowledge in the future by providing simpler, faster and more efficient techniques.

CYBERINFRASTRUCTURE, DATA, AND LIBRARIES

A Cyberinfrastructure Primer for Librarians

E-Science, cyberinfrastructure – these ideas are at the heart of the great ambitions and promise of science in the new century. The last several decades of network-and computer-enabled work in science have produced untold amounts of data, leading to the challenge of developing practices to manage and provide access to this data. Along with oceans of data and technology, changes in the conduct and nature of science – notably new collaborative and computational science practices – present both novel requirements and exciting opportunities to succeed in meeting this challenge. A global effort is emerging to take collective responsibility for a growing yet still vulnerable investment in scientific data as a permanent part of scientific research communications and practices.

Today, everyone with a role in the traditional infrastructure of scientific research and communication is jockeying for a role in the emerging landscape of scientific data: national libraries; research funding agencies; universities and research libraries; and giants of the software and publishing industries. As roles and responsibilities get sorted out, librarians are testing the waters to identify what present and future roles they may have in these developments; but these are early days, and it is still unclear what those roles may be.

For information professionals, getting to know the concepts and issues raised in the name of cyberinfrastructure and E-Science is no mean feat. There has been an outpouring of lengthy reports addressing and framing their challenges, and the result is a ferment of ideas, vocabularies, organizations and strategies. Becoming literate in cyberinfrastructure means understanding cyberinfrastructure, E-Science, collaboratories, collaboration science, computational and grid science, data curation, the Semantic Web, open data, data archiving, digital preservation, and data management, and how they relate to each other.

While this learning curve is one factor, a second challenge adds to the difficulty that librarians have engaging in these issues: data science and data management are an awkward fit with the text-oriented constructs and systems that still dominate library relationships with science communication and publishing. Most librarians are much less familiar with the data-generating research phases of the scientific research cycle than with post-research phases of reporting, communication and publication.

Finally, add to these challenges the technical background needed to understand, even at a general level, the technologies that may be used in data management. Language itself becomes a barrier to understanding. When used in discussions of E-Science, a vocabulary familiar to librarians (archival, curation, stewardship, provenance) takes on new or specialized meaning.

Despite these challenges, the library profession has been eager to grapple with the new issues presented by scientific data as a part of the scholarly record. Major professional organizations, among them the American Society for Information Science & Technology (ASIS&T), the American Library Association (ALA), and the Association of Research Libraries (ARL), are sponsoring or leading activities with a focus on cyberinfrastructure and scientific data. A major milestone in this growing interest is the initiative launched in 2006 by ARL, a Task Force on E-Science. The purposes of this ongoing E-Science initiative include exploring and addressing gaps in awareness and understanding within the profession; as well as positioning research libraries alongside research funding agencies and research universities and organizations, as contributors and partners in dealing with the immense challenges of managing and preserving access to digital scientific data.

Shortly after the Task Force was established, ARL and the National Science Foundation (NSF) co-sponsored an invitational workshop in October 2006 on the topic of digital data stewardship. An executive summary of the workshop was published reaching a broad audience of library leaders and professionals. Yet even this brief and relatively accessible article, focused on the roles of libraries and librarians in E-Science, presumes a fairly high level of general understanding of the relevant issues and vocabulary as well as familiarity with a host of stakeholders engaged in the field of digital data management.

The following two-part article is offered to help open up the discussion with library practitioners working directly with research faculty and graduate students, advising on issues of scholarly communication, and concerned with providing relevant data services in the context of relatively well-established library-based data support programmes in GIS, social science data, and bioinformatics. Part 1 provides a primer for librarians on cyberinfrastructure, including an overview of major issues and readings to help locate the issues in the larger national and global framework, as well as an introduction to emerging critiques of global cyberinfrastructure theory. Part 2 offers an overview and analysis of current theories about the roles libraries and librarians can have associated with the multiple dimensions of cyberinfrastructure.

A Cyberinfrastructure Primer for Librarians

At a research university, a professor collects data on protein crystal measurements. This data is very valuable because getting protein to crystallize is difficult: it may take a week, or it may take fifteen years. Repeating experiments is non-trivial. The resulting raw data files are huge: they include 360 images – one from each angle. Data formats change as instrumentation changes – constantly. The professor saves the raw data in the latest file format, on the latest storage media – currently CD-ROM. She provides detailed instructions to graduating students on how to pass the data back to her, but there is no central storage service for this kind of data product.

Once the data is captured, the raw data is processed (analyzed) into a form that is widely used by researchers (although this form, too, changes over time). Submitting data to an international data bank requires one such conversion. But once submitted, there is no easy way to reverse engineer that format back to the working format that makes it usable for other researchers. Also, it becomes important to publish data quickly because otherwise researchers will not be able to use the original data as different detectors do not talk each other's language, and these programmes are constantly changing.

The sketch above illustrates several of the problems facing scientists in data-rich, data-driven science. Instruments and arrays yield vast amounts of data, and increasingly the data itself becomes the subject of research and re-use through computational manipulations. In many fields these activities take place in local settings that are subject to rapid and continual changes in instrumentation and digital media standards. Support is lacking for long-term storage, for retrieval of usable formats and derivatives, and for sharing data in forms suitable for reuse or for use in different research settings. Where standards and practices for publishing research results in textual form are well-established and supported, managing access to data has the feel of a vast frontier with pockets of homesteaders and small settlements, and a few well-supplied and well-guarded nodes. And yet, data is the currency of science, even if publications are still the currency of tenure. To be able to exchange data, communicate it, mine it, reuse it, and review it is essential to scientific productivity, collaboration, and to discovery itself.

Setting the Stage: Supercomputers, Informatics and Grid Science, and the Rise of Cyberinfrastructure

By the late 1990's, the use of computers to handle manipulations of very large data sets was well-established. National computational science infrastructure took three primary forms: local high performance computing (HPC) centres– located at most research universities; supercomputing capabilities located in national laboratories; and a small number of distributed supercomputing nodes that provided supercomputing capabilities on demand to scientists around the country. At about the same time, the rise of genomic science offered a template for a new approach to problems in life science, using collaborative efforts to gather pieces of data in standard and well-understood ways, thereby building up shared data resources – the genomes of several organisms – culminating in the sequencing of the human genome in April 2003.

At the end of the last century this inter-networked and distributed infrastructure began to evolve towards what became known as "grid computing." The grid offered a new way of accessing centralized supercomputing capabilities; at the same time it provided a more distributed computational architecture that reduced reliance on supercomputing centres. Grid computing – sharing computational resources across a decentralized and heterogeneous computing and institutional network – had its origins in the 1970's, but it became a major element of scientific computing infrastructure with the emergence of the Globus Toolkit in 2002.

At about the same time, a new kind of data science initiative emerged that didn't require high performance or parallel computing, but helped provide an important model for data sharing: the PDB (Protein Data Bank, a shared data bank of protein structures.

Gradually these and similar developments came to be referred to as "cyberinfrastructure" in the U.S., and elsewhere as "E-Science" – mostly in Europe and the U.K. A focus on creating an infrastructure of computing hardware, software, networks, and services began gradually to give way to a new interest in data reuse, followed by a concern for the long-term stewardship of the data being produced. Public research funding organizations were worried about their investment in data produced through publicly funded research, especially when it had long-term, authoritative and reference value within a research community.

Similar concerns were emerging among scientists and engineers who had begun to understand that data management over time and across heterogeneous data sources posed an increasingly complex and unaddressed research problem. Meanwhile, the growing dependence of all social, academic, and cultural sectors on digital data created a new awareness of the vulnerability of digital data, and the need to create both technical and social models to assure the persistence and integrity of important digital data over time.

Cyberinfrastructure and E-Science

After 2000, a number of workshops, reports, and related publications dealing with cyberinfrastructure began to appear from the NSF. Of these perhaps the best known is

Revolutionizing Science and Engineering Through Cyberinfrastructure (also referred to as the Atkins report), published in January 2003. As defined by the authors of the Atkins report, "cyberinfrastructure" refers to a comprehensive and integrated system of hardware, networks, software, and middleware, designed to support a range of advanced data acquisition, storage, management, integration, mining, and visualization over the Internet:

"The term...cyberinfrastructure refers to infrastructure based upon distributed computer, information, and communication technology. If *infrastructure* is required for an *industrial* economy, then we could say that *cyberinfrastructure* is required for a *knowledge* economy."

An important outcome of the Atkins report was the creation by the NSF of a new Office for Cyberinfrastructure (OCI). Since its establishment, the OCI has already issued a number of calls to action, vision, and other planning documents. The Atkins report also marked recognition of a broader change in the role of computing in science at all scales. For one thing, the emerging cyberinfrastructure was clearly something with human and social dimensions as well as technical ones. Both the Atkins report and another draft NSF report that followed in early 2006, *Cyberinfrastructure Vision for 21 Century Discovery*, called for steps to develop the workforce that would be needed to create and sustain cyberinfrastructure. This workforce would include data scientists, a new type of professional with both domain science expertise and high-level computational skills; and also social scientists trained to understand the human factors relevant to the use of technology-mediated collaborative tools.

The broadening implications of cyberinfrastructure were echoed in a publication by Microsoft Research issued later the same year, *Towards 2020 Science*. Written by a panel of scientists, this report argued that computer science concepts, tools, and theorems have the potential for having "a profound impact on science. It is a leap from the application of computing to support scientists to 'do' science (*i.e.*, 'computational science') to the integration of computer science...into the very fabric of science". The Microsoft report notes that the new paradigm will bring with it the challenge of "end-to-end scientific data management, from data acquisition and data integration, to data treatment, provenance and persistence."

The Microsoft report claims that a new paradigm will bring with it the challenge of "end-to-end scientific data management, from data acquisition and data integration, to data treatment, provenance and persistence." It also predicts a paradigm shift in scientific publishing, from the "traditional sequence of 'experiment › analysis › publication'" to "'experiment › data organisation › analysis › publication'".

Data archiving and Preservation

While these ideas about cyberinfrastructure were forming, a different, if overlapping array of reports began to chart another challenge of digitally based research: the problem of preserving digital content. Given the staggering output of digital data and digital records, the problem had several daunting aspects. On the one hand, there was the problem of what "preservation" means in the digital realm. It seemed clear already that in the absence of practices for refreshing and migrating both data and relevant retrieval software, digital records of all kinds were threatened with loss. Some began to refer to the threat of a "digital dark age." Early prophets of this threat had begun to warn of this a decade earlier. While keeping digital objects usable was one concern of the digital preservationists, there were others, including capture (archiving) and selection, as well as providing sufficient metadata or other descriptive or administrative information to ensure adequate (as well as legal) access and retrieval over the long term. Several years ago, major government organizations worldwide began to outline the scale of the digital archiving problem, while calling for the development of needed technical, social, and business models. Internationally, these included the National Library of Australia in the 1990's; UNESCO, with its 2003 *Charter on the Preservation of Digital Heritage*; JISC in the UK, with its 2003 *E-Science Curation Report*; and, in Canada, the National Consultation on Access to Scientific Research Data 2005 report.

In the US, the Library of Congress and the National Archives both began to convene stakeholders and develop research programmes to create "national infrastructure for long-term preservation of digital information." In 2004 the Library of Congress began to fund research through its DIGARCH programme, in partnership with the NSF, as part of its new National Digital Information Preservation Programme (NDIPP). After pursuing related research beginning in 1998, in 2005 the National Archives (NARA) awarded a major contract to Lockheed Martin to build a permanent archive of federal electronic records. With these and other partner organizations, the NSF continues to play a key role in shaping U.S. discourse and strategies for digital preservation. The National Science Board (NSB) issued an important report in 2005 on *Long-Lived Data Collections*, and in late 2006 the NSF funded a workshop with the Association of Research Libraries, documented in its report, *To Stand the Test of Time: Long Term Stewardship of Digital Data Sets in Science and Engineering*. For libraries, this report was significant for the explicit case it made for the role of U.S. research libraries in future cyberinfrastructure.

As diverse as these reports have been in their focus and provenance, common threads can be found across all of them. With varying emphasis, each has called for more education on the issues; for collaborative action by cross-sector partnerships of academe, government, industry, and others; and for enabling public policies (*e.g.*, requirements to provide data management plans as a condition of receiving government grants), as well as research funding to support, encourage, and improve preservation tools, standards, and practices: in short, to fund infrastructure.

Curation, Access, and Interoperability

If preservation in the narrowest sense means keeping the bits safe, and safely reusable, the promise as well as the challenge of digital *curation* is a more encompassing concept that embraces preservation as one element of digital archiving. Curation, according to the UK-based Digital Curation Centre, means "maintaining and adding value to a trusted body of digital information for current and future use; specifically....the active management and appraisal of data over the life-cycle of scholarly and scientific materials."

A major effort in the arena of curation is to develop metadata practices and standards that will do several important things: first, they must make data understandable by computers; second, they must support discovery across heterogeneous data collections; and third, they must manage all of this across data scales, from the small to the immense.

One of the keys to making all this possible, many believe, is expressing data using a data model called RDF (Resource Description Format). The promise of RDF is to encode data in a standard that is highly flexible and yields significant economies of scale. Adopting RDF in turn supports the development of the Semantic Web, an effort incubated within the W3C (World Wide Web Consortium).

The promise of the RDF standard in combination with the Semantic Web is to make it possible for meaningful data in documents to be processed and extracted by computers. That in turn makes it easier to exchange data within and across research domains (*e.g.*, between geology and chemistry). Indeed, the huge scale of data production makes it essential that metadata be generated and captured by automated means, even if human expertise is needed to develop cross-walks, annotations, or other descriptive information that will contribute to its value and usability. Ideally metadata will be captured as a by-product of the natural data production life cycle, *e.g.*, at the point the data is actually created. But to do this means to understand, at a fairly finely-grained and socially nuanced level, what the actual life cycle of data production is like.

Services and the Data Life Cycle

Librarians have long been familiar with canonical representations of the life cycle of scientific activities that result in publications, as well as (separate) representations of the various stages of scholarly communication and publishing. Given these two somewhat stable frameworks, it was relatively easy to describe the flow from experiment to results, with the outcome being the generation of primary and eventually secondary literature such as indexes, abstracts, handbooks, encyclopedias, and textbooks.

While some library services, including GIS and social science data services, operate in the top half of this framework in the pre-publication phase, for the most part libraries have assembled, managed, and served artifacts of various genres mostly from the "published" or bottom half of this framework.

Scientific data exists mostly in the pre-publication phase, and only a small sub-set of data is transferred across the divide into the publication phase. Here data – usually in highly reduced form – appears as tables or graphs embedded within a textual report of the scientific work. The demand for systems to capture, steward, and reuse scientific data clearly violates this old demarcation. Librarians in particular have not traditionally been involved in the production of scientific information prior to the publication of results. Yet if data produced through the conduct of science is to become a target of derivative works (for data mining, discovery and other reuse), then standards such as RDF, and systems and ontologies developed as part of the Semantic Web and other annotation systems, will be necessary.

To develop these systems will require a more complete and nuanced understanding of the data life cycle. One well-developed model for understanding this cycle is the "life cycle model" developed by Hunter, which follows the workflow of data from conception to final product. Several strengths of this model are that it allows for the possibility that a data set will grow; it supports the ability to track the evolution of data over time; and it includes the data source (provenance) as an integral aspect of the data.

To some extent, generalizations about data production in science can be useful. As can be seen in the story at the beginning of this article, data production in science may be characterized in several phases and flavours. To begin with there is "raw data" – data as it comes directly from the scientific instrument. There may be stages of validating and selecting the data. Then the data may be subjected to any number of standard or ad hoc processes that calibrate it – that translate it into a more general schema (*e.g.*, sky maps, catalogs). Another way of abstracting the nature of data is to contrast particular knowledge with "properties in general" – data abstracted or generalized to a level of understanding.

The 2005 National Science Board (NSB) report entitled *Long-Lived Digital Data Collections* suggests that data can be differentiated based on its nature, *e.g.*, numbers, images, video or audio streams, software and software versioning information, algorithms, equations, animations, or models/simulations; and also by their origins: whether they are observational, computational, or experimental. These latter distinctions are crucial when it comes to making choices for archiving and preservation. Observational data (*e.g.*, observations of ocean temperature on a specific date) are essentially historical and cannot be reproduced, and so may be primary candidates for indefinite archiving. Computational data may require archiving complete information about the computer model and the execution (*e.g.*, hardware, software, input data), but not of the data results themselves – which can in theory be reproduced. Experimental data may not be easily reproduced, given both cost considerations and the complexity of all the experimental variables. These factors (cost and reproducibility) will be relevant to preservation policies for experimental data. If data is processed for a variety of purposes (as in our illustration of the chemist's work), a variety of derivative products may also merit preservation.

In the life sciences, scientists have been encouraged to share their data with others – yet no one expects them to share all their data, in all its pre-processed and post-processed forms. The National Institutes of Health (NIH) has developed data sharing guidelines that offer some important distinctions between different categories of scientific data in relation to whether it is important that they be shared. The NIH requires that their grantees share "final research data," consisting of records "necessary to document and support research findings." This category therefore falls in between the summary tables and graphs normally found in research articles, and the preliminary records such as laboratory notebooks, partial dataset, and other artifacts of the research process. The NSB, following the NIH, has also distinguished between data collected by individual researchers ("research collections"), or in the context of collaborative research ("resource collections"), or research that produces a shared, curated resource ("reference collections").

While the data life cycle is essential to understanding the needs and services for data curation and stewardship, the fact that most data is digital adds another dimension to the consideration of life cycle: the digital life cycle. Digital curation – the activities that assure that digital resources are managed and preserved for discovery, access, and reuse – is a concern that overlaps widely with data curation, since it is essential to understand both the data life cycle and the digital life cycle if the investment and opportunities represented by digital scientific data are not to be lost.

In short, models of data life cycles suggest the need for a wide range of supportive services, including repository services (for data that is stable and where sharing is a goal); a variety of metadata production services appropriate to the anticipated use and reuse of the data within and across the originating and interested research domains; discovery and data-mining services that provide essential linkages and pattern finding tools; and preservation services that assure long-term access for reuse.

Policy Tools

Not all services and tools supporting cyberinfrastructure are technological. The social nature of science and the network of interested stakeholders in the future of access to scientific data make it essential to develop social and policy tools to support this future. One of the most significant policy tools to be developed to aid in the effort to ensure access to digital scientific data is the attachment of data management and data sharing requirements to government research funding.

Since 2003 the NIH has required applicants seeking $500,000 or more in direct costs to include a plan, in their application, for sharing their final research data. In *Long Lived Data Collections*, the NSB recommended requiring that applicants for NSF funds include a data management plan that would be subject to peer review. In addition, specific NSF units, such as the Division of Ocean Sciences, and the NSF Arctic System Science programme have for years had their own published policies on data sharing and management. In addition, some research communities have addressed this issue, creating data policies and guidelines.

The establishment in 2007 by the National Science and Technology Council of an Interagency Working Group (IWG) on Digital Data promises to bring about a great increase in sharing data policies and practices, as well as aiming at creating an "open interoperable framework to ensure reliable preservation and effective access to digital data for research, development, and education in science, technology, and engineering".

This is very good progress, because in the absence of such requirements, as we have learned at least in the social sciences, very little data survives over even short periods of time. The primary exception is data that has been deposited in well-understood community-based data repositories.

Another policy need is for standards and practices for *citing* data. Standard citation practices in scientific communication have developed for every conceivable type of textual publication, and these, along with web-based linking standards, are what make immensely popular and effective services such as SFX possible. Similar standards do not exist for most scientific data, although there are a few exceptions, such as the data publishing practices of the American Geophysical Union and the well-established social-science data archiving practices of the ICPSR.

In the UK, the eBank project (funded by JISC and led in part by UKOLN, the UK Office for Library and Information Networking), has been working on the problem of creating links between publications and datasets referred to in those publications, using citation and citation schemes (URIs) such as DOIs, PURLs, and handles.

A different approach is being adopted in Germany, where the German Science Foundation has been sponsoring a general-purpose data repository and registration system since 2005, as well as a project on the "Publication and Citation of Scientific Primary Data (STD-DOI)". A goal of this system is to make data citable as publications using DOIs assigned by one of several data publishing agencies, while the German National Library of Science and Technology (TIB) acts as a DOI registration agency for primary scientific information.

Finally, another aspect of social policy regarding data is the development of practices and mechanisms to provide appropriate access control mechanisms. While data sharing and open data practices may serve the public interest, there are cases either where privacy requires some access limitation, or where there are intellectual property restrictions on its sharing. Funding agencies address these issues in relationship to data sharing requirements. For example, the NIH notes that applicants are expected to address if, or how, they will exercise intellectual property rights while making data available to a broader research community.

Business Models

A growing concern of research funding agencies is finding workable business models for supporting the massive and evidently complicated new line of business that digital scientific data management represents. The business model for distributing, curating, and preserving textual representations of scientific findings, including published articles, papers, technical reports, and the like – is well understood and reasonably stable. While far from perfect, that system comprises an ecology of institutional players, from societies and commercial publishers to national and university libraries and archives. These partners maintain a system that can be reasonably counted on to sustain usable access to the published record of science over the long term.

The same can't be said, yet, for digital data. As can be seen from the review of issues above, national funding agencies and national libraries have played a very large role in framing the problem and bringing parties together to create the social and economic infrastructure that is as clearly needed as the technical one. But the problem is immense and, like the data itself, heterogeneous and distributed across a system at many scales. It seems only logical that a business model for data will likewise be both distributed and federated, a new ecology of institutional arrangements.

Those will almost certainly include research libraries, whose funding structure is tied to even longer-lived institutions – universities – yet who have collaborated well and diversified their revenue streams to include private and grant funding. At the same time, research libraries have urged the NSF to involve economic and social science experts in developing models for sustainable digital data stewardship. A danger is that, given what some refer to as the "Google effect" (the expectation that good infrastructure can be free), there will be a reluctance to devote scarce public or research dollars to create and sustain programmes of long-term data stewardship. There is therefore an urgent need to articulate a strong case for investing in data commons controlled and shaped by research communities, not by commercial interests.

A Rebalancing Act: Local and Global Cyberinfastructure

Accounts of cyberinfrastructure that prevail today are strongly influenced by their technological roots in high performance computing, and tend to idealize distintermediated solutions for optimizing data flow and transfer to general end-users. These solutions express assumptions that knowledge is a direct result of more and better access to data; many of these solutions will naturally be centred on large-scale data centres, not libraries. However these solutions tend to emphasize global, large-scale data-taking and data-management enterprises, and these neither exhaust nor address the full extent of science data production and use in knowledge-making. Complementing these solutions are others that focus on local knowledge-making and local data centres:

"Paying attention to the growth of local knowledge-making provinces is a strategy for changing how we think about generalizations and network federation. Considering local and global arenas as distinct yet interdependent, allows a local data centre to be transformed, to be seen as a new-age information environment where design and communication efforts are understood as knowledge work... A key information age challenge is creating a modular system of decentralized, heterogeneous information environments that function as learning arenas across the digital landscape."

Librarians interested in what their roles will be in the future cyberinfrastructures of science may find their skills and capabilities give them a natural and even crucial role in building and supporting the information infrastructures of local data centres – a role that draws on and adapts the mediating practices of the library profession to the world of data. In the second part of this article, the roles of libraries and librarians in cyberinfrastructures in light of current developments are explored further.

Bibliography

Alfred Aho, John Hopcroft, and Jeffrey Ullman: *Data Structures and Algorithms*, Addison-Wesley, 1983.

Bazirjian, Rosann: *The Acquisitions Librarian*, New York: Haworth, 1995.

Cargill, Jennifer: *Technical Services Today and Tomorrow of Library and Mass Communicatioin,* Michael Gorman. Englewood, Colo.: Libraries Unlimited, 1990.

Dennis S. Arnon. Scrimshaw: *Electronic Publishing: Origination, Dissemination and Library*, 1993.

Magrill, Rose Mary, and John Corbin: *Acquisitions Management and Collection Development in Libraries,* Chicago: ALA, 1989.

Mark S. Ackerman and Roy T. Fielding: *Proceedings of the Second Annual Conference on the Theory and Practice of Digital Libraries*, 1995.

Paul S. Adler and Terry Winograd: *Usability : turning technologies into tools and Library*, Oxford University Press, 1992.

Ricardo Baeza-Yates and Berthier Ribeiro-Neto: *Modern Information Retrieval of Library Science*, Addison-Wesley-Longman, 1999.

Strauch, Katina, and Bruce Strauch: *The Acquisitions Librarian,* New York: Haworth, 1990.

Schmidt, Karen A.: *Understanding the Business of Library Acquisitions,* Ann Arbor: Books on Demand, 1990.

Index

M

N

O

P

R

T

V

□□□